Edward Vernon-Harcourt

The Last Aristocratic Archbishop of York

1757–1847

— TONY VERNON-HARCOURT —

Sacristy
Press

Sacristy Press
PO Box 612, Durham, DH1 9HT

www.sacristy.co.uk

First published in 2023 by Sacristy Press, Durham

Sacristy Limited, registered in England & Wales, number 7565667

British Library Cataloguing-in-Publication Data
A catalogue record for the book is available from the British Library

ISBN 978-1-78959-316-7

Contents

Preface

Edward Vernon-Harcourt was Archbishop of York from 1807 to 1847. He died still in office at the age of 90. He is the second of only two Archbishops of York to hold the office for 40 years. The first was Walter de Gray, who was Archbishop of York from 1215 until his death in 1255.

Walter de Gray was supported by King John but had to pay the pope the immense sum of £10,000 to ratify the appointment. His episcopacy was a success: "He found the province a barren wilderness. He left it a fruitful garden." Like his successor some 600 years later he had to deal with issues such as plurality, non-residence and clergy education. De Gray purchased the village of St Andrewthorpe and constructed the first house for the archbishop, at what is now known as Bishopthorpe.[1]

Opinions on Archbishop Harcourt are more mixed. *The Times*' obituary immediately following his death stated he bore his "high dignities with meekness, exercised the large powers with which the law invested him with as much usefulness and justice as might be expected from a man of moderate learning and average intellect . . . he descends to his tomb not only with the reputation of a blameless life but the still high fame of benevolence and simplicity of character."[2] Charles Greville wrote in his diary for 8 November 1847: "He was in no way remarkable except for the wonderful felicity of his whole life . . . he had many friends and no enemies, was universally esteemed and respected, and beloved by his own family."[3]

---

[1] W. H. Dixon and James Raine, *Fasti Eboracences*, Volume 1 (London: Longman Green, 1863), pp. 279, 283 and 291. Canon Dixon was one of Archbishop Harcourt's domestic chaplains.

[2] *The Times*, 8 November 1847.

[3] Lytton Strachey and Roger Fulford, *Greville Memoirs Volume 5* (London: Macmillan, 1938), pp. 464–5, 8 November 1847.

A. M. G. Stephenson, writing in 1967, described the Archbishop's four decades at York as "years of episcopal stagnation: the archiepiscopate of Vernon-Harcourt is remembered for the ease and affluence amid which he lived rather than for any great advancement which he brought to the church in Yorkshire." Stephenson expressed doubts that he ever visited many parts of his diocese and concluded: "In Vernon-Harcourt we have a perfect example of a man with no deep vocation to the ministry, of mediocre ability and no special scholarship."[4]

By contrast, the *Oxford Dictionary of National Biography* notes that Vernon-Harcourt "was scrupulously attentive to the duties of the primacy". It compliments him for his frequent ordination and confirmation tours and notes that he was a constructive conservative who helped the Church of England come to terms with the extensive changes of the 1830s and 1840s.[5]

Such widely diverging views of the Archbishop's life and work made me curious to find out more. Where did the truth lie? How did he spend his days? I could only hope to find out by doing my own research. Archbishop Harcourt was my great-great-great grandfather.

Tony Vernon-Harcourt, Lord Vernon

---

[4]   A. M. G. Stephenson, *Archbishop Vernon Harcourt, Studies in Church History IV, Volume 58* (Cambridge: Cambridge University Press for Ecclesiastical History Society, 1967), pp. 143–54.

[5]   Nigel Aston, *Harcourt [formerly Venables-Vernon], Edward, Archbishop of York*, Oxford Dictionary of National Biography, 3 January 2008, accessed 31 July 2023.

For Cherry, Charlotte, Simon, Edward and Oliver

1

Early years (1757–91)

Edward Venables Vernon was born on 10 October 1757 at Sudbury Hall in Derbyshire, the third surviving son of a Member of Parliament and major landowner. As the youngest of eight surviving children, he would need to carve out a career for himself. His success would depend on his family, his friendships and his marriage as well as his innate abilities. Edward was fortunate that his family was well connected. Through his education he made valuable friendships. His links to the aristocratic and politically powerful men of his time were extended through a successful marriage.

Edward's parents

Edward's father was George Venables Vernon, one of two MPs for the Borough of Derby; the other was Lord Frederick Cavendish, a member of the Duke of Devonshire's family. The Vernons of Sudbury had succeeded to the Kinderton estates in Cheshire in 1715, and Edward's father had inherited Sudbury from his father in 1719. As an MP for Derby, George was much beholden to the Duke of Devonshire. He had told Lord George Cavendish in January 1756 he was "resolved not to take part in anything of consequence" until he knew Devonshire's opinion.[1]

George Venables Vernon believed he was eligible for a peerage and applied to the prime minister, the Duke of Newcastle, on 20 March 1760.

---

[1] Lord George Cavendish to the Duke of Devonshire, Devonshire MSS, 20 January 1756, quoted in *The History of Parliament: the House of Commons 1754–1790*, accessed 20 November 2022.

He referred to assurances he had had from the Duke of Devonshire, by whose advice he had come into Parliament: "I am sure the Duke of Devonshire will answer for my principles and pardon my saying that I think I have been of service, and may be of greater, as my interests in Derbyshire, Staffordshire, Cheshire and Sussex are not inconsiderable, and his Majesty's favour will strengthen them."[2] His efforts were at first unsuccessful. Newcastle wrote to the king asking for a number of peerages, including one for George Venables Vernon, but the king declined. However, in October 1761, George received Newcastle's parliamentary whip through the Duke of Devonshire. Two months later he was told he was to be awarded a peerage, probably through the influence of his wife's brother, Earl Harcourt, who had been governor to George III when Prince of Wales and in 1761 negotiated the marriage between the young king and Princess Charlotte of Mecklenburg-Strelitz.[3] George became Baron Vernon of Kinderton on 12 May 1762.

Edward's mother was Martha Harcourt, George's third wife. Martha's grandfather had been Lord Chancellor to Queen Anne and the first Viscount Harcourt. Her father died before his father and the title passed to Martha's brother, who was created the first Earl Harcourt in 1749. Martha and George married in April 1744.

Edward's siblings

Edward was George and Martha's last child. His parents were elderly for the time—his mother 42 and his father 49 at his birth. Edward's success in life was to be influenced as much by some of his siblings as by his parents. His father died in 1780 when he was only 23. His mother lived to the age of 79.

---

[2]   British Library, Add. MS 32903, f. 412, quoted in George Venables Vernon's biography in *The History of Parliament: the House of Commons*, accessed 20 November 2022.

[3]   George Venables Vernon's biography in *History of Parliament: the House of Commons 1754–1790*, accessed 20 November 2022.

Above: Sudbury Hall, Edward's family home

Left: George Venables Vernon, 1st Lord Vernon, Edward's Father

Right: Martha Harcourt, Lady Vernon, third wife of George Venables Vernon, sister of 1st Earl Harcourt and Edward's mother

Left: Edward Venables Vernon as a young man

Right: Elizabeth Venables Vernon, Countess Harcourt, Edward's elder sister and wife of the 2nd Earl Harcourt, her first cousin

When Edward was born, there were two surviving children of his father's first marriage to Mary, daughter of Lord Howard of Effingham, and five surviving children from his marriage to Martha. Of his father's other five sons, three had died young, including Martha's younger son William, who had died aged five the year before Edward was born.

Edward's eldest half-brother was, like their father, named George Venables Vernon. He was born on 9 May 1735 and, three months before Edward's birth, had married Louisa, daughter and heiress to the fourth Lord Mansell, who had extensive properties in Glamorgan. Following the death of his father in 1780, George became the second Lord Vernon and would play a role in promoting Edward's career.

Edward's half-sister Mary was 21 at his birth. On 5 January 1763, she married George Adams, MP for Saltash in Devon and subsequently from 1768 for one of the two Lichfield seats. On the death of his uncle, Adams changed his name to Anson, when he inherited the Anson estates including Shugborough Hall in Staffordshire. His eldest son was created Viscount Anson and his grandson the first Earl of Lichfield.

Of Martha's six surviving children, probably the most important for Edward's future was his sister Elizabeth. Aged 11 when Edward was born, in October 1765 she married her first cousin, Viscount Nuneham, the eldest son of her mother's brother, the first Earl Harcourt. Elizabeth and her husband were important to Edward as contacts at Court. In July 1784, Elizabeth, now Countess Harcourt, was appointed a Lady of the Bedchamber to Queen Charlotte. Her husband, who had become the second Earl Harcourt in 1777, was appointed Master of the Horse to the queen in 1791.[4] An unusually close friendship developed between Elizabeth and her husband and George III and Queen Charlotte. It was Elizabeth's husband who entailed the Harcourt estates to Edward. Elizabeth and Earl Harcourt had no children.

Henry, Martha's eldest son, was 10 at the time of Edward's birth. In 1779 he married Elizabeth Sedley, the natural daughter and heiress of Sir Charles Sedley. Sir Charles left the Nuthall Temple estates in Nottinghamshire to his daughter. Henry took the name Sedley on his marriage, then reverted back to Vernon on succeeding to the Vernon title as the third Lord Vernon on the death of his half-brother George in 1813. Henry's marriage strengthened the Vernon links to two other powerful Nottinghamshire families, the Dukes of Newcastle at Clumber and the Dukes of Portland at Welbeck. Such connections would be useful to Edward in his future career.

Closer in age to Edward were his three sisters—Catherine (known as Kitty) aged eight, Martha (called Patty) aged six and Anne, aged three at his birth. Patty was to follow her sister Elizabeth to Court. She was appointed as a Woman of the Bedchamber to the Princess of Wales by the Prince of Wales, the future George IV, who only wanted daughters of peers to serve the princess. The post was worth £200 a year tax free, "an equipage at the times of waiting and a share of the Princess's wardrobe".[5]

Education

No record remains of Edward's early education. It is likely that the rector of Sudbury played a part: Dr John Addenbrooke (1691–1776) was also dean of Lichfield and lived principally at Sudbury. Writing to Edward's sister Elizabeth from Sudbury in May 1765, he congratulated her on her engagement to her cousin Viscount Nuneham and stated: "Mr Edward is very well and desires his duty and love. I have not yet informed him that he is in a fair way of having another brother."[6] Edward was eight at the time.

Some three years later Elizabeth, now Viscountess Nuneham, wrote to Addenbrooke to say she and Lord Nuneham were not going abroad with Earl Harcourt, who had been appointed ambassador to France. Addenbrooke replied that, as compensation for not going to France, "you will oftener see your little brother Edward. He is designed for

---

[5]   Countess Harcourt to her sister Patty, 21 September (no year), *Harcourt Papers* (HP), Vol. XI, p. 99. The 14 volumes of *The Harcourt Papers* were edited by Edward William Harcourt and printed in Oxford between 1880 and 1905 for private circulation.

[6]   Dean Addenbrooke to Miss Vernon, 22 May 1765, HP, Vol. XI, p. 50. Viscount Nuneham would be Edward's brother-in-law following Elizabeth's marriage.

Westminster at Lady Day, and seems very desirous to be there as soon as he can. He'll do very well, I think, wherever he is."[7]

Westminster School was probably the most prestigious public school at the time and popular with both the Vernon and Harcourt families. Edward's brothers George and Henry and his cousin and future brother-in-law, Lord Nuneham, had attended Westminster. Edward was 11 when he first travelled there, arriving on 5 April 1769. There were 217 boys in the school. Numbers rose to 252 by 1772. The headmaster was Dr Smith, a former King's Scholar at the school, who had become headmaster in 1764 and continued in the role until 1788. Edward boarded at Jones's house in Dean's Yard.

Edward's journey to school "was occasionally performed on horseback, the young gentleman on his palfrey being followed by his mounted groom with saddlebags".[8] Edward liked the school and in due course sent six of his sons there. He regularly attended the annual anniversary dinner and was a steward for the dinner in 1799 and 1809. He was to be a steward again in 1848 but did not live to perform the role. He gave £300 to the fund for a new dormitory in 1846.

Edward's father was told by the school in October 1772 that Edward was "ripe for University". His sister Kitty wrote from Bath on 22 December 1772, "We expect Edward today; he has now taken leave of Westminster and I imagine is at this moment the happiest of human beings."[9] His father decided he was too young at 15 to go up to Christ Church, Oxford. Edward remained at Sudbury Hall in Derbyshire for two years and "took an active part in the management of his father's hounds".[10]

Edward matriculated on 2 July 1774, but did not take up residence at Christ Church until 16 January 1775. [11] He was first examined on

---

[7]   Dean Addenbrooke to Viscountess Nuneham, 12 January 1769, HP, Vol. XI, p. 52.

[8]   HP, Vol. XII, p. 1.

[9]   Catherine Vernon to Dean Addenbrooke, 22 December 1772, Nottingham University Archives, Addenbrooke letters, MS 107/5/8.

[10]   HP, Vol XII, p. 2.

[11]   *Alumni Oxoniensis* 1715–1886 (London: Foster, 1888). The Harcourt Papers give the date as 8 July.

Xenophon's *Memorabilia* that year during Hilary term.[12] According to the *Gentleman's Magazine* of January 1820, in Dr Bagot's time "all found it expedient to beware of going to the examination table unprepared". Dr Bagot was sub-dean of Christ Church when Edward went up and dean from 1777. At this time, the Oxford year was divided into four terms, so there were four "Collections" each year.[13] Edward's final assessment took place in the Michaelmas term 1777. He transferred to law on 24 October 1778.

The links between Christ Church and Westminster school were strong. Dr Markham, who was dean when Edward arrived, had been headmaster of Westminster.[14] Markham reformed the system of education at Christ Church. He organized for Noblemen and Gentleman Commoners to be taught alongside Commoners and Servitors and follow the same curriculum. From 1774, Noblemen and Gentleman Commoners had to present Collections like all other undergraduates. Status affected many aspects of Oxford life including academic dress. Each category sat at separate tables in the dining hall. Some sets of rooms were reserved for Noblemen and Gentlemen Commoners. Markham also enhanced the system of public lectures in the College.[15]

From 1774 to 1778, Edward held the Vernon studentship. Most Christ Church students, the nearest equivalent to fellows in other Oxford

---

12   Christ Church Archives, li.b.2, p. 137.

13   A Collection is a form of examination or assessment undertaken by the college to monitor a student's progress. The term continues in use at Oxford today.

14   Markham was elected to a Westminster studentship at Christ Church in 1738, was a tutor for ten years and a college lecturer from 1747 to 1750. He was appointed headmaster of Westminster in 1753 and designed an integrated system of education between Westminster and Christ Church. He had been appointed Dean of Christ Church in 1767 and served till 1776, when he was appointed Archbishop of York. He was also Bishop of Chester from 1771 to 1776. Edward was to be Markham's successor at York.

15   The lecturers in Edward's time included William Jackson, Thomas Pettingall (Senior Censor) and John Randolph, who would in due course become Bishop of Oxford. Randolph was Edward's tutor.

Colleges, were appointed by the canons, who formed Christ Church's governing body. In 1601, by Act of Parliament, Thomas Venables of Kinderton had acquired the right to appoint one of the 100 Christ Church students. The studentship was created as part of the settlement of a long-running dispute between the College and the Venables family. When Sir Peter Venables died in 1679, the right passed to his daughter Anne and then via her cousin Anne Piggott, who was the first wife of Henry Vernon of Sudbury, to their son, George Venables Vernon, Edward's father.[16]

In spite of his status as the son of a peer, Edward seems to have taken some time to get an appropriate set of rooms. His sister Kitty wrote to Dean Addenbrooke at Sudbury on 18 February 1775, "We heard from Oxford this week. Edward goes on very well but is not yet got into chambers of his own; which he is desirous to obtain, as he will not till then think himself thoroughly established."[17]

Edward also wrote to Dean Addenbrooke on 28 May to let him know how he was settling in. He had at last found some suitable rooms:

> As I know you will wish to hear how I like my situation at Oxford, I have taken the liberty to trouble you with a letter now that I am able to give some satisfactory accounts during the first two months I passed here. My time was almost constantly employed in getting into rooms and being immediately turned out again; after an infinity of trouble, I have at length taken possession of some which I may call my own at least for a considerable time. The different scene of life I am now engaged in to whatever yet has been appears highly agreeable. Our college is very full. Many are obliged to take up their quarters in different parts of town. Dr Bagot is at present our sub-dean and acts in that capacity so entirely like a gentleman that, although remarkably strict, yet

---

[16]   When Edward relinquished his studentship, his place was taken by Joshua Powell (1778–91) and then by two members of the Anson family, Henry (1791–8) and Frederick (1798–1800). Henry and Frederick were Edward's nephews, children of his half-sister Mary.

[17]   Catherine Vernon to Dean Addenbrooke, 18 February 1775, Addenbrooke letters 107/5/4.

he is beloved and respected by all the sensible young men of the college.

I hope you have got through the winter tolerably well and have not been much troubled with your old complaints.

I am at present going through a course of mathematical lectures and have finished the fifth book of Euclid. Our lecturer is Mr Jackson who is esteemed universally and uncommonly clever in that science.[18]

I shall now conclude with desiring you to believe that I am ever with great truth most sincerely and affectionately yours

Edward Venables Vernon

I hope you will excuse this scrawl.[19]

When Bagot took over from Markham as dean in 1777, he found discipline needed further improvement. With the help of John Randolph, who was now one of the censors, the problems were overcome. Following Markham and Bagot's reforms, "learning had been made a duty, a pleasure and even a fashion" at Christ Church.[20]

Edward appears to have enjoyed his time at Oxford. His sister Kitty wrote on 27 April 1777 from London: "Edward came to town last Thursday. He is quite well again, is vastly grown and has very much the air of an Oxford scholar."[21] His sister Patty wrote a few days later that Edward was still with the family but about to return to Oxford: "He seems to like his situation extremely and has the additional satisfaction of thinking it will every day improve upon him."[22]

---

[18] William Jackson was educated at Westminster. He was the brother of Cyril Jackson, a future dean of Christ Church. From 1769 to 1783, he held the College mathematical lectureship.

[19] E. V. Vernon to Dean Addenbrooke, 28 May [1775], Addenbrooke letters 107/3.

[20] H. L. Thompson, *Christ Church* (London: F. E. Robinson, 1900), p. 167.

[21] Catherine Vernon to Dean Addenbrooke, 27 April 1777, Addenbrooke letters 107/7/3.

[22] Martha Vernon to Dean Addenbrooke, 4 May 1777, Addenbrooke letters 107/5/14.

Edward made some important lifelong friendships at Christ Church. Thomas Grenville had come up to Christ Church the year before Edward. Thomas had "a genial, humorous disposition, but also studious habits". Edward considered he was greatly beholden to him for good example and advice.[23] Both Thomas Grenville and Edward lived to the age of 90 with all their faculties intact. The Grenvilles were an important political family. Thomas's younger brother William, subsequently Lord Grenville, was to be Speaker of the House of Commons and Prime Minister. Thomas's elder brother George Grenville was also a statesman and on two occasions Lord Lieutenant of Ireland; he was created the first Marquess of Buckingham.

By June 1776, Thomas had moved on to Lincoln's Inn to study law. In a reply to a letter from Edward, he stated: "the satisfaction you express at the amicable intercourse between you and [Randolph] gives me the greatest pleasure; but it would be doing you little justice to allow you to consider yourself indebted, in the least degree, for that to any circumstance but your own manners and disposition." Thomas was clearly sure that Randolph, who was tutor to both Edward and Thomas, enjoyed a good relationship with Edward. Thomas went on to say he thought Edward would enjoy the *Logical* works of Aristotle "more than any book you ever looked into". He concluded by saying he thought he was unlikely to get to Oxford for admission (to a degree) and asked Edward to remember him to their friends.[24]

Another significant lifelong friend from Christ Church was George Granville Leveson Gower, Viscount Trentham, the eldest son of Earl Gower. He matriculated on 2 May 1775, and his time at Christ Church therefore coincided closely with Edward's. In the first six months of 1781, after both had completed their studies, Edward and George travelled together through France and Germany to Venice.[25] George was brother to Lady Anne Leveson Gower, Edward's future wife.

---

[23] HP, Vol. XII, pp. 6–7.

[24] Thomas Grenville to E. V. Vernon, 14 June 1776, HP, Vol. XII, pp. 8–9.

[25] James Loch, *Memoir of George Granville, first Duke of Sutherland* (London, 1834, for private circulation). The Harcourt Papers also mention a European visit but give no date.

By the spring of 1777, Edward was considering a move to All Souls to study law. His friend Thomas Grenville wrote to him from Lincoln's Inn in April 1777: "Your views of All Souls are pretty strong symptoms of a change of situation; and although the actual distance between this town and All Souls College is much the same with the distance to Christ Church, yet I shall consider you there as half way, at least, on your road to Lincoln's Inn." He asked Edward to give his love to his younger brother, "the ardour of whose studies could, I am sure alone, prevent him from living in a perpetual state of ignorance of his friends".[26]

All Souls in the eighteenth century was not a place of great academic distinction. Its 40 fellows had to have studied for three years elsewhere in Oxford and be aged between 18 and 25 on election. Between 1750 and the reform of the statutes in 1857, more than half of the fellows elected were kin of the founder and nearly as many came from Christ Church.[27] Edward was following a well-trodden path and was one of the few eighteenth-century fellows to have a distinguished career.

Edward had largely finished his studies at All Souls by the end of 1780, for he went on his tour of Europe with George Viscount Trentham in the first six months of 1781. He deferred completing the formalities for five years till 1786, by which time he was well established in his clerical career. The *Oxford Mail* of Saturday 29 April 1786 announced: "On Thursday [26 April] Hon. and Rev. Edward Venables Vernon, Canon of Christchurch, was admitted to the degree of Bachelor of Civil Law from which he went out Grand Compounder."[28] The following week several papers, including the *Oxford Mail* and the *Bath Chronicle*, reported that

---

[26] Thomas Grenville to E. V. Vernon, 25 April 1777, HP, Vol. XII, pp. 10–11.

[27] All Souls College website, accessed April 2020.

[28] Grand Compounders were degree candidates who possessed property with a value of more than £300 a year or had a benefice rated in the King's Books at £40 a year. Grand Compounders were required to pay extra for their degrees—£30 rather than £7 for a BA and £40 rather than £14 for an MA. In return for their higher fee, they were entitled to wear a bright red gown and to process next to the Vice Chancellor. Because of their bright garb, they were referred to as "University Tulips". As a member of an aristocratic family, Edward would have been required to take his degrees in this manner.

Edward had on 4 May been admitted to the degree of Doctor of Civil Law, for which once more he went out Grand Compounder.[29]

Family life

At Sudbury Hall, family life centred on hunting, shooting and racing. Balls and concerts often took place during race meetings.[30] Sudbury was sometimes the setting for concerts and theatricals. The *Derby Mercury* of 31 July 1783 recorded that Lord Vernon, Edward's eldest brother, was staying at Burghley House with Lord Exeter, and that "their evenings are generally dedicated to music". The music was provided by professionals of the highest standing including noted singers of the day—Knyvett, Hanson and Oswald. The party was going on to "Lord Vernon's seat at Sudbury". Edward had a good knowledge of music, and in later life, he was to help

---

[29]   The *Oxford Dictionary of National Biography* (accessed 13 October 2021) has the year 1780 for Edward's BCL and 1786 for DCL. *A Catalogue of all Graduates in the University of Oxford between 10 October 1659 and 10 October 1800* (Oxford: Clarendon Press, 1801) gives 27 April 1786 for BCL and 4 May 1786 for DCL as do newspapers of the time. *Derby Mercury,* 29 April 1786; *Reading Mercury,* 8 May 1786; *Stamford Mercury,* 12 May 1786. It seems likely that it was convenient for him to be admitted to both degrees on a single visit to Oxford.

[30]   One such special event was the coming of age of the fifth Duke of Devonshire. The duke made his first visit to Derby in August 1770 some months after his 21st birthday. Accompanied by his uncles, Lords George, Frederick and John and his brother, Lord Richard Cavendish, he gave a "grand entertainment" at three inns in Derby—the George, the King's Head and the Greyhound. The nobility, gentry and tradesmen of the town were invited. The duke opened the dancing with Edward's eldest unmarried sister, Catherine, who was the same age as the duke. The duke's sister was married to the Duke of Portland. Some years later the Duke of Devonshire married Georgiana, the somewhat notorious daughter of the future Earl Spencer. Georgiana was, like Edward, only 12 at this time. Neither were, therefore, likely to have been present at the ball.

develop the music festivals in Carlisle and York. As Archbishop of York, he was invited to be a Director of the Ancient Concerts, where he was required to plan concert programmes.[31]

Shooting and hunting were activities that all three Vernon brothers, George, Henry and Edward, enjoyed.[32] Early in the century, the country around Sudbury had been hunted by the Talbots of Ingestre, but by 1773 the Vernon family had its own pack of foxhounds maintained solely by Edward's father. This arrangement continued under Edward's brother George, when he inherited in 1780. The land hunted stretched from Cannock Chase through Shipley, Foremark and Bretby to Hopwas Hays, and the Sudbury huntsman, Sam Lawley, was highly regarded.

Edward's love of foxhunting is shown in a humorous account of a hunt in Needwood Forest in January 1777. He wrote: "The army, consisting of 60 privates and three officers [The huntsman and two whippers-in], aided by a numerous band of Volunteer officers who had joined the camp the previous evening, were, by direction of the Commander-in-Chief, drawn up on the heights of Needwood about 9 o'clock on 23 January. In less than an hour of their being formed in this manner, in spite of the utmost vigilance of the officers, a triple division of the forces took place, owing to the impetuosity of the privates and their eagerness to engage at all events." With the assistance of one of the volunteer officers, the veteran Lieutenant General Fitzherbert, the privates were brought back together and the enemy succumbed. This was the conclusion of the campaign, "as the Commander-in-Chief talks of removing soon into winter quarters". (Lord Vernon was going to London.)[33]

The Vernon family also had a pack of buckhounds, which were much valued. An advertisement appeared in the *Derby Mercury* of 15 March 1776 offering a reward for the recovery of a buck hound of light colour. "He has a blemish on one claw of his near foot and has a little white on the end of his tail. He answers to the name of Forrester. If returned to John Morgan, Keeper to Lord Vernon, the finder will receive half a guinea."

---

[31]   See Chapter 6.

[32]   Their names appear in the lists published annually in the *Derby Mercury* of those holding licences to kill game.

[33]   The full account is reproduced in HP, Vol. XII, pp. 2–6.

If Edward's winters were engaged in hunting and shooting, one of his summer interests was racing. The two local racecourses were at Lichfield and Derby.[34] Members of the Vernon family were closely associated with the city of Lichfield, a two-member parliamentary seat effectively controlled by the Anson and Leveson Gower families. Edward's father had been a Lichfield MP from 1741 to 1747 and had been steward of Lichfield Races in 1761 with Lord Frederick Cavendish. From 1770 till his death in 1789, Edward's brother-in-law George Anson was one of the two MPs for the city of Lichfield. It is not therefore surprising that Edward, with his interest in and knowledge of horses, was invited to be one of two stewards. What is less usual is that he was only 19 at the time. His fellow steward was Noel Hill, later Lord Berwick of Attingham, who was aged 32. The Hills owned Shenstone Park near Lichfield.

The precise duties of the stewards varied from course to course, but Edward and Noel Hill will have had overall responsibility for the organization and running of the races and the entertainments associated with them. A clerk would be appointed to keep the books, collect subscriptions and entry fees and deal with traders. The stewards would have to find the prize money and encourage subscribers to meet the costs of preparing the course. Entry fees were given to the second horse in a race. The stewards were required to settle disputes, a huge responsibility when large bets were involved. If the income was insufficient, the stewards

---

[34]   Racing was important politically, socially and commercially in the second half of the eighteenth century. To the local MP with a limited electorate, racing provided an opportunity for him to demonstrate his support for the local gentry and freeholders. The races would be accompanied by balls, concerts, dinners and other entertainments to attract men, women and families. Commercially the races were valued for the trade they brought to the local community, particularly by the innkeepers, who provided accommodation and food for visitors and their horses. Gambling was hugely popular in the eighteenth century and betting on horses involved significant sums. The races were open to all for no charge, though the aristocracy and gentry, as subscribers, would watch from a grandstand or their coach. See Mike Huggins, *Horse Racing and British Society in the Long Eighteenth Century* (Woodbridge: Boydell Press, 2018), pp. 37–78 and pp. 175–98.

would be expected to cover the loss. Lichfield often ran at a loss in the 1770s.

The following letter from Edward, dated 7 June 1777, indicates that the choice of dates for Lichfield Races was a matter of some dispute. Edward had returned to Christ Church and found a letter from the Clerk to the Lichfield Races awaiting his attention. Edward then wrote to George Hand Junior, who was a member of a leading Lichfield family. Hand's father was a clergyman and his uncle a respected lawyer in the city. Edward wrote:

> Upon my return to Oxford last night, I found your letters. I had before heard of the dispute between Lord Paget and the Corporation of Lichfield, but that being adjusted, I was in daily expectation of seeing the advertisement in the papers. I am extremely sorry that Mr Inge and Lord Donegal's wishes with respect to the races should meet with the least opposition from me, yet I do not think that the days can now be altered with any degree of propriety, as several persons have from my information made their disposition for the above mentioned time and, were it to be now changed, they would in all probability be put to great inconvenience: besides this, if you recollect, some of the heats last year, when the races were the first week in September, were run absolutely in the dark and certainly there would be a greater probability of the same inconvenience arising this year if the races were to be fixed for a period when the season is more advanced. Mr Hill [Edward's fellow Steward], when I consulted with him in London upon the affair, assured me that it was a matter of perfect indifference to him and begged that I would finally settle the time; in consequence of his desire, I not only wrote to you, but applied also to the Duke of Ancaster, for his permission that the King's Plate might be run for on the 26th day of August.
>
> I am not myself sufficiently conversant in these matters to know whether the objections I have stated against the alteration you propose ought to have any weight. You will readily acquit me of any imputation of consulting my own convenience when I inform you that I shall be in Derbyshire from the middle of

July till the end of October, and consequently either of the times
proposed would be agreeable to me. My Brother [Lord Vernon]
is now at Sudbury and, being nearer the spot, will be better able
to form an opinion from circumstances than I could do, who am
at a distance. I wish therefore that you would consult him, and
settle the time of the races finally according to his determination.
I beg my compliments to Mr Inge, & am Sir your humble servant
Edward Venables Vernon.[35]

Edward had good reason to be reluctant to change the dates, which would
have been published in *Weatherby's Racing Calendar*. More importantly
he had safety concerns: some of the heats might be run in the dark.
Ultimately Edward had his way, and the races took place on 26, 27 and
28 August as originally planned. The races were to be accompanied by
balls, ordinaries, concerts and public breakfasts.[36]

The Vernon family were also closely involved with Derby Races and
participated in the entertainments which took place in the evenings. The
ball on the Thursday evening after racing in September 1774 was attended
by the Duke and Duchess of Devonshire and their family, including the
Duchess's mother Countess Spencer and her brother Lord Althorp. Also
attending were Lord Vernon and the Hon. Mr and Miss Vernon.[37]

In 1778, Edward's elder brother George was a steward at Derby
Races. Edward followed his brother as steward in 1780. He served

---

[35]   Edward Venables Vernon to G. Hand Junior, 7 June 1777, private collection.
       The advertisement for the Lichfield races appeared in the *Derby Mercury*, 8
       August 1777, and a number of other publications.

[36]   Huggins, *Horse Racing and British Society in the Long Eighteenth* Century,
       p. 71 and pp. 76–8. Ordinaries were meals organized typically in the early
       afternoon before racing started, usually at one or more local inns. Sometimes
       they were just for gentlemen or ladies, but some allowed mixed attendance.
       Public breakfasts became fashionable from the 1750s. Cocking or cock
       fighting was also offered at the Swan Pit. It remained popular till about 1800
       and the prizes and bets were often greater than those at the races. The entry
       fees to the cock fights provided income for the innkeeper.

[37]   *Derby Mercury*, 8 September 1774. The two younger Vernons are not named.

with Richard Fitzherbert from Somersal Herbert, a village about two miles from Sudbury. Racing took place on Tuesday 8 and Wednesday 9 August on Sinfin Moor. Perhaps aware of problems of previous years, the advertisement made plain that racing would start at four o'clock precisely, "it having been unanimously agreed".[38] The rules of racing were not yet laid down nationally, although those used at Newmarket were widely copied. The stewards therefore needed to explain in the advertisement how much of the entry fees would go to the second horse in a race and how many entries were required for the race to run. The advertisement made clear that the King's Plate, worth £100, would be run to the nationally agreed King's Plate Articles or rules. The stewards exercised their discretion on the rules for other races. Edward's interest in horses and racing continued throughout his life. Although he did not think it appropriate to attend York races when archbishop, his coach would take his family and guests to the meetings.

There is a delightful and probably apocryphal tale of a meeting between Edward when archbishop and a clergyman in his diocese who had no love of racing and thought to curry favour with the Archbishop by reporting another priest, a Mr W, who had entered a horse at Whitby races. "You don't mean to say," exclaimed the Archbishop with well-feigned astonishment. "I do indeed," said his informant. "But," rejoined the Archbishop hopefully, "you doubtless have only heard this said of him, and the probabilities are that there is no truth in the report." The clergyman replied: "I am sorry to say I know it for a fact." The Archbishop continued: "You know that Mr W is fond of horses. He may have entered the horse merely to test its capabilities and without any thought of competing in the stakes." The clergyman replied: "I am only grieved to say that Mr W's conduct will not bear that interpretation." "You are quite certain of this?" asked the Archbishop. "Yes, your Grace, quite certain." "Very well then," continued the Archbishop, "I'll bet you a guinea he wins. Mr W is such a judge of the horse and he has such blood

---

[38]   *Derby Mercury*, 16 June 1780 and later issues.

in his stables, that if he entered a horse to win, he will win. There now, here is my guinea."[39]

Ordination and marriage

It was not uncommon for the younger son of a peer to be ordained. With Edward's wide connections, it would be a sensible career. He would have a basic income of about £200 a year from the family living at Sudbury, which he would hope to supplement with additional clerical appointments. Fortunately for Edward, the practice of holding several clerical appointments at the same time was still acceptable. The day-to-day duties of the role of rector of Sudbury could be delegated to a curate on £30 to £50 a year, which salary Edward or the Vernon family would have to find.

When Dean Addenbrooke died in February 1776 and left the living of Sudbury vacant, Edward was 18. It is, however, clear from a letter Edward's father wrote to the dean's brother, Edward Addenbrooke, that a decision had already been made for Edward to be ordained. Lord Vernon wrote on 17 May 1776: "I have fixed upon George Fletcher to be the locum tenens for my son and he is to accept a curate of my nomination."[40] Fletcher had been Lord Vernon's personal chaplain since 1762. He was also rector of two nearby parishes, Cubley with Marston Montgomery and Barton Blount, the latter position worth £23 a year. He gave up this position but continued as rector of Cubley in plurality with the rectory of Sudbury. He resigned the Sudbury living in 1780 and for a year the position was held by George Talbot, who was also rector of Ingestre, Staffordshire.

Edward was ordained deacon at Cuddesdon by John Butler, Bishop of Oxford, on 8 July 1781, shortly after his European journey with Viscount

---

[39]   Rev. M. C. F. Morris, *Yorkshire Reminiscences* (London: H. Milford, 1922), pp. 320–1.

[40]   Lord Vernon to Edward Addenbrooke, 17 May 1776, Addenbrooke Letters 1/13.

Trentham.[41] Three months later on 14 October he was ordained priest by the Bishop of Peterborough, John Hinchcliffe, in the chapel at Buxton, Derbyshire. He was instituted as rector of Sudbury by the Bishop of Lichfield and Coventry on 24 April 1782.

Edward's first preferment preceded his arrival at Sudbury. On 12 December 1781, he was appointed Chaplain in Ordinary to King George III. There were 48 chaplains. Four were assigned to each month of the year and each would serve for one week. Their duties included preaching at the Chapel Royal on Sundays and festivals. They would read morning and evening prayers with the king and his family in his private chapel and might join him for dinner. Although the role was unpaid, the position enabled the priest to get to know the king, a considerable advantage when it came to preferment in the Church of England.

Around this time Edward met his future wife, Lady Anne Leveson Gower. Lady Anne was the sister of Edward's friend and travelling companion, George Viscount Trentham. George and Anne were two of the eight surviving children of Granville Leveson Gower, Earl Gower, later Marquess of Stafford. George was some three years older than his sister Anne and they were two of the four children of Lord Gower's marriage to Louisa Egerton, daughter of the first Duke of Bridgewater. Anne's mother had died a few months after her birth and Anne seems to have developed a good relationship with her stepmother Susanna, Countess Gower, who was the daughter of the Earl of Galloway.

After George and Edward's return from Europe, George and his sister Anne went to Ireland to stay with their elder sister Caroline, who was married to the Earl of Carlisle. Lord Carlisle was Lord Lieutenant of Ireland. Anne's stepmother, Countess Gower, wrote to Anne at Dublin Castle from Trentham, the Leveson Gower family house in Staffordshire:

> I am glad you have found an acquaintance *a votre gout*. I have no
> doubt of her being reasonable and well behaved since you like her

---

[41] Butler was Bishop of Oxford from 1777–88 and was familiarly known as "Dr Pig and Castle" from an inn at Bridgenorth whose wealthy heiress he married (S. L. Ollard and Gordon Crosse (eds), *A Dictionary of English Church History*, 2nd rev. edn (London: A.R. Mowbray 1919).

Leveson Gower Children—Lady Anne, Edward's wife, on the right with her half-siblings Lady Georgiana, Lady Susan, Hon. Granville and Lady Charlotte, the five younger children of Granville Leveson Gower, 2nd Earl Gower

... I am sorry, my dear, that you had not (when you wrote) been at Church. I beg of you neglect that duty as little as possible. Habit is a great deal, and by leaving off public worship for a little while, it soon becomes troublesome and we make ourselves believe it to be unnecessary ... I know my dear Nanny the goodness of your dispositions and what a well-ordered mind you have; I only fear that dissipation and example may weaken your good ideas. Take care to go to Church when you possibly can.[42]

Countess Gower wrote to Lady Anne a week later: "I rejoice to know they made a ball for you and I love you for not going without a chaperone. Lady Carlisle says that Lord Trentham seems to like Ireland. Don't let him stay longer than is necessary for your sister's lying in ... I am glad you have been at Chapel; pray my dear when you can, let nothing prevent that. Your papa is vastly well. The little ones often talk of their dear Nanny."[43] Lady Anne had a half-brother, Granville Leveson Gower, who was 12 years younger than her and aged eight at this time. Her three half-sisters, Georgiana, Charlotte and Susan, were then 12, ten and nine. Anne was therefore used to a large family. Through the marriages of her seven siblings, Lady Anne's and therefore Edward's connections to other aristocratic families were to be greatly strengthened.

While Edward and Lady Anne's friendship was developing, Edward was starting to make a name for himself as a preacher. A Mrs McCartney wrote to Edward's sister Elizabeth on 11 October 1781, a few days before he was made a priest. Mrs McCartney had met Edward at the Harcourts' house in Bath, a popular resort for the aristocracy: "Lord Vernon [Edward's half-brother George] loves all his family, particularly my friend Edward, which delights me; and I am much delighted he is pleased with his profession. I have no doubt of his excelling in whatever situation, but I rather he had been placed where his good sense and

---

42   Countess Gower to Lady Anne Leveson Gower, 3 November 1781, HP, Vol. XII, pp. 276–7.

43   Countess Gower to Lady Anne Leveson Gower, 8 November 1781, HP, Vol. XII, pp 278–9.

agreeableness had more play, but, if he is pleased, that is everything. He and the Bishop of Peterborough will put me in conceit with parsons."[44]

Early in 1782 Mrs McCartney wrote again to Elizabeth from Bath: "I hear great fame of Edward as a Divine. I wish he were here. We have a great choice of heiresses." In May, she wrote: "I confess I have not the grace to mend, though my friend Edward has given us an excellent sermon, so excellently delivered that I was stopped by several strangers to inquire who the charming man was. I felt pleased at the opportunity of expiating on his merit, and I am sure your ladyship will not accuse me of partiality or flattery, when I tell you the Bishop of Peterborough joins with me that he is an honour to his family."[45] John Hinchcliffe, Bishop of Peterborough and Master of Trinity College, Cambridge, was renowned as an orator.

In September 1783, Edward was invited to preach the sermon at the anniversary of the institution of the General Hospital, Nottingham. "The sermon was preached by the Rev. Edward Venables Vernon, brother to Lord Vernon and one of His Majesty's Chaplains in Ordinary, from Galatians VI verse 2 'Bear ye one another's burdens and so fulfil the laws of Christ'. Collections were taken by Lord Middleton and the Hon. Henry Sedley [Edward's brother]. £172 13s 2d was raised for the hospital."[46]

On 5 February 1784, Lady Anne and Edward were married at Earl Gower's house in Whitehall by special licence. Lord Gower approved of his son-in-law. He wrote to Edward: "I am much obliged to you for your kind and affectionate letter. It breathes the emotions of a mind formed to ensure the happiness of my daughter, who, I am persuaded, will prove as amiable a wife as I experienced her as a daughter. The love you bear each other, the affections and friendships of your relations on both sides, will, I am confident add more permanent and solid happiness than thousands and tens of thousands of pounds. God in externals never placed content. I assure you on my honour, I gave my daughter to you

---

[44]   Mrs McCartney to Countess Harcourt, 11 September 1781, HP, Vol. XII. p. 18.

[45]   Mrs McCartney to Countess Harcourt, 11 October 1781, 8 January and 13 May 1782, HP, Vol. XII, pp 18–19.

[46]   *Derby Mercury*, 9 September 1783.

with more satisfaction than I should have done to the first grandee of the kingdom whose character was not as decidedly good as your own."[47]

Mrs McCartney had met Lady Anne at Bath and liked her. She thought Lord Gower's high opinion of Edward was justified and was delighted he preferred his daughter's happiness to great wealth. The young couple started married life with a settlement of about £15,000, of which £10,000 came from Earl Gower and Lady Anne's late mother and around £5,000 from Edward and his family. The trustees were Lady Anne's brother George, Viscount Trentham, Edward's brother Henry Sedley, and Earl Gower.[48] Interest rates were around 4 per cent at this time, so this capital sum would add in the order of £600 a year to Edward's income of about £200 from the Sudbury living.

Edward and Lady Anne started their married life in the Sudbury rectory. In 1687, Edward's great-grandfather George Vernon had exchanged parts of the glebe lands close to Sudbury Hall, including the old timber-framed parsonage, for ground a little further away but adjoining other glebe land. He had built a new rectory and barn for the then rector. This was the house Edward and Lady Anne and their children occupied.[49] Their first child, George Granville, was born 18 months after their marriage, on 7 August 1785. Five more of their 16 children were born before Edward was promoted to Bishop of Carlisle in 1791.

Shortly after his first son's birth, Edward conducted the marriage of his friend George Viscount Trentham to the Countess of Sutherland, who was aged 20. The *Derby Mercury* of 8 September 1785 stated: "On Sunday [4 September] was married by special licence at Lady Sutherland's house in Manchester Square, Rt. Hon. George Granville Leveson Gower [Viscount Trentham] to Lady Elizabeth Gordon, Countess of Sutherland,

---

[47]　Earl Gower to Edward Vernon, 10 February 1784, HP, Vol. XII, p. 20.

[48]　Derbyshire Archives, D410M/Box31B/1824 and Staffordshire Archives, D593/D/1/2.

[49]　Cherry Ann Knott, *George Vernon, 1636–1702, 'who built this house', Sudbury Hall, Derbyshire* (Stroud: Tun House Publishing, 2010), p. 637. The house was at the far end of the village from the hall. It was replaced by a later Victorian rectory, now largely demolished.

by Rt. Rev. Edward Venables Vernon, brother to Lord Vernon and rector of Sudbury and brother-in-law to Lord Trentham. After the ceremony the new married couple set off with a grand retinue to her Ladyship's villa in Hertfordshire."

Preferment in the Church

One of the most coveted positions in the Church of England was membership of a cathedral chapter. Cathedral incomes were substantial and the canons or prebendaries (the names were interchangeable) were well remunerated for limited duties. Many such positions were political appointments and a useful means by which a politician might reward his supporters and their families. Much later in life Edward was to be involved in diverting the income from cathedral canonries to support under-remunerated clergy in poorer parishes. Now he wished to obtain such posts for himself.

Edward's brother Lord Vernon acted on his behalf. Lord John Cavendish wrote to his neighbour the third Duke of Portland: "Lord Vernon has written to me to apply to you for the canonry of Christ Church for his brother. I answered him that it was yours, but that I would inform you of his request and that I was sure you were very well disposed to serve his brother."[50] Henry Sedley, Edward's other brother, who was now living at Nuthall in Nottinghamshire and friendly with the Duke of Portland, may have played a part in asking for his support. The formal announcement of Edward's appointment appeared in the *Oxford Mail* of 1 October 1785: "The King has been pleased to grant the Rev. and Hon. Edward Venables Vernon, Chaplain in Ordinary to His Majesty, the place and dignity of a Canon in Christ Church Cathedral vacated by the death of the Hon. Edward Seymour Conway." Edward was installed as a canon of Christ Church, Oxford, two weeks later on 15 October.

The Dukes of Portland, Devonshire and Newcastle were all Whigs, although party allegiances were fluid. Edward's father had been a Tory

---

[50] Lord John Cavendish to the third Duke of Portland, 4 September 1783, Nottingham University Archives, PWF 267/3.

but transferred his allegiance to the Whig Duke of Devonshire. A Whig ministry led by the Duke of Newcastle held power when Lord Vernon received his peerage. Now in 1785 the administration was led by William Pitt "The Younger", a Tory. Fortunately for Edward the Leveson Gowers were Tories and Edward's father-in-law Earl Gower was Lord President of the Council in Pitt's administration. This meant that Edward was able to obtain a second canonry. He was appointed a prebendary of Gloucester Cathedral at the chapter meeting on 12 November 1785. The prebend was in the gift of the king, who would take advice from his ministers.

The ceremony for installing a new canon or prebend was similar in both cathedrals and took place during morning service. In Gloucester, the new prebendary met the dean and chapter in the chapter room before the service and took the oath. He then waited in the chapter room with the chapter clerk till the first lesson had been read, when the dean and clergy, accompanied by the choir, came to the chapter room, collected the new prebendary and processed back into the cathedral. The chapter clerk read the mandate and the dean conducted the prebendary to his stall and endowed him with "all manner of rights, profits, emoluments, houses, privileges and appurtenances applicable to the office".[51] At Christ Church, Edward had to wait in the North Chapel till the first lesson had been read. After the ceremony, the dean took him first to the chapter house to show him his place and then to the "mansion house of the said canonry and put him into the real and actual possession thereof".[52] Edward now had the use of a substantial house in Oxford and another in Gloucester in addition to the rectory in Sudbury.

The two canonries were somewhat different in terms of duties and financial rewards. At Christ Church, the dean and chapter were responsible not just for running the cathedral but also for managing the college. There were regular monthly chapter meetings to discuss both cathedral and college business. Edward would sometimes attend, particularly in the spring, but most frequently he would give his proxy to the dean, Cyril Jackson, brother of his former lecturer William Jackson. As a canon, Edward would have the right from time to time to nominate

---

[51]   Gloucester Cathedral Archives, Chapter Act Book No. 4, 1775–1807.

[52]   Christ Church Archives, Chapter Book, pp. 502–5.

canoneer students at the college, and in 1788 he nominated his nephew Charles Anson, the son of his sister Mary. Edward was not required to be in residence for a specific number of days in the year, although he would be required to take services from time to time.

At Gloucester, responsibilities were organized rather differently. Prebendaries were required to be in residence for two months every year. The allocation of residencies was decided at a chapter meeting every June for the subsequent 12 months from Michaelmas. The allocation of residencies varied from year to year. In 1796, Edward would have been expected to take over the months of April and May, which had been given to his predecessor. In most subsequent years, Edward was given either the months of June and July or August and September.

Gloucester Cathedral had some difficulty in getting all prebendaries to comply with the residency requirements. A chapter meeting of 20 November 1784 insisted residency "must be performed by [the prebendary] residing in his own prebendal house" and "by attending divine service in church once a day at least for one and twenty days successively". The prebendary could not be absent from the prebendal house above one day in any one week. Prebendaries were allowed to exchange dates with other prebendaries, but it was up to each to ensure his dates were covered. Records do not exist to show how regularly Edward fulfilled his residency requirements, but he was seldom present at chapter meetings and regularly gave his proxy to the dean.[53]

Edward was in residence in Gloucester in September 1787 and July 1788. 1787 was the year in which the Three Choirs Festival took place at Gloucester from 12–15 September and raised money for the widows and orphans of poor clergy. On the Wednesday, there was an opening service at which the three choirs sang Handel's *Te Deum* and the *Coronation Anthems*. Edward preached the sermon, choosing the same text from Galatians 6:2 that he had used five years earlier in Nottingham: "Bear ye one another's burdens, and so fulfil the law of Christ."[54]

---

[53]   Gloucester Cathedral Archives, Chapter Act Book No. 4, 1775–1807.

[54]   *Oxford Journal*, 18 August 1787. The other two choirs came from Worcester and Hereford Cathedrals.

In the summer of 1788, George III was unwell, the start of his first major bout of ill health. His doctor advised him to visit Cheltenham to take the waters. During their stay, the king and queen and their three elder daughters visited Worcester for the Three Choirs Festival and then Gloucester on 28 July. Edward's sister Elizabeth Lady Harcourt accompanied them. The party was received by the bishop and his wife at the Palace, before going to the cathedral, where they were welcomed by the dean and the "Hon. and Rev. Dr Vernon and the minor canons".[55]

The rewards from Edward's two posts were somewhat different. As a prebendary of Gloucester, he received a flat fee of £120 paid annually, plus the use of a house. For his first year, he was appointed sub-dean and received an additional £10. This was a one-year appointment and never repeated.

At Christ Church, the rewards were more substantial and complex. The income for the canons fluctuated with the profits from the landed estate, but probably averaged about £400 a year. Every canon received a basic £5 a quarter, which was supplemented by entry fines and dividends. In the Lady Day quarter of 1786, Edward received £22 8s 0d from entry fines, £32 10s 2¼d from "improvements", £9 7s 6d from meadow hay profits, in addition to his basic £5. Out of this income, he had to pay 6s for lamp lights, £2 10s 3d towards window tax, 10s for wine and 5s as his share of the Christmas box for the canon's cook. His net "pay" was therefore £65 14s 5¼d. He received £180 10s 5½d in the Christmas quarter of the same year. It is clear that the Christ Church canonry was significantly more financially rewarding and probably less demanding in terms of time than the Gloucester prebend. The Christ Church post also gave him the chance to reward friends and family through his right to appoint canoneer students. It is perhaps therefore no surprise that, when promoted to the bishopric of Carlisle, he decided he would prefer to retain the Christ Church role, if he could not keep both.

---

55   *Oxford Journal*, 2 August 1788.

Rector of Sudbury

As rector of Sudbury, Edward was supported by a curate. From his appointment in September 1781 till 1785 the register of baptisms, marriages and burials is largely in his handwriting and signed "EV Vernon Rector". From 1785 to 1788, the registers were kept by Joshua Powell, Curate. Following Powell's departure in the late summer of 1789, George Haggitt took the role. Haggitt was a graduate of Pembroke College, Cambridge, and was ordained deacon only the day before he joined Edward at Sudbury. George Haggitt's father was rector of Rushton in Northamptonshire, so George would have had some understanding of the duties of a curate. His brother was rector of Nuneham Courtenay and chaplain to Earl Harcourt. Haggitt was ordained priest in 1791 and continued to serve the people of Sudbury as curate when Edward became Bishop of Carlisle. He was still in post when Edward resigned as rector in 1803.

Edward baptized his sons at All Saints' Church, Sudbury. George, who was born in August 1785, was followed by Edward in February 1787, Leveson in May 1788, William in June 1789, Frederick in June 1790 and Henry in July 1791. All were baptized approximately a month after birth.

Lady Anne may have accompanied Edward when he was undertaking his duties at Oxford and Gloucester or for the king at the Chapel Royal, but coach journeys would have been most uncomfortable when pregnant. Edward is recorded as preaching before George III at the Chapel Royal in Lent 1791. On 7 July of the same year, he was in Oxford preaching at the anniversary service of the governors of the Radcliffe Infirmary. The service was held at St Peter-in-the-East, as the roof of the usual church, St Mary's, was under repair. £1,081 8s 6d was raised from collections and other events.[56] Hopefully he was with Lady Anne for the birth of Henry, their sixth son, two weeks later.

Edward retained his licence to shoot game whilst rector of Sudbury but decided it was not appropriate for a clergyman to hunt. He was a Justice of the Peace and was often asked to marry friends. In July 1789 he performed the ceremony when Mr Dicken of Heylins Park, near

---

[56] *Oxford Journal*, 18 June 1791.

Burton-on-Trent, married a Miss Fitzherbert of Somersal Herbert. When Louisa, the then only daughter of his half-brother George, second Lord Vernon, died in the south of France, he conducted her burial at Sudbury Church on 19 March 1786.

A happier occasion will have been George's second marriage to Jane Georgiana Fauquier on 25 May 1786. They were married by Edward at her father's house in Stratton Street in London. The marriage was a success and produced two daughters, one of whom died young. George's first marriage had been an unhappy one. Three of their four children had died as infants. The couple had proved to be incompatible. She accused him of being bad-tempered, while his friends put the blame on her. They lived apart for many years till her death in January 1786.

Edward was involved in Sudbury village celebrations. On Thursday, 23 April 1789, King George III's recovery from his first serious illness was marked with bonfires. Two whole sheep were roasted, and a "considerable quantity of ale" was provided by the rector and his brother Lord Vernon. The hall, the rectory and other houses in the village were illuminated and "exhibited several transparencies". The evening concluded with festive harmony.[57]

By the summer of 1791, the press was full of speculation that Edward was to be made a bishop. On 11 June, the *Oxford Journal* was sure he would be appointed Bishop of Lichfield and Coventry: "Lord Stafford [Edward's father-in-law] has been working indefatigably to secure this appointment." *The Derbyshire and Nottinghamshire Advertiser*, the *Chester Chronicle* and the *Newcastle Courant* on 17 June said: "It was settled—Dr Vernon would go to Lincoln." However, a week later it was announced that Dr Vernon was to be appointed to the see of Carlisle.

William Pitt wrote from 10 Downing Street on 23 June 1791: "I have great pleasure in acquainting you that, in consequence of the wish expressed by Lord Stafford, I have had the honour of recommending you to succeed to the bishopric of Carlisle . . . and that his Majesty has been graciously pleased to approve of the appointment. I beg leave to offer you

---

[57] *Derby Mercury*, 2 April 1789.

my congratulations on this occasion and have the honour to be, Sir, your most obedient humble servant W Pitt."[58]

Edward was formally elected to the see of Carlisle by the dean and chapter of Carlisle Cathedral on 28 September 1791. His delight at his promotion must have been tempered by some political concerns. Pitt and his father-in-law were Tories and would expect henceforth his political support. His aristocratic friends in Derbyshire and Nottinghamshire and his Grenville friends from Oxford days were Whigs and would also hope for his endorsement in the House of Lords. He could not avoid an issue by not attending. It was accepted practice for bishops to attend and, where they could not be present, give proxies to other bishops who could attend.

---

[58]   W. Pitt to Dr Vernon, 23 June 1791, HP, Vol. XII, p. 24.

2

Bishop of Carlisle (1791–1807)

Edward Vernon's pleasure at becoming Bishop of Carlisle also brought concern about his future income. If the newspapers had been correct and he had been made Bishop of Lincoln, he would have received about £4,000 a year. If, as he had hoped, he had been offered Durham, he would have received about £6,000 a year.[1] Enquiries to the outgoing Bishop of Carlisle indicated the see had an income of around £1,400 a year. This might be enough to maintain his growing family and even the Bishop of Carlisle's palace of Rose Castle, but it would not be sufficient to enable him to live appropriately in London when Parliament was sitting.

The bishop elect's first tasks were to thank the king and review his financial position. On 13 July, three weeks after receiving his offer letter from the prime minister, William Pitt the Younger, he went with his father-in-law, the Marquis of Stafford, to be presented formally to George III and kiss his hand. He followed this meeting with a letter to Pitt explaining his financial predicament:

> I find from Dr Douglas that the income of the Bishoprick of Carlisle, after the necessary deductions, is about £1,400. It would ill become me, after the very kind manner in which you were pleased to express yourself, when I had the honour of waiting on you, to presume to dictate anything with regard to my present preferments. It is however my wish to retain the living

---

[1]   Earl Gower and Sutherland to the Bishop of Carlisle, 8 February 1795, refers to a dispute between Lord Lambton and the Dean of Durham and states: "Had you therefore obtained the object of your ambition, you would have had to contend with [Lord Lambton]." *Harcourt Papers* (HP), vol. XII, p. 33.

of Sudbury and the canonry of Christ Church; and I am willing to flatter myself that a large family and expensive journeys, together with the rank and character which it will be expected for me to maintain, both in my diocese and in London, may be considered some plea for what I have suggested. I shall only add that, whatever may be your determination on this point, I shall always retain the most grateful sense of the favours you have already conferred on me."[2]

Edward had consulted his friend, the Bishop of Peterborough, before writing to Pitt. Dr Hinchcliffe appears to have discouraged him from writing, but recognized his predicament and was delighted when Pitt agreed to Edward's request: "It is not an imputation to the fair sex only, that they ask advice and, in the end, follow their own inclination. Happy it would be for them could the friend consulted say afterwards, as I do to you, I am glad you preferred your own opinion. The habits of life which a bishop must adopt, besides that you are getting of a child annually, cannot be maintained under two or three and twenty hundred pounds a year; and, if you preserve your form ten or a dozen years longer, half your bishoprick will go in breeches and shoes." Hinchcliffe concluded his letter by saying he planned to call in to Sudbury during the summer and hoped he would be able to assist at Edward's consecration.[3] As a result of Pitt's consent, Edward retained around £400 a year from the Christ Church canonry and £200 a year from the Sudbury living. With the £1,400 from the bishopric of Carlisle, this would give a total of about £2,000, before taking account of £600 income from the marriage settlement. He gave up the canonry at Gloucester, worth £120 a year.

Edward also received a congratulatory letter from his old friend and brother-in-law, now Earl Gower and Sutherland, who was ambassador in Paris during the early stages of the French Revolution. He wrote:

I direct this letter, my letter of congratulations, to *your Lordship* at Oxford … I am extremely pleased with the thoughts of

---

[2]   E. V. Vernon to the Rt. Hon. William Pitt, 15 July 1791, HP, Vol. XII, pp. 26–7.

[3]   Bishop of Peterborough to EVV, 26 July 1791, HP, Vol. XII, pp. 27–8.

someday hearing you deliver a good moral discourse, when the
silence of faction will permit you to confine yourself to morality
ex Cathedra at Carlisle, after having partaken of an excellent
episcopal breakfast at your palace, where Lady Sutherland and
I hope always to be hospitably received on our way to Scotland.

He hoped the bishop and Lady Anne would on some occasion come with
them to Dunrobin, the Sutherland mansion in northern Scotland. Lady
Sutherland sent her congratulations and love to Lady Anne.[4]

London, October 1791 to May 1792

From October 1791 till May 1792 Edward, as the new Bishop of Carlisle,
stayed largely in London. In October, his father-in-law, the Marquess
of Stafford, gave a dinner at his London house for Edward and Lady
Anne. Other guests included Lady Anne's sisters and their husbands,
the Earl and Countess of Carlisle and the Marquess and Marchioness of
Worcester. The Marquess was a Tory MP and married to Lady Charlotte
Leveson Gower; on his father's death he became Duke of Beaufort.

A month later Edward attended a Dining Room at St James's Palace,
where he did homage to King George III. The following day, 4 November
1791, he was consecrated by the Archbishop of York at the Chapel Royal.
A week later, he attended a levee at St James's Palace.[5] He also received
a letter from Prime Minister Pitt asking Edward if, as a canon of Christ
Church, he could secure a studentship for a young man from Bath known
to Lord Bayham.[6] Edward was familiarizing himself with Court life and
his obligations, as a newly appointed bishop, to the politician who had
secured his appointment. He acquired a house at 17 Albemarle Street for

---

[4]   Earl Gower Sutherland to E. V. Vernon, 22 July 1791, HP, Vol. XII, pp. 25–6.

[5]   The levee was a formal reception at St James's Palace at which officials,
diplomates and members of the services were presented to the king.
Introduced by Charles II, the practice continued till 1939.

[6]   W. Pitt to the Bishop of Carlisle, 5 November 1791, HP, Vol. XII, p. 28.

his London home. His brother-in-law Earl Gower occupied 16 Albemarle Street.

On the way to Sudbury for Christmas, Edward and Lady Anne visited his sister and brother-in-law, Lord and Lady Harcourt, at Nuneham. Lord Granville Leveson Gower, Lady Anne's half-brother, was at Christ Church and invited to dinner. He wrote to his mother, Lady Stafford:

> I should certainly have gone to Blanford Park [the Duke of Beaufort's House] the middle of this week had I not been under an engagement to visit the worthy folks at Nuneham. Morpeth [Earl of Carlisle's son] and I went there on Wednesday, dined and slept there. The party consisted of Lord and Lady Harcourt, the Bishop and Lady Anne, the Dowager Lady Vernon and her daughters Anne and Pat—all very respectable and worthy people, but not those who give a very agreeable or lively turn to conversation, but the extreme civility we experienced was a compensation for the dryness of the party. The Bishop and Lady Anne dine at the Deanery [Christ Church] today, where I am also invited. I can assure you the short cassock and wig give him *l'air bien serieux et episcopal.*[7]

The bishop and Lady Anne reached Sudbury in mid-December, where on Sunday 18 he conducted his first ordination. The four deacons, who were all for parishes in Cumbria, can hardly have welcomed the cost and time involved in travelling to Sudbury: William Kilner was a graduate of Queen's College, Oxford and would be earning £30 a year as curate at Dufton; his three fellow ordinands were destined for parishes in the Eden valley and would receive £20 a year.

Returning to London in the middle of January 1792, the bishop attended the king's birthday parade in his own coach: "The body was olive green with the arms and mitre on the mantle. The lining was of a

---

[7]   Lord Granville Leveson Gower to Lady Stafford, December 1791, in Castalia Countess Granville (ed.), *Lord Granville Leveson Gower: Private Correspondence 1781 to 1821*, Vol. I (London: John Murray, 1916), p. 35.

light mixture with the arms woven into the lace."[8] At the end of January, he preached at St Margaret's Westminster on behalf of the Humane Society. He asked Lord Grenville's advice as to whether he should mention that the king supported the society's plans to build a pavilion near the Serpentine to give help to those rescued from the water. Lord Grenville advised against mention of the king's support as it had been an "accidental conversation" at a levee.[9] A month later, the bishop was invited to preach at St James's Piccadilly on behalf of The Society of Ancient Britons. This was a charity which supported the education of poor children of Welsh descent. The advertisement noted that the bishop would speak in English and admission was by ticket only. Preaching in connection with charity fundraising was to be a regular part of the new bishop's London season.

On Sunday 4 March, he ordained ten deacons and five priests at the Chapel Royal on behalf of the Archbishops of Canterbury and York and the Bishops of London, Rochester and Chester. While in London he made a number of clergy appointments to posts in his gift as Bishop of Carlisle.

The pattern of life which Dr Vernon had established in the first few months of his episcopate was to persist for the rest of his life. He would have to spend about half the year in London, interspersed with visits to Sudbury, Oxford and his wife's family home at Trentham. He would typically be in his diocese at Rose Castle for Christmas and New Year and from June to October. He was the first Bishop of Carlisle to treat Rose Castle as his principal family home.

---

[8]   *The Times*, 18 January 1792.

[9]   Lord Grenville to the Bishop of Carlisle, 8 Feb 1792, British Library Add. MS 59003, f. 159 and f. 160.

The eighteenth-century bishop and politics

James Boswell wrote in his biography of Dr Samuel Johnson: "No man can be made a bishop for his learning or piety; his only chance for promotion is being connected with somebody who has a parliamentary interest."[10] Johnson died in 1784.

The link between ecclesiastical preferment and parliamentary interest was of particular importance in the eighteenth century. Bishops seldom held ministerial office, but their influence on parliamentary proceedings was considerable. The votes of the 26 English bishops were important in a House of Lords with, in 1780, 224 members, of which typically about 120–45 attended. Parliament sat from November to May and bishops were expected to attend. The proxy system enabled bishops from more distant dioceses to vote by giving their proxies to another bishop, but proxies were not allowed for committees. Bishops had therefore to be in London for much of the period between November and May.[11] Their work in their dioceses took place largely between June and October, although Edward made a point of being in his diocese over Christmas.

Because bishops were recommended by government ministers to the sovereign, the bench was divided on political lines. As his appointment had been made by Pitt, the Bishop of Carlisle would be expected to support Pitt in the House of Lords. It would be in his interest to do so if he hoped for translation to a more valuable see. For Edward, this would prove awkward when parliamentary factions split, and Pitt and his allies favoured different policies from those of his father-in-law.

In his diocese, the bishop might be expected to report to government ministers on public opinion. At the time Edward became Bishop of Carlisle, there was a great fear that the French Revolution could influence behaviour in Britain, and the Church of England was valued by the government for the moral guidance it provided. It in turn valued its established and privileged status at a time when non-conformity was growing and there were calls for Catholic emancipation.

---

[10]   Quoted in Norman Sykes, *Church and State in England in the XVIII Century* (Cambridge: Cambridge University Press, 1934), p. 41.

[11]   Sykes, *Church and State in England in the XVIII Century*, pp. 46 and 64.

In December 1792, Lord Grenville, who was Foreign Secretary in Pitt's government, asked the Bishop of Carlisle to come to London to attend the House of Lords. The bishop replied he thought he would be more useful to the government if he remained in Carlisle:

> Pains have been taken to excite a spirit of disaffection amongst the manufacturers in Carlisle and its vicinity, but I have the pleasure to add that such attempts have not hitherto been attended with the smallest success, so far from it that on Sunday last when I preached in the cathedral, a report having been spread that the object of my discourse would be to explain the necessity of subordination in society and to recommend obedience to the laws, the church was prodigiously crowded; and upon my entrance, the organist, to gratify what appeared to be the general wish and opinion of the congregation, played God Save the King.

The bishop went on to say that the disposition of the people was not yet perverted, but a seditious pamphlet had since been circulated entitled "The Call to Freedom". The bishop believed it was the result of a drunken frolic and that the authors were now ashamed of it. He also mentioned that the audience at an exhibition in Whitehaven a few days previously demanded "God Save the King".[12]

The bishop was expected to be hospitable to the laity and the clergy and to know and be known to the owners of the great estates in his Carlisle diocese. The most influential local landowner was James, Earl of Lonsdale, who lived at Lowther Castle, south of Penrith. He used much of his huge income of £45,000 a year to control many of the local parliamentary seats in the Whig interest. He died in 1802 without children, and his estates were inherited by a cousin William, Viscount Lowther, who was created Earl of Lonsdale in 1807.

The second major landowner in the area was the bishop's brother-in-law, the Earl of Carlisle, who owned the Naworth estate at Brampton, east of Carlisle. The main family house was Castle Howard near York.

---

[12] Bishop of Carlisle to Lord Grenville, 6 December 1792, British Library Add. MS 59003, f. 162.

Naworth was used for shooting parties, to which the bishop was invited. One day, when it was proposed that a diversion should be organized so that the bishop could view Hadrian's Wall, he is said to have replied: "Never mind the wall; show me the grouse."[13] When it came to politics, the Lonsdale and Carlisle interests did not always coincide, and Edward sometimes found himself caught in the middle.

Other local families whom he knew and entertained included the Howards at Corby Castle on the river Eden, the Grahams at Netherby and the Wallaces at Featherstone Castle. The bishop was also involved with the local MPs. Walter Spencer Stanhope, MP for Carlisle 1802–12 and a cousin of Lord Lonsdale, said of the bishop: "What a picturesque sight he invariably presented in his full bottomed wig and bright purple coat. The good Bishop, although extremely stately, was gifted with a keen sense of humour and could enjoy a spice of frivolity when he could indulge in it without detracting from his dignity."[14]

Rose Castle

Rose Castle, in the parish of Dalston, is about eight miles south of Carlisle and had been the home of the Bishops of Carlisle since 1270. It stands on high ground overlooking the Caldew Valley. A priority for the new bishop was to improve the house to meet the needs of his growing family. Repairs and improvements commenced in March 1792 and continued until August. The main reception rooms and six bedrooms were painted. An additional staircase was inserted and improvements made to the stables, coach house and farmyard. In 1793 and 1794, farm fields were fenced and gates were replaced; land was improved and new offices and a joiner's shop created.

---

[13] Frederick Leveson Gower, *Bygone Years* (London: John Murray, 1905), p. 17. Frederick was the bishop's nephew.

[14] Marianne Spencer Stanhope to her brother John Spencer Stanhope, 4 December 1805, A. M. W. Stirling, *The Letter-Bag of Lady Elizabeth Spencer Stanhope*, Vol. 1 (London, New York: J. Lane, 1913), p. 36.

ROSE CASTLE.

The Seat of the Hon.ble & R.t Rev.d E.V Vernon L.L.D
Lord Bishop of Carlisle

Rose Castle, the Bishop of Carlisle's home in Edward's time

During the two-year period 1795–6, over £500 was spent on a series of major improvements. Steps were renewed, the walls in the hall plastered, the dining room enlarged and its ceiling replaced. A new passage was cut through the nine-foot-six-inch walls of the thirteenth-century tower to improve communication. Smaller repairs and alterations continued in subsequent years to meet the needs of the bishop's expanding family and support staff. He improved the garden in 1800 by bringing soil from the woods and bought shrubs from Keswick and Scotland. In 1805, almost £300 was spent on enlarging the drawing room and installing a marble fireplace. In 1806, a register office and a steward's office were created in what is now Rose Castle farm.

During his 13 years as Bishop of Carlisle, Dr Vernon spent a total of £2,235 8s 10d on the building, gardens and farm. £1,506 12s was recovered from the sale of timber, leaving the bishop to find £728 16s 10d from his own funds. He spent a further £30 on bath stoves in various rooms and paid £29 10s to Mr Watson of Dalston Mills for losses on timber supplies.[15]

Samuel Taylor Coleridge and William and Dorothy Wordsworth visited Rose Castle in August 1803. William and Dorothy's father John had been agent to James, Earl of Lonsdale, but the Earl had never paid John Wordsworth the £5,000 he was owed. The debt was only settled when his cousin William Lowther succeeded and became a close friend of William Wordsworth. Dorothy wrote in her *Journals*: "Passed Rose Castle upon the Caldew, an ancient building of red stone with sloping gardens, an ivied gateway, velvet lawns, old garden wall, trim flower beds with stately and luxuriant flowers. We walked up to the house and stood some minutes watching the swallows that flew about restlessly." Coleridge wrote: "All, all perfect—cottage comfort and ancestral dignity." [16] The bishop's gardener, Mr Jordan, had died in March 1801, but he must have been replaced with someone of equal talent.

---

15   Carlisle Diocese Bishop's General Register, Carlisle Diocesan Archives, DRC 1/8; Canon David Weston, *Rose Castle and the Bishops of Carlisle 1133–2012* (Carlisle: Cumberland & Westmoreland Antiquarian and Archaeological Society, 2013), p. 87.

16   Quoted in Weston, *Rose Castle and the Bishops of Carlisle*, p. 88.

Local landowners and clergy enjoyed visits to Rose Castle. William Lord Lonsdale stayed on his way from Lowther Castle to civic functions in Carlisle. Isaac Milner, the Dean of Carlisle and a noted evangelical, was a regular summer visitor. His niece wrote:

> Perhaps one of his greatest joys was to spend a few quiet days at Rose Castle with his friend the Bishop of Carlisle. The mode of living there was such as suited his taste. There was no pomp, no oppressive style. He used to saunter about the meadows and hay fields while engaged in conversation with his host, and, as he more than once told his friend after he became Archbishop of York, he liked the simplicity of Rose Castle a great deal better than the splendour of Bishopthorpe.[17]

Milner was by all accounts an entertaining guest. He spent two months a year in residence as Dean of Carlisle. His main role was president of Queens' College, Cambridge.

There were regular visits from Lady Anne's large family and from others on their way north. Her brother George, the Earl Gower and Sutherland, and his wife the Countess of Sutherland, as well as Lady Anne's eldest sister Louisa and her husband Sir Archibald Macdonald, the Lord Chief Baron, stayed en route to Scotland. The Earl of Carlisle and his wife, Lady Anne's sister Caroline, visited when staying at Naworth. The visits were reciprocated, with the bishop and his family regularly staying at Castle Howard. Lord Castlereagh, sometime Secretary of State for War and Foreign Secretary, stayed in August 1806 on his way to his house in Ireland. Castlereagh was a supporter of William Pitt and a friend of Lord Lowther.

After they had left home, Edward and Lady Anne's older children saw Rose Castle as the main family home. When writing to each other, letters would usually be sent to Rose Castle rather than to their school or college or to the London house. With at times up to 15 children there and many visitors, it is difficult to think Rose Castle was a very peaceful place.

---

17   Mary Milner, *Life of Isaac Milner, Dean of Carlisle* (London and Cambridge: J. W. Palmer, J. J. Deighton, 1842), p. 327.

Episcopal duties

Carlisle diocese was established in 1133, and its geographical area was designed to coincide with the lands of the Earl of Carlisle. The diocese had just 127 benefices; only Rochester was smaller, with 94. In terms of population, it was the second smallest, with about 125,000. It covered only the northern portions of the counties of Cumberland and Westmoreland, stretching down the coast to the River Derwent just north of Workington.[18] Because of its modest size, the bishop was able to get to know his clergy in a way which would not have been possible in a large diocese such as York.

The bishop was supported by a single archdeacon for the whole of the diocese. William Paley had been appointed to the role by a previous Bishop of Carlisle in 1782. Paley was educated at Giggleswick School, where his father was headmaster, and Christ's College, Cambridge, where he became a Fellow. He was rector of Dalston, the parish for Rose Castle, till 1793, when he exchanged the living for the more valuable one of Stanwix, which was in the gift of the Bishop of Carlisle. Dalston was worth about £50 a year and Stanwix £132 12s.[19] Paley was at the same time rector of Addingham, rector of Great Salkeld, chancellor of the Carlisle diocese and a canon of Carlisle Cathedral. He was supported by curates in all three parishes. He resigned from the parishes in 1795 on his appointment as rector of Bishop Wearmouth in Durham but continued to live in Carlisle and remained archdeacon.

Paley's duties as archdeacon were light and his chief contribution to the life of the Church was as the author of *Principles of Moral and Political Philosophy*, which ran to many editions, and *View of Evidences of Christianity*. The bishop took a considerable interest in Paley's writings

---

[18] Clergy of the Church of England database (CCEd), Carlisle diocese description. The figures come from a survey of 1829–30. The population would probably have been smaller in EVH's time.

[19] Archdeacon Paley to the Bishop of Carlisle, undated, HP, Vol. XII, p. 93.

and, for the 1793 edition of *Moral and Political Philosophy*, suggested changes which Paley adopted and submitted to him for approval.[20]

Paley also discussed the nature of evangelical doctrines with him. Dean Isaac Milner of Carlisle Cathedral was a noted evangelical preacher. Paley, according to Milner's biographer, mentioned Milner's great powers to the bishop: "I told the Bishop of Carlisle that about evangelical doctrines themselves I must leave him to judge, but if he chose to hear them used with great ability and placed in the most striking point of view, he must go and hear our dean."[21] No doubt evangelical doctrines were discussed during the bishop and Milner's walks at Rose Castle. Edward was content to appoint evangelical clergymen and found them generally hard working.

The Bishop of Carlisle was fortunate that he had the patronage of 20 out of the 127 livings in his diocese. He also had the patronage of a further ten livings: five in Lincoln diocese, three in Durham and two in Lichfield and Coventry. One of those he chose to assist was the Revd Joseph Dacre Carlyle, the son of a Carlisle doctor, who was Professor of Arabic at Cambridge. Carlyle was perpetual curate of St Cuthbert's in Carlisle, a canon of Carlisle Cathedral and rector of Kirklinton. In 1792, the bishop offered Carlyle the more valuable rectory of Torpenhow in exchange for Kirklinton. The dean and chapter of Carlisle Cathedral then added Castle Sowerby to his portfolio in 1793. The parishes relied on the services of curates for day-to-day clerical support, for Carlyle not only had his duties in Cambridge to consider, but also decided in 1799 to join Lord Elgin as his chaplain on Elgin's expedition to Constantinople. Carlyle did not return to Carlisle until the autumn of 1801.[22]

Carlyle was another regular visitor to Rose Castle, and the bishop and Carlyle exchanged lengthy letters throughout Carlyle's expedition to Turkey and the Middle East. Carlyle wrote from Constantinople of his

---

[20]　Archdeacon Paley to the Bishop of Carlisle, 1 November 1793, HP, Vol. XII, pp, 30–2.

[21]　Milner, *Life of Isaac Milner*, p. 116.

[22]　St Cuthbert's in Carlisle, Torpenhow and Castle Sowerby all had curates for the duration of Carlyle's expedition. *Clergy of the Church of England database*, accessed 26 April 2023.

first stop in Lisbon: "The filthiness of the place is beyond all conception. I have it in my nostrils at this moment." After Gibraltar, the party stopped at Palermo, where they found Lord Nelson, Sir William and Lady Hamilton and the Nepalese Court, which was "no very brilliant spectacle". With his knowledge of Arabic, Carlyle was able to make a large collection of Arabic poetry, which he subsequently published. Carlyle much appreciated the bishop's letters and repeatedly stated how he missed Cumberland: "How do I long to thank you in person for the kind sentiments [your letter] contains! How do I wish once more to participate in the quiet comforts of your domestic circle! Once more to enjoy the green fields and the blue mountains that stretch themselves before your windows."[23]

Carlyle did not entirely forget his parishes whilst on his expedition. His sister had written to him to say that his curate at Castle Sowerby, Robert Nicholas French, had obtained a living in Derbyshire. Carlyle wrote to the bishop:

> I much regret the loss of a representative who was so much approved by your Lordship and who, by every account, was deserving of your approbation. I trust your Lordship has fixed upon a successor as you liked ... I fancy your Lordship would think it right for him to engage to teach the school as long as he remained on the Curacy. In that case I would wish to increase the salary four or five pounds, or perhaps it would be better to give him the additional sum specifically on account of teaching the school."[24]

William Tiffin, who succeeded French, received £30 a year for the curacy. What extra he received for teaching is not recorded. Carlyle was clearly aware that the bishop had met his curate, a sign that Edward took trouble to know his clergy.

One of the principal methods by which a bishop might learn more about his clergy was through a visitation. Meetings were organized

---

[23]   J. D. Carlyle to the Bishop of Carlisle, ten letters dated 14 November 1799 to 24 July 1801, HP, Vol. XII, pp. 45–91.

[24]   J. D. Carlyle to the Bishop of Carlisle, 14 January 1801, HP, Vol. XII, pp. 80–1.

around the diocese and the clergyman's presence or absence noted. The meetings enabled the bishop to check that the clergy had the appropriate documentation covering ordination, institution, licence and, where the rector or vicar held more than one living, a dispensation from the Archbishop. Dr Edward Vernon, as already noted, had a dispensation to allow him to continue as rector of Sudbury. The bishop could also ask such supplementary questions as he thought appropriate to ensure he had a full picture of his diocese.

Edward's first visitation as Bishop of Carlisle took place in June 1792. It was his practice to hold confirmations at the same time. The advertisement for his second visitation three years later appeared in the *Cumberland Pacquet* on 17 March 1795 and explains how matters were organized. The clergy were given three months' notice.

Visitation

The Bishop of Carlisle intends to hold his VISITATION at CARLISLE on Monday Eighth June 1795, at PENRITH on Tuesday Ninth, at APPLEBY on Wednesday Tenth, at WIGTON on Friday Twelfth. The Bishop will also confirm on the days aforementioned and all those who may wish to be confirmed must bring with them a Certificate of them having been examined and approved by the ministers of their respective parishes. It is required that no minister will grant such certificates to persons under the age of fourteen years.

Taking account of the speed a coach could travel and the distances involved, the bishop, even if he stayed overnight, would not have had much time to meet the clergy individually. Assuming a quarter of the clergy attended each location, there would have been up to 30 incumbents at each place, plus perhaps 20 curates. The numbers confirmed would have been substantial. For example, between 1,400 and 1,500 people were confirmed at Carlisle in June 1801 after the bishop delivered "an excellent charge to his reverend brethren".[25]

June 1801 was a busy month for the Bishop of Carlisle. Having completed the fourth day of his visitation and confirmations at Penrith on Wednesday 17 June for his own diocese, he travelled swiftly to Yorkshire to start a series of eight days of confirmations for the Archbishop of York. He was in Stokesley on Friday 19, Whitby Saturday 20, Scarborough Sunday 21, Bridlington Monday 22, Beverley Tuesday 23, and Hull Wednesday 24. He had two days of travel and recovery on Thursday 25 and Friday 26, before undertaking confirmations in Malton on Saturday 27 and Thirsk on Sunday 28. The number of confirmation candidates was large. Over 3,000 were confirmed at Whitby and Beverley and over 4,000 in Hull, including the 17 sons and daughters of a farmer from Holderness. From Friday 10 June to Sunday 28 June, he had an almost continuous stream of engagements, for he had included an ordination at Rose Castle on Sunday 12 June between his visitation days in his own diocese.[26]

In his final letter from Naples in July 1801, Carlyle expressed regret that he would not be back in time for the bishop's visitation: "Your Lordship's visitation will no doubt be over before I can reach the diocese. If it were not, with what pleasure should I accompany you! How different would the journey be through our green and quiet fields from most of the countries I have recently gone through."[27] As chancellor for the Diocese of Carlisle, Carlyle should have accompanied the bishop on his visitation. Shortly after Carlyle's return Edward used his patronage to appoint Carlyle as vicar of St Nicholas, Newcastle. Carlyle died there in 1804.

The bishop was also able to get to know his neighbours and his clergy by holding public days at Rose Castle. These were advertised in the press. The timing varied each year, but the public days were always four days in July, August or early September. In theory anyone could come, but they took place during the working week. Each day was a week apart.

---

[25]   *Carlisle Journal*, 13 June 1801.

[26]   *Hull Pacquet*, 5 May 1801; *Carlisle Journal*, 2 May 1801; *Ipswich Journal*, 4 July 1801. The bishop's charges were not published.

[27]   J. D. Carlyle to the Bishop of Carlisle, 24 July 1801, HP, Vol. XII, p. 91.

In 1801 the days were Thursday 9, 16, 23 and 30 July. Every clergyman had the chance to come and meet his bishop informally if he so wished.

A further major responsibility for a bishop was ordination. Through this process he would get to know the new deacons and priests coming into his diocese and could assess their quality. In his time as Bishop of Carlisle, Edward Vernon conducted 44 services of ordination. Most ordinations were public occasions advertised in the press. The advertisements had a standard format. Candidates were required to send papers to the bishop a fortnight before the ordination, which invariably took place on a Sunday in Rose Castle chapel. They were also obliged to attend for an examination at 10 a.m. on the Thursday prior to ordination. The numbers ordained ranged from two to a maximum of 12, typically seven to eight.

In his early years as Bishop of Carlisle, from 1792 to 1794, Edward took four ordinations at the Chapel Royal in the early months of the year for other bishops. In later years, he took three at Rose Castle for other bishops. On one occasion, he ordained a deacon for the East India Company. Private unadvertised ordinations took place at both Rose Castle and on three occasions at Sudbury. These private ordinations were often for family members, such as his Anson nephews, or sons of friends, including Edward Hinchcliffe, son of his friend, the Bishop of Peterborough.

Excluding those ordained for other bishops, Dr Vernon ordained 95 deacons and 85 priests for his diocese. The overwhelming majority were literates—that is, they did not have a degree from Oxford or Cambridge University. Such candidates would in most instances have received training from an experienced clergyman, who supplemented his income by assisting candidates with their post-school education. For example, the Revd John Robinson, master of Ravenstonedale Free Grammar School, advertised his services and mentioned references could be obtained from the Revd Walter Fletcher, vicar of Dalston and domestic chaplain to the Bishop of Carlisle.

Of the 95 deacons ordained by Dr Vernon, information on their education was provided for 79. Only 19, or 24 per cent, had university degrees. Of the 73 priests for which data was available, 23, or 32 per cent, had a degree. The Diocese of Carlisle had a higher proportion of non-graduates than, for example, York at this period. A number of factors affected the ability of the Diocese of Carlisle to attract graduates, including its geographical isolation and the generally low level of remuneration. Few incumbents could afford to pay a curate. The register entry for 8 September 1800 noted that Thomas Singleton was to be assistant curate at Allhallows, near Aspatria: "The Curate Mr Chambers is too poor to pay a curate and too infirm to officiate himself." Chambers had been at All Hallows for 43 years.[28]

Legislation passed in 1714 laid down the minimum stipend for a curate of £20 and a maximum of £50. It was up to the bishops to ensure curates were adequately rewarded. Information on remuneration levels in Carlisle diocese was available for 65 of the 95 deacons. The table below indicates that remuneration increased during Dr Vernon's time there. The most common stipend was £20 a year between 1791 and 1799, with one deacon receiving only £15. Some may have been able to supplement their salary with teaching at the local school or being provided with accommodation. By the time Dr Vernon moved on to York, the most common salary was £30, with one fortunate curate receiving £50.[29]

Deacons' stipends in the Diocese of Carlisle 1791 to 1807

Year Band	Under £25	£25–£29	£30–£39	£40 or more	Totals
1791–5	10	0	3	1	14
1796–9	12	5	1	1	19
1800–3	7	4	4	4	19
1804–7	0	3	6	4	13
Totals	29	12	14	10	65

---

[28] Chambers was a literate and had been licensed as a deacon in 1757 and priested in 1759. *Clergy of the Church of England database*, accessed 23 April 2023.

[29] Information on deacons' stipends is taken from the Ordination Returns in Bishop's Register, Carlisle Diocesan Archives, DRC/1/8.

Preaching

As a bishop, Dr Vernon was frequently asked to preach on behalf of charities during the London season. Most of his engagements were for charities concerned with the welfare of women and children. In March 1793, he preached the anniversary sermon for the Lying-in Charity, which assisted poor married women giving birth at home. The Prince of Wales was a patron and attended the service at which Bishop Vernon preached. In 1796, he preached in the chapel of the Asylum for Female Orphans and in 1798 at St Martin-in-the-Fields for the Westminster General Dispensary, which benefited the poor of Westminster. In April 1800, and again in April 1805, he preached for the Freemasons' Charity for children, and in 1803 for the Ladies' Charity school, which taught 51 poor girls and helped them find work.

As a chaplain to the king, Bishop Vernon continued to preach every year at the Chapel Royal, usually in Lent. On Sunday 27 February 1803, he preached on the text 1 Peter 3:15: "But sanctify the Lord in your hearts; and be ready always to give an answer to every man that asketh you a reason of the hope that is in you with meekness and fear." His friend Lord Grenville attended as well as Lord Woodhouse, Lord Folkestone and the Marchioness of Bath, along with other members of the aristocracy. King George, Queen Charlotte and their daughters did not attend, as the king thought he had caught a cold in the chapel, which he believed had brought on his last serious illness.[30]

The bishop was also required to take his turn to preach before the Lords at Westminster Abbey. On 30 January 1794, his sermon had to mark the anniversary of the martyrdom of King Charles I. He chose as his text Ecclesiastes 7:8: "Better is the end of a thing than the beginning thereof; and the patient in spirit is better than the proud in spirit." The House of Lords met at one o'clock, and the Lord Chancellor, Earls Kellie and Morton, and nine bishops processed to the Abbey to hear the Bishop of Carlisle's words.

Creating an appropriate sermon to commemorate the execution of Charles I was difficult, particularly during the French Revolution.

---

[30] *British Press*, 28 February 1803.

Dr Vernon stated that, if our passions and our resentments cannot be indulged with impunity in private life, "it would surely be strange should we permit ourselves to think that they may be so indulged, if not with absolute impunity, yet at least with less hazard in the conflicts of political parties and civil dissensions". He accepted that the causes of alarm to the nation in Charles I's time were many, but that these causes did not justify overthrowing the constitution. He drew parallels with the ongoing French Revolution: "If the miseries which our fathers were doomed to suffer have not yet been sufficient to teach us righteousness and wisdom, let us at least learn those lessons from the still more dreadful miseries of our neighbours." He concluded: "For ourselves let us bow before our God with humility and fear . . . And beg devoutly that he would never punish us by a renewal of those delusions or suffer us to be again so tempted." As for the French government, he accepted it was necessary to seek security through war but that people should be reminded that the religion which they had rejected had taught them to pray for their happiness and peace. The sermon ended: "Pity and forgive the infatuation of thy miserable and fallen creatures."[31]

In line with custom at the time, the sermon was published, and Edward sent copies to friends. Lord Thurlow wrote: "I think the idea was justly conceived and neatly applied to the occasion. This unavoidably lies a little too near to political discussion, which the Sermon, however, keeps at a proper distance." However, not everyone agreed. His brother-in-law Earl Gower and Sutherland commented: "I have read your sermon with some attention, and I find in it much to commend, and no part of it liable to criticism. Mr Curwen must be a hypercritic if it meets with his censure." Mr Curwen was probably John Christian Curwen, who lived at Workington Hall and was an MP for Carlisle at the time.[32]

The sermon to mark King Charles I's martyrdom was Edward's only published sermon for this period in his life. Although it is not possible

---

[31]　Edward Vernon Harcourt, Lord Bishop of Carlisle, *A sermon preached before the Lords Spiritual and Temporal at the Abbey Church of St Peter, Westminster, 30 January 1794* (London: R. Faulder, 1794).

[32]　Lord Thurlow to the Bishop of Carlisle, 13 March 1794, and Earl Gower and Sutherland to the Bishop of Carlisle, 8 February 1795, HP, Vol. XII, pp. 32–4.

to make a judgement about the quality of his preaching from a single sermon, it seems unlikely he would have been invited to preach on behalf of charities unless his preaching drew in a sizable congregation. He mentions in the letter to Lord Grenville quoted above that Carlisle Cathedral was well filled when he preached and, prior to his appointment as a bishop, his preaching was well regarded in Bath. It seems reasonable to conclude he was a competent preacher.

Family life

The whole family did not go to Rose Castle until the summer of 1794, when the initial building work was completed. Lady Anne wrote from there to her eldest son, George, in September 1793. George, who had just celebrated his eighth birthday, was staying with his maternal grandparents at Trentham: "I am sure my dear boy will not give us reason to repent of having indulged him, by taking him there, instead of leaving him at home, and that he will be as obedient and attentive to his grandpa, grandmamma and his aunts, as if we were there ourselves." Lady Anne described Rose Castle to George: "This is a charming place, with very pleasant fields for you to walk and ride in, and we have fixed upon comfortable apartments for you and your brothers; but we shall have some trouble in getting you all here next year, for it was with great difficulty that we performed our journey in two days and a half, altho' we travelled till between ten and eleven o'clock at night."[33] Lady Anne had been to Rose Castle in August 1792 with the baby Granville, for he was baptized at Dalston Church on 26 August following his birth on 20 July. Their eighth son, Octavius, was born on Christmas Day 1793 at Rose Castle and baptized at Dalston on 20 January 1794.

When, therefore, all eight boys first came to Rose Castle in the summer of 1794, George was nine, Edward seven, Leveson six, William just five, Frederick four, Henry nearly three, Granville one and Octavius

---

[33] Lady Anne Vernon to her son George Vernon, 15 September 1793, HP, Vol. XII, p. 286.

six months. For the next 13 years, it was to be home to the growing family. Lady Anne gave birth to another eight children during this period.

The bishop and Lady Anne were fortunate that only one of their 16 children died shortly after birth. Their ninth child and first daughter, Caroline, was born 18 June 1795 and baptized at Dalston 14 July. Anne was born 23 November 1796; Charles two years later on 9 November 1798, and Francis three years later on 7 January 1801. Louisa Elisabeth was born on 2 February 1802, lived only a few days and was buried at Dalston. Their eleventh son and fourteenth child Egerton was born 15 months later on 12 May 1803. Two more daughters completed the family—Louisa Augusta, born on 23 November 1804 and Georgiana, born on 29 June 1807. By that date, George was 22 and MP for Lichfield, Lady Anne was 46 and the bishop rising 50.

The bishop was closely involved with his sons' education and maintained a well-ordered routine for the children. Writing to his eldest son George in October 1796, when George was at Westminster, he stated he had received a letter from the headmaster: "He says you are come to Westminster for your holidays; do not however imagine that he means to reflect upon you by that expression, very far from it, for I am sure he is satisfied by your diligence and attention to your school business; all he intended to insinuate was that you were worked harder at home than at school."[34]

In a subsequent letter a month later, the bishop wrote to George to tell him how he and his brother Edward, who was also at Westminster, should behave when visiting their uncle and aunt in their London house:

> As you are now in the habit of going occasionally to the Chief Baron's, it is very necessary I should mention [something] to you. I mean that the Chief Baron and Lady Louisa having the same ideas about education as your mama and myself, have accustomed their children to unite amusement with education, and of course to devote some part of every evening to instruction.

---

[34] The Bishop of Carlisle to George Vernon, 11 October 1796, HP, Vol. XII, pp. 37–8.

Their father feared that George and Edward's visits might interrupt this plan and advised the boys to read books or maps for part of the evening and not to play all the time with their cousins.[35]

Dr Vernon's surviving letters do not just discuss schoolwork and behaviour. For example, he wrote to George (aged ten) on 17 June 1796 to say that the boys' rabbits had not multiplied as much as expected, "but you will probably find a pretty large stock when you come home in August". He told George: "Your lamb is become a mother and perhaps next year will become a grandmother, as her present offspring is a female." He noted that George's pony had become fat, as it only got exercise when the coachman took William riding. Dr Vernon mentioned in a subsequent letter that the family planned to go on holiday to the Cumberland coast at Allonby or Maryport for a fortnight and asked whether George and Edward would like to go with them or prefer to stay at Rose Castle. If the two boys did not want to come, the family would go before the school holidays.[36]

Dr Vernon appears to have had an open and confident relationship with his children. Writing to George in March 1797 when Leveson was three months short of his ninth birthday, he expressed his anxiety about Leveson:

> I have not yet determined what to do with Leveson; he has gained so much since he has been with me, that I am perfectly persuaded he would acquire more real knowledge of Latin, French etc. in one month at home than six at school; were his requirements to exactly [match] those of a parrot, to say things by rote, without at all understanding the sense of what he said.

His father complained that Leveson had a glorious disregard for any distinction of cases, tenses, moods and voices. He seemed to have been taught a few things over and over again, though his father admitted he

---

[35] The Bishop of Carlisle to George Vernon, 22 November 1796, HP, Vol. XII, pp. 39–40.

[36] The Bishop of Carlisle to George Vernon, 17 June 1796, HP, Vol. XII, pp. 34–6.

was "pretty perfect in the Westminster Latin syntax and could translate a collect or two or two or three verses of a psalm into Latin". Dr Vernon did not begrudge the time he had spent on teaching Leveson but concluded he needed to return to school "to be routed and bustled about".[37]

The boys were asked at the age of about ten or eleven whether or not they wished to be ordained. Their father realized there was a limit to his patronage. George chose the diplomatic service. Edward and Leveson both said they wanted to be ordained. William, the fourth son, who also wanted to be ordained, was told to make his selection between the army and the navy. He chose the navy without having any great liking for the calling. His three older brothers followed their father to Westminster. George, Edward and Leveson were all Captains of School and went on, like their father, to Christ Church, Oxford. William was sent to sea as a midshipman in 1801 at the age of 12. He joined his ship in Plymouth, staying on the way with his aunt, Lady Georgiana Eliot, another of his mother's sisters, and Mr Eliot at Port Eliot.

The Vernon brothers enjoyed corresponding with each other. Both George and Edward wrote to William from Westminster. Edward sent the seven-year-old William some Latin verse he had composed. William wrote back to George with a translation of Edward's verse into English and told him he would translate the rest of the poem, if he would send it to him. The older boys much missed William when he went to sea. Leveson wrote to his mother: "I felt the loss of him most severely. In the holidays he was a never-failing source of amusement to us. He had a perpetual fund of conversation. He used to amuse us by relating the things that had happened in our absence [at Westminster] and was for ever inventing new schemes."[38]

Of the remaining seven sons, four—Granville, Henry, Charles and Egerton—went to Westminster. Only Henry was not Captain of School. Frederick and Octavius followed William into the navy at the age of 12. Francis went to Sandhurst in preparation for a career in the army. The boys who did not go to Westminster were schooled locally with

---

[37]   The Bishop of Carlisle to George Vernon, 12 March 1797, HP, Vol. XII, pp. 42–4.

[38]   Leveson Vernon to Lady Anne Vernon, undated, HP, Vol. XIII, p. 49.

the Revd John Fawcett. He was headmaster of Carlisle Free Grammar School from June 1795 until August 1803 and also took private pupils. Fawcett had local connections, as his cousins lived at Scaleby Castle. He was assistant curate and then perpetual curate of St Cuthbert's, a major church in Carlisle in the gift of the dean and chapter of the cathedral. He was appointed by Dean Milner and became the leader of the evangelical party in Carlisle. His evangelical leanings did not stop the bishop from entrusting the education of Frederick and Octavius to his care. William and Henry may also have been sent to the Grammar School or to Fawcett as private pupils, but this is not corroborated in the surviving family correspondence or in the Carlisle Free Grammar School records.[39]

When William was away at sea, his father took trouble to keep him up to date with family news. Writing to him from Rose Castle in October 1804, he advised him:

> His beloved mother will, I trust, present you with a little brother or sister before the departure of the December packet, in which case you may expect to hear from me [Louisa Augusta was born 23 November 1804]. George and Edward are both at Oxford. George extremely grown; of Edward's size there never was any doubt; the latter writes verses remarkably well, *d'ailleurs* is an incomparable scholar; so is George but not equal to him as a poet. Leveson is greatly improved in mind and attainments, and is a truly honest fellow. Frederick is on the 'Latona' ... and is excessively fond of the profession. Henry and Granville at Westminster—both doing well, but Granville the better scholar, though a year younger. Octavius at Mr Fawcett's apparently as clownish as you please. Charles, Francis and Egerton are severally promising for their age; Charles evidently very quiet. Caroline just what she was, as engaging as ever, only taller and stouter. Anne altered only by being grown. Caroline has begun learning music and takes great pains to improve herself in it.

Their father concluded by saying how thankful he was to hear William had fully recovered from his illness—he had had yellow fever. His tutor on board the ship had written to the bishop to report on William's health and education. The bishop suggested the tutor, Mr Jenkins, should visit them in London on his return.[40]

Edward, who was now at Christ Church but spending the summer at Rose, wrote to his brother William in July 1805: "Considering the anxiety we are all in for news from your quarter of the globe, your correspondence would not be less acceptable for being more frequent [William was in Jamaica at the time]. Edward reported on his sisters: "Anne's knee is almost well; Caroline is getting on very well with her music, but between you and I (tho' I dare not say it openly) she will never sing, she has not an idea of it." Edward asked whether William was still studying Latin and Greek or was now concentrating on English literature. He wrote his father had discouraged him from writing poetry because it might interfere with his classical studies. Edward stated: "[The Muse] is the only Lady whose hand I am ambitious to obtain." He asked William to send him anything he had written. He hoped he had received the letter George had written and thanked him for the letter he sent to Leveson.[41]

Lady Anne also wrote regularly to her children when away from home to give them news from Rose Castle. She told George about a carriage accident:

> Your papa preached this morning at Raughton Head [the nearest church to Rose Castle] and the coachman told two of the maids that, if they would walk that way, he would give them a ride home. Jenny, housemaid, was one of the favoured nymphs; in order to display her grandeur to the humble foot walkers, she meant to make a most noble bow and in so doing, thrust her head through the glass.

---

40 The Bishop of Carlisle to W. Vernon, 25 October 1804, HP, Vol. XII, pp. 101–2.
41 E. Vernon to W. Vernon, 28 July 1805, HP, Vol. XII, pp. 107–8.

The housemaid was not hurt, but what was unfortunate was that there was no carriage glass obtainable in the locality to make a quick repair.[42]

Lady Anne also kept William up to date on family matters and political developments. In her letter of May 1804, she told William she wished she could send him a copy of a caricature of Lord Grenville endeavouring with a pitchfork to cram Mr Fox down the king's throat. In June 1805, she commented that the improvements to the drawing room, stairs and passage to the nurseries at Rose were complete, but decorating and furnishing was not yet done, so the family could not get any benefit yet from the improvements. She noted all the family was well, except Anne, whose lameness was causing concern. Her education was suffering, and she had to be constantly out of doors. The treatments she was having for her knee were very time consuming—warm salt and water had to be poured onto the knee from eight feet several times a day. Lady Anne was herself teaching Charles, but she had secured a 17-year-old governess for Caroline, as she had not the time with Anne's illness to teach Caroline herself. She and the governess both agreed on "the proper system of education". The younger children sometimes went with their parents to London, where tutors were engaged for subjects such as history, geography, music and dancing.

It is very evident that both Bishop Vernon and his wife were directly involved with the upbringing of their children whilst the family lived at Rose Castle. They made time to teach them personally and wrote regularly to them when away from home to give both family and political news. The children in their turn wrote regularly to their parents and siblings discussing their educational progress or, in the case of William and Frederick, providing vivid accounts of their life at sea. The bishop and Lady Anne enjoyed a close and open relationship with their children, something perhaps not so common amongst their aristocratic peers at this time. The children enjoyed a rich and varied life with their siblings and their many first cousins. Many years later William had a discussion with his sister Louisa just before his wedding and concluded they had 78 first cousins.[43]

---

[42]   Lady Anne Vernon to George Vernon, 9 April 1797, HP, Vol. XII, p. 291.

[43]   William Vernon to Matilda Gooch, 18 May 1824, HP, Vol. XIII, p. 163.

The unfortunate affair of Mr Ching's lozenges

In December 1798, Dr Vernon, as Bishop of Carlisle, wrote a letter which was thereafter widely used to promote a potentially fatal medicine. From January 1799 until he was promoted in 1807, an apothecary, Mr Ching, arranged for the letter (below) to appear in numerous newspapers throughout the country. The letter appeared amongst other regular correspondence and did not seem to be an advertisement.

> From the Hon. & Right Reverend THE LORD BISHOP OF CARLISLE, to Mr. CHING, Apothecary, Cheapside, London
> Sir,
> I readily embrace the opportunity your letter affords me, of adding my testimony to that of the Lord Chief Baron in favour of your Worm Medicine; my eldest son having, a few months ago, derived very material benefit from the use of it. He had been unwell several weeks prior to his taking it, appeared pale and emaciated, was languid and complained of pain in his head and side. The Lord Chief Baron, who had accidentally seen him in this state, fortunately recommended to me the trial of your Lozenges and, that no time might be lost, or any mistake occur in obtaining the genuine Medicine, sent me three doses of it.[44] The first of these occasioned a visible amendment, and—after the second dose, every unpleasant symptom disappeared; but I judged it right to give the third, as the two former had agreed so uncommonly well—From that time my son has been in perfect health, and I certainly attribute his cure wholly to the efficacy of the Worm Lozenges. I have since recommended your lozenges in several instances, wherein I have the satisfaction to assure you they have uniformly been of great service. I ought to add, that from the nature of the effect produced by them in my son's case, I apprehend his complaints to have arisen from an obstruction between the stomach and viscera.

---

[44] Sir Archibald Macdonald, the Lord Chief Baron, was married to Lady Anne's sister Louisa.

I am, Sir, your obedient Servant, E. CARLISLE.
Rose Castle 7 December 1798

Mr. Ching's advertisements were usually placed in the papers on the same day as the bishop's letter appeared. These contained endorsements from many members of the aristocracy including the Duchesses of Rutland and Leeds and the Countesses of Shaftesbury, Cork, Derby and Darnley. However, it was only the bishop's letter which was widely reproduced. The advertisements concluded: "Undeniably they have saved the lives of many thousand children; and for adults are at all times the best opening physic; being so innocent as neither to injure the delicate female or the most tender infant."

The statement in the advertisement was untrue. Although the salesmen were told to deny it, the pills contained white panacea of mercury or calomel. Panacea of mercury was widely used as a medicine in the eighteenth century. A small quantity of calomel might not be unduly harmful. However, mixing techniques were often inadequate, and a single pill might contain a large dose of calomel.[45]

To the embarrassment of the bishop, it was widely reported in December 1803 that a three-year-old boy had died 28 days after being given the lozenges. His mouth ulcerated, his teeth dropped out, and his feet and whole body were flushed and spotted. The coroner blamed Mr Ching's lozenges. The editor of the *Medical Observer* wrote to the bishop, who replied: "In answer to your inquiries I have to say Ching's Lozenges were recommended to me by the Lord Chief Baron and at his request I informed Mr Ching of the good effects produced in my son's case—but I never authorised Mr Ching to publish my letter on the subject. I am fully

---

[45] The contents of the two pills were as follows: The yellow pills were made from 1lb of white panacea of mercury combined with 2 lbs of white sugar, ½ oz of saffron and a pint of spring water. The brown pills were composed of 3.5 lbs of jalap, 7 oz of white panacea and 9 lbs of sugar. Spring water was added in sufficient quantity to make it possible to combine the ingredients and roll the lozenges out. Jalap is a strong cathartic drug made from the root of a convolvulus type plant and designed to clear out the intestines.

aware that calomel is one of the principal ingredients of the lozenges."[46] In spite of the coroner's verdict, Mr Ching's successor continued to produce the pills and give his salesmen copies of the bishop's letter to hand out to customers.

The final years as Bishop of Carlisle, 1804–7

Bishop Vernon's final four years in the Diocese of Carlisle were marked by political controversy and sadness. He became embroiled in a complex dispute about parliamentary candidates for the Carlisle seats. As a result of a policy disagreement with the Grenville faction, he was considered by them to have behaved badly. Tragedy also struck the bishop and Lady Anne with the death of their second son Edward, whilst an undergraduate at Christ Church, Oxford.

The family's financial circumstances had markedly improved during 1803. Lady Anne's uncle, the third Duke of Bridgewater, died in March 1803 and left her and her two full sisters £10,000 each. Lady Anne's father, her husband's most faithful supporter, the Marquess of Stafford, died in October 1803 and left her £3,000. This additional capital enabled the bishop to afford to pass the Sudbury family living to his nephew, Fredrick Anson, but he himself retained the valuable canonry of Christ Church.

Bishop Vernon added to his responsibilities by becoming, with his sister-in-law's husband, Sir Archibald Macdonald, one of three trustees of the Bridgewater estates, including the canal and mines. The third trustee was Robert Haldane Bradshaw, the manager. The income from the enterprise went to Dr Vernon's brother-in-law, the new Marquess of Stafford and, on his death, to his second son Francis and his heirs, provided Francis changed his name to Egerton. If Francis had no heir, the properties would go to the Chief Baron's family and, if he had no male heir, to Bishop Vernon's family.

The bishop and Lady Anne were at Rose Castle in January 1804. In the first week of the year, the bishop's chaplain, William Carey, was married in Carlisle Cathedral to a Miss Sheepshanks, the daughter of a prebendary

---

46   *Medical Observer*, 30 August 1806, p. 150.

of the cathedral. Carey had been to Westminster and Christ Church, and in 1803 had been appointed headmaster of Westminster. Carey later became Bishop of Exeter and subsequently Bishop of St Asaph.

Lady Anne was also playing her part in local events. On the anniversary of Queen Charlotte's birthday in January 1804, she presented the colours to the Loyal Carlisle Volunteers. Lady Anne arrived on Castle Green at two o'clock in the bishop's coach to be greeted by "perhaps the greatest concourse of people that ever witnessed a public spectacle in this part of the kingdom". In her speech she stated: "I am persuaded should the enemy be daring enough to attempt the execution of his boasted menaces and so far succeed as to pollute our shores with a foreign army, the Loyal Carlisle Volunteers will be among the foremost to brave every danger to our king and country." After the colours were handed over, the major in charge made a rousing speech of thanks. Guns were fired and the band played "many loyal tunes". As the crowd dispersed, the soldiers marched to the cathedral, where the colours were placed on the altar. The chaplain, Carey, delivered a sermon to a full congregation, and Bishop Vernon gave a blessing. The company moved on to an assembly, where dancing commenced at 10 p.m. Celebrations continued until five the following morning.[47]

The Bishop of Carlisle's fame was now sufficient for his portrait to be offered for sale to the public. Mr R. Cribb of 288 Holborn announced in the *Morning Chronicle* of 20 February 1804: "Most animated portrait of the Hon. & Rt. Rev. Edward Venables Vernon LLD, Lord Bishop of Carlisle, engraved by Mr Charles Turner, from a picture by John Hoppner RA; size of plate 20 inches by 14 inches; proof impression £1 1s; prints 10/6." The portrait from which the engraving was made hangs in Christ Church College, Oxford.

---

[47]   *Carlisle Journal*, Saturday 21 January 1804.

Episcopal duties

The bishop's round of episcopal duties remained largely unchanged. His 1804 visitations were held over four days between 5 and 11 June at Carlisle, Penrith, Wigton and Appleby. Confirmations took place before each visitation. Two deacons and four priests were ordained in Rose Castle chapel on 3 June 1804, and similar regular ordinations took place there over the next three years. The only significant difference was that deacons were now usually paid £30 to £40 a year in comparison with £20 to £30 some ten years earlier when Bishop Vernon first arrived in the diocese. Four public open days remained the norm every summer.

One sign of how things might change for a diocesan bishop in the new century was the Residence Act of 1803. There was a growing concern in the Church of England that pastoral care was inadequate if the incumbent was not resident. The new act required bishops to make an annual return to the Privy Council of non-resident incumbents in their diocese. It may not have been entirely coincidental that Bishop Vernon resigned from the Sudbury living about this time.[48] The figures for the Diocese of Carlisle showed that 52 incumbents were non-resident in 1804–5, 54 in 1805–6, and 50 in 1806–7. These figures indicate that around 40 per cent of the parishes had no resident incumbent. Many will have been served by a resident curate, as was the case with the Revd J. D. Carlyle, who had curates in all his three parishes when he went on an expedition to the Middle East.[49] The reasons for non-residence in 1806–7 were: residence in other benefices (19), literary or ecclesiastical appointments (11), no parsonage house (7), infirmity (6), diocesan or cathedral office (6) and no licence (1).[50]

Dr Vernon also lost two friends in the clergy. The Revd J. D. Carlyle, whom he had appointed to the vicarage of Newcastle, died in April 1804. Carlyle had remained vicar general or chancellor of the Carlisle diocese

---

[48]   The CCEd gives two alternative dates for Edward's resignation as rector of Sudbury—18 December 1802 and 2 April 1803.

[49]   See note 22 above.

[50]   Non-residence returns to Houses of Parliament 1804–5, 1805–6, 1806–7, published May 1808, FP Porteus 15, f. 81, Lambeth Palace Archives.

while at Newcastle. Dr Vernon appointed Dr Browne Grisdale in his place. Grisdale was rector of Bowness, a lecturer at Carlisle Cathedral and a prebendary of Salisbury. He had been headmaster of Carlisle Grammar School until 1795 and chaplain to the Earl of Lonsdale till Lonsdale's death in 1802.

A year later in May 1805 Bishop Vernon's friend William Paley died in Lincoln. Paley had continued as the sole archdeacon of Carlisle in the diocese after moving to be rector of Bishop Wearmouth in Durham. According to the *Lancaster Gazette* of 7 July 1804 and some three other newspapers, the bishop appointed the Revd Phineas Pett as Paley's replacement. Pett was another Westminster and Christ Church alumnus and principal of St Mary's Hall, Oxford, and he had been the bishop's chaplain. Pett never appears to have taken up his duties for, on 8 February 1805, the Revd Charles Anson, Bishop Vernon's nephew, was installed as archdeacon and "on Sunday performed the usual ceremonies of the Church".[51] Anson was appointed rector of Great Salkeld, a living which traditionally went with the archdeaconry. He was also rector of the Anson family living of Lyng in Norfolk. He remained archdeacon of Carlisle till his death in 1827.

Political difficulties

On the political front, Dr Vernon was asked by Lord Carlisle in September 1804 to contact Lord Lowther to ascertain whether there would be support for Carlisle's eldest son Lord Morpeth to be a candidate for one of the Cumberland county seats in Parliament. There had been discussions some two years previously about John Christian Curwen taking the place of the current member, Sir Henry Fletcher, when the latter retired. Lord Carlisle had heard from Bishop Vernon that Fletcher was ill and wanted to know if Lord Lowther would support Lord Morpeth as an MP for Cumberland. The other current member was John Lowther, Lord Lowther's brother.

---

[51] *Carlisle Journal*, 16 February 1805.

Bishop Vernon wrote to Lord Lowther to seek his views. Somehow Lord Lowther gained the impression from Vernon's letter that Lord Carlisle thought the seat was Lord Morpeth's by right. Vernon replied that neither Lord Carlisle nor his son Lord Morpeth "consider their success certain". He explained Lord Morpeth was his nephew by marriage and indicated that Lord Carlisle had thought Lord Morpeth's candidacy might be welcomed. Bishop Vernon reminded Lowther that Lord Morpeth had an income of about £12,000 from his interests in the county of Cumbria and was well connected by friendship and marriage. He indicated Morpeth would not proceed if he did not have the residents' support. Lowther thought Vernon had instigated Morpeth's candidacy, and the bishop had to make clear he had not. He had learnt from the Duke of Portland and William Pitt as well as others that all had agreed to support Sir Henry Fletcher until he retired. Bishop Vernon had only been in touch with Lord Carlisle because he had heard Fletcher was dying. He declared he did not want to parade his good opinions of Lord Morpeth too openly, as Morpeth was his wife's nephew. He hoped there would be no diminution of his friendship with Lord Lowther whatever happened about representation.[52]

Fletcher did not die and continued to represent the seat till the election of 1806, when he was still reluctant to retire. Lord Carlisle remained concerned that his son would not be offered the seat. Lowther now favoured Morpeth over Fletcher. Curwen, who now had a Carlisle seat, tried to get Fletcher to remain to discourage Morpeth. Curwen hoped to exchange his Carlisle seat for the county seat. Lowther then expressed some doubts to Bishop Vernon regarding his support for Morpeth and Vernon began to think it might be time for a compromise and Morpeth would have to wait. Lowther then told Fletcher he would not support him and that the agreement reached with Lowther's predecessor no longer held good. The nomination meeting on 6 November was the crucial test. Without Lowther's support, Fletcher began to waver and, at the nomination meeting, it was clear Morpeth's supporters had the majority. Fletcher decided not to fight an election and withdrew. Morpeth held

---

[52] Twelve letters from the Bishop of Carlisle to Viscount Lowther, 10 September to 7 November 1804, Carlisle Archives DLONS L1/2/3 and L1/2/6 A.

one of the two Cumberland seats from 1806 to 1820.[53] Bishop Vernon's efforts on behalf of his nephew had been successful.

Bishop Vernon had been fearful that his correspondence supporting Lord Morpeth's candidacy in the autumn of 1804 might have damaged his friendship with Lord Lowther. This was not the case, for in October 1805 Lowther invited him to stay at Whitehaven Castle. The purpose of the visit was to go down a coal mine:

> On Friday Viscount Lowther and the Lord Bishop descended into the coal works with two engineers. Their Lordships visited Kells pit, one hundred and eighteen fathoms deep and went through all the workings including three quarters of a mile under the sea. Their Lordships were in the mine for five hours viewing the outstanding monuments to human skill, intrepidity and perseverance.[54]

Edward Vernon's death

Two months later in January 1806, the bishop and Lady Anne had to cope with the death of their second son Edward and the near death of his eldest brother George. The cause of the boys' illness was believed to be scarlet fever. Both were undergraduates at Christ Church, Oxford; their parents were at Rose Castle. Dr Cyril Jackson, Dean of Christ Church, wrote to Bishop Vernon on the morning of Saturday 25 January:

> God comfort and support you and support the afflicted mother of him who was one of the delights of my life also, but of whom we were deprived about two this morning. And God also knows how soon I may have occasion to afflict you again, for, indeed, the night has been very bad for his poor brother.

---

53 The *History of Parliament: House of Commons 1790–1820*, Cumberland Constituency, accessed 31 July 2023.

54 *Lancaster Gazette*, Saturday 2 November 1805.

Later that same evening Jackson wrote again about George: "I dread to say it, and yet I just in honesty say, that hope has left me." Jackson was wrong and George survived.

It was never clearly established where the boys picked up the infection. They had come to Oxford on the coach from Carlisle the previous Friday. Jackson speculated that the infection had been caught on the coach. George in one of his deliriums had called out: "Edward, do let down the windows, this coach smells so ill." Jackson suggested Bishop Vernon try to find out if anyone on the coach also became ill. George was not informed of his brother's death, for fear it would put back his recovery. The dean discouraged the bishop and Lady Anne from coming to Oxford, for they would have been unable to help or to visit George.[55]

Edward was buried in the Latin Chapel at Christ Church with his pall carried by six King's Scholars. Jackson wrote:

> The grief of all through the service operated differently. Some struggled almost convulsively against it, though the tears streamed down their cheeks. One in particular sunk under it; his head was bent down and his sobs were dreadful. I made a strong effort to exert myself. I just got out the words, "Be comforted and for God's sake compose yourself" or something like it and I had hold of his hand. By a sort of impulse, the hands of all the others were laid on ours, and one sobbed out these words (which now sound in my ears) "Over this grave". I could by strong exertion repeat "Over this grave, we will all remember it."

Jackson concluded: "Let your tears flow, it is the road to consolation. Mine have not yet ceased. But still remember one dear and valuable child is given back to you; one brand is plucked out of the fire. God bless and support you."

Bishop Vernon wrote to Sir Archibald Macdonald:

---

55   Five letters from Cyril Jackson to the Bishop of Carlisle, 25 January 1806 and undated, HP, Vol. XII, pp. 112–27.

We endeavour to look forward, but we cannot forget poor
Edward. Talents, scholarship, goodness of heart and early piety,
he possessed in a very uncommon degree; and it is the highest
consolation to us to think that no young man was ever better
prepared to submit to so awful a dispensation. That he is now
happy I have not the smallest doubt. Still, we must grieve for
him. Praised however be to God, who has not suffered us to be
tempted above what, by his succour, we have been enabled to
bear. We prayed for Him for support. He did support us.[56]

Bishop Vernon and Lady Anne wrote to friends to explain what had
happened to their son Edward. Dean Milner wrote back encouraging
them not to be afraid to talk about Edward. If people suggested that time
will work a cure, Milner recommended the answer should be: "We hope
not; we have learnt something which we should never have learnt in
complete prosperity, and which we would not unlearn for all the world."[57]

William did not learn of his brother's death until late April. He wrote
to his brother George and to Lady Anne from Port Royal in Jamaica. To
his mother he wrote:

In the midst of the deepest, the most heartfelt affliction, it affords
me some consolation to observe the resignation and wonderful
fortitude with which religion has enabled you to support yourself
under a shock the severest in the world. I shall do my utmost to
follow the bright example you have set me, though I confess my
heart is wrung with the bitterest sensations of grief, for I loved
Edward most affectionately.

In his letter to George, William realized George would feel especially
bereft, as Edward had been his constant companion throughout his life.

---

[56]   The Bishop of Carlisle to the Chief Baron Sir Archibald Macdonald, undated,
      HP, Vol. XII, p. 111.

[57]   Dr Milner Dean of Carlisle to the Bishop of Carlisle, 16 February 1806, HP,
      Vol. XII, p. 131.

William feared for his mother's health and the shock it would have been to their father.[58]

George wrote back to William to thank him for his letters and hoped William would return shortly to England, so that they could be at Rose Castle together. George wrote: "The subject [of Edward's death] is too painful for me to enter on now and to my mind fit only for solitary and melancholy reflection, but you will find them feeling differently at Rose Castle and rather willing than otherwise to converse about it."[59] Their father and mother seem to have taken Dean Milner's advice to talk about Edward.

Edward's death had profound implications for William's future. He was now able to consider the possibility of giving up his naval career, which he did not much enjoy, and becoming a priest. His father wrote to both William and to Captain Bligh to ask for their thoughts on William being ordained. Captain Bligh replied: "William appears to retain a decided predilection for the clerical profession . . . I think he will qualify himself better than the generality of candidates for ordination."[60] William decided to be ordained: he retired from the navy and was matriculated at Christ Church in April 1807.

More political difficulties

In the midst of his grief at Edward's death and his concern for William's future, Bishop Vernon had to contend with a political dilemma somewhat more severe than the choice of a candidate for a Carlisle county seat. The problem arose when William Pitt returned in January 1804 as head of a new administration, which included the Duke of Portland and the Earl of Harrowby, who was married to Lady Anne's youngest half-sister Susan. The new Pitt administration excluded the followers of Grenville

---

[58]   William Vernon to Lady Anne and to George Vernon, 26 and 27 April 1806, HP, Vol. XII, pp. 126–8.

[59]   George Vernon to William Vernon, 17 September 1806, HP, Vol XIII, p. 6.

[60]   The Bishop of Carlisle and Captain Bligh, 26 March 1806 and 9 June 1806, HP, Vol. XIII, pp. 129–32.

and Fox and Bishop Vernon's brother-in-law Lord Stafford. The bishop felt an ongoing obligation to Pitt, who might yet offer him translation to a more lucrative bishopric. His loyalties were divided.

William Pitt the Younger died in office on 23 January 1806. The following day Bishop Vernon wrote to Lord Stafford to say he was now able to follow his political line. He offered Lord Stafford two livings which he had previously made available to Pitt, as Leveson was too young to be considered, being only 17 at the time. A few weeks later, Bishop Vernon wrote to Lord Grenville, who was shortly to be the replacement head of the government, to state he had planned to give his proxy to the Bishop of Bangor, but, as he could not attend, he would entrust his proxy to the Bishop of Oxford and ask him to support Lord Grenville's administration. Bishop Vernon offered to attend in person if Grenville at any time thought it necessary, but asked Grenville to give him plenty of notice due to the time it took to get from his "Siberian residence" to London.[61]

All was satisfactory until April 1807, when Lord Stafford put down a motion in the House of Lords which, in effect, condemned George III for failing to support Catholic emancipation and in particular the right of Irish Roman Catholics to sit in the House of Commons. Bishop Vernon had always opposed Catholic emancipation, which he saw as a threat to the established Church. On 6 April 1807 he wrote to the Bishop of Bangor, who held his proxy:

> Attached to Lord Stafford by the strongest ties of gratitude and affection, and by a friendship of nearly forty years, I cannot however join him in approving the conduct of the late ministry in the proceedings which lead to their dismissal [Grenville's administration had fallen in March 1807]; but it would be so painful to my feelings to vote against a motion brought forward by himself, and in support of Lord Grenville, that I must request you not to give my proxy on the occasion. On questions not

---

[61]   The Bishop of Carlisle to the 2nd Marquis of Stafford, Leveson Gower papers, Staffordshire Archives, D868/11/37, 57–58, 65–68; the Bishop of Carlisle to Lord Grenville, British Library, Add. MS 59003, ff. 164, 166, 167, 169 and 171.

connected to this unfortunate business I shall be as anxious as
yourself to prove my attachment to Lord Grenville.[62]

Lord Stafford, whose motion was heavily defeated, made it plain to the
Bishop of Carlisle that he disapproved of the latter's conduct. Stafford
suggested Bishop Vernon should discuss the situation with his son
George, who in 1806 aged 21 had become MP for Lichfield, a seat in the
gift of Lord Stafford and the Anson family. George had been encouraged
to take the seat by his uncle Lord Harcourt. The decision had been
made without consulting his father, who was at Rose Castle. George
had supported a motion in the House of Commons which had similar
objectives to Lord Stafford's motion in the Lords. Bishop Vernon and his
eldest son therefore held opposing views.

The bishop wrote to George:

> I have this instance received a letter from Lord Stafford, in which
> he expresses his opinion of what I have done and refers me to
> you for his opinion of what I ought to do. I grieve to find he is
> dissatisfied with my conduct, and I fear he will be still more so
> when I add that, after reading the actual resolutions proposed
> on Monday, I do not regret that my proxy was withholden ... I
> have endeavoured, in a trying moment, to acquit myself of what
> I owed to my public station, to my private feelings and to my
> connections. That I have failed in answering the expectations of
> the latter is a subject of the truest concern to me, but I should not
> have possessed the approbation of my own heart if I had acted
> differently; and as the reserve of exercising my own judgement
> on all questions which *I may consider* [Dr Vernon's emphasis]
> connected with Religion renders inadmissible my offer of
> support to Lord Grenville, I have only to lament that such is his
> determination, and to submit to the consequences of it.

---

[62]   The Bishop of Carlisle to the Bishop of Bangor, 6 April 1807, HP, Vol. XII, p. 135.

As a postscript, the bishop wrote: "I hope Lord Grenville will see ... that it is possible even for his *oldest and best friend* to differ with him in opinion and that he will forgive this difference."[63] Although Bishop Vernon and Lord Grenville continued to be on opposite sides over Catholic emancipation, they were reconciled by 1809, when the bishop actively supported Lord Grenville's candidacy for chancellor of Oxford University.

James Sack, in his book *The Grenvillites 1801–1829*, argued that Dr Vernon's failure to support Lord Stafford was a cynical ploy to secure a better clerical appointment. Sack wrote:

> When the Talents [Grenville's Ministry] fell, [the Bishop of Carlisle] affirmed his support for Grenville on all non-Catholic issues; but on Stafford's motion regarding the change of ministers, he declined to vote at all. Grenville, according to [Lord] Carlisle, was furious at what he considered to be time serving and Carlisle made it clear to his brother-in-law that his options with the opposition were for ever closed. Vernon then supported Portland and received his reward several months later through translation to the archiepiscopal see of York.[64]

The letter the bishop wrote to his son George makes it plain that his vote on Lord Stafford's motion was a matter of conscience. The refusal of Lord Grenville and Lord Stafford to accept Bishop Vernon's future support left him no choice but to vote with the Duke of Portland's administration.

---

[63] The Bishop of Carlisle to his son George Vernon, dated "Friday evening", probably Friday 17 April 1807, HP, Vol. XII, p. 136.

[64] James J Sack, *The Grenvillites 1801–1829: Party Politics and Factionalism in the Age of Pitt and Liverpool* (Urbana, IL and London: University of Illinois Press, 1979), p. 105.

Supporting the elderly Archbishop of York

In late September and early October 1807, the Bishop of Carlisle undertook a series of confirmations and an ordination for the 88-year-old Archbishop of York. The programme was similar to that he had undertaken for the archbishop in the summer of 1801 and involved visits to Thirsk, Malton, York, Hull, Beverley, Bridlington, Scarborough and Whitby. At York Minster 6371 candidates were confirmed and 5383 at Hull, where the day was wet and the candidates had to wait in the rain for the church to open at 9 a.m. for a 10 a.m. service. Over 11 days, from 23 September to 3 October, Bishop Vernon had only two days off.

The Bishop was the lead patron of the first music festival at Carlisle on 9–11 September. It was organized to celebrate the installation of a new organ in the cathedral. Three Handel oratorios were performed in the cathedral. Two concerts were held in the assembly rooms, as well as a ball. All the local gentry patronized the festival including Lord Lowther, who had recently been made Earl of Lonsdale, Sir James Graham and J. C. Curwen, the local MP who had tried to prevent Lord Morpeth taking a Carlisle County seat. The festival was advertised in Newcastle and York as well as locally. Tickets for all five concerts were 11s 6d or 3s per concert. Singers were brought from London, Bath and Manchester and there was a full orchestra. According to the press the cathedral was well filled, but Dean Milner's biographer suggested that Carlisle was not a musical city and the festival was a failure.[65]

Translation to York

On 3 November 1807, the Archbishop of York died at his London residence. Two days later most papers suggested that the Bishop of Carlisle would be appointed to York. The *Ipswich Journal*, however, thought the appointment might go to Dr Stuart, Archbishop of Armagh, in which case the Bishop of Carlisle would go to Ireland. Only 13 days

---

[65] *Newcastle Courant*, 22 August 1807; *Carlisle Journal*, 16 and 21 September 1807; Mary Milner, *Life of Isaac Milner*, p. 351.

after Archbishop Markham died, the Bishop of Carlisle received a letter from the Duke of Portland, then prime minister, offering him the archbishopric of York. The editor of the Harcourt papers wrote: "Bishop Vernon was promoted by his old patron to the Archbishopric of York. He was at that time of the age of 50, and being remarkably healthy and vigorous, felt himself equal to undertaking the extensive and laborious duties of a Diocese which then included almost all the large county of York and also that of Nottinghamshire."[66]

The Duke of Portland, after informing Bishop Vernon of George III's assent to his appointment, wrote:

> I beg leave to congratulate you upon this distinguished mark of his Majesty's favour, and to assure you of the pleasure it affords me to have been instrumental to an event which promises to contribute so much to the happiness of a family for which I have always professed sentiments of the most perfect regard.

On receipt of the letter, Bishop Vernon set out from Carlisle to London. He called en route at the duke's house in Buckinghamshire to offer his thanks, but Portland was already in London. Bishop Vernon had advised him he would attend a levee at the Queen's Palace in order to kiss George III's hand. The Duke of Portland wrote back to tell Bishop Vernon that it was not enough just to attend the levee. He must ask for an audience with the king, "which I am persuaded would be graciously accepted by him".[67]

Bishop Vernon had achieved recognition and financial security. His annual income would in future be in the order of £12,000 to £14,000, almost ten times that of the bishopric of Carlisle, and he could afford to resign the canonry of Christ Church. As Archbishop of York, he was number two in the hierarchy of the Church of England and would have to play a more prominent role in the House of Lords. The number of clergy and the number of parishes for which he would be responsible

---

66   HP, Vol. XII, p. 141.

67   Duke of Portland to the Bishop of Carlisle, 16 November and 24 November 1807, HP, Vol. XII, pp. 143–5.

would increase almost tenfold. He would have less time for his family of 14, and his younger children would not get the close involvement in their education that the older boys had enjoyed. Lady Anne, no longer burdened with regular childbirth, would be freer to be involved in the new archbishop's life in York and London.

3

Becoming archbishop (1808–9)

Edward Venables Vernon's basic pattern of life did not change following his appointment as Archbishop of York, but his workload increased substantially. He would continue to spend around half the year in London, where he was expected to attend Court and the House of Lords. He would have some four months a year based at his palace at Bishopthorpe, typically a month at Christmas and around three months in the summer. The increase in his wealth enabled him to provide for his family as he had always wished, but he would not be able to spend as much time educating his younger children as he had done with the older boys. He did not make his official entry to his new diocese until June 1808, some seven months after his appointment.

London, 1808

Following a final family Christmas at Rose Castle, the new archbishop travelled to London via York. He stayed the night of 12 January 1808 at Bishopthorpe, presumably with a view to checking how his large family could be accommodated. In London, the family continued to live at 17 Albemarle Street until 1810 when they moved to 45 Grosvenor Square, a house he and his family occupied as their London home for the rest of his life.

On 20 January 1808, Archbishop Vernon attended a levee at St James's Palace, where he paid homage to King George III and was sworn in to the Privy Council. He was appointed Lord High Almoner, an honorary post where the work was largely undertaken by the salaried sub almoner. On the following day in his absence, he was officially placed in his seat in

York Minster with a canon taking the Archbishop's part.[1] On 5 February, he took the oath and was introduced to the House of Lords by the Bishops of Bangor and Bristol.

In addition to appearances at Court and in the House of Lords, the new archbishop gave dinners and attended numerous functions. One Saturday in March he attended the annual Westminster School Grand Dinner. He sat on the headmaster's right and his sister-in-law's husband, the Lord Chief Baron, on the headmaster's left. The Archbishop was appointed a steward for the next annual dinner. The following morning, Saturday 19 March, he consecrated his successor as Bishop of Carlisle in the Chapel Royal. In early May, his London engagements included attending the Royal Academy Grand Annual Dinner, an event he tried to attend every year. Later in the month he dined with Frederick, Duke of York, George III's second son. He and members of his family enjoyed the weekly *Concerts of Antient Music* in the Hanover Square Rooms.[2] Patronized by the king and the royal dukes, the Archbishop was to become a director of the concerts in 1811.

In early February 1808, the Archbishop received a letter from 28 members of the clergy of the deanery of Westmoreland. They offered their congratulations on his new role and thanked him for his work in the diocese of Carlisle:

> It would be unbecoming in any order of men, it would be peculiarly so in ours, to obtrude on your Grace the language of adulation. But, My Lord, contemplating with Veneration the uniform vigilance and dignified benignity that has marked your episcopal jurisdiction in this diocese, we cannot suppress our expressions of regret at your departure, and of gratitude for your unremitting attention and paternal regard to the interests of the

---

[1]   Dr Vernon was the last Archbishop of York to be enthroned by proxy. His successor was enthroned in person on 13 January 1848.

[2]   The Hanover Square rooms were in the south-east corner of Hanover Square and were London's chief concert hall from 1774 for the next 100 years. The *Concerts of Antient Music* were held there from 1804.

Church in a deportment and example which throws transcendent
lustre and invigorates the great cause of morality and religion.

The letter concludes with good wishes to the Archbishop and his family
for happiness and a long life.[3]

The Archbishop was delighted to receive the congratulations of his
former clergy:

> Any mark of attention from a clergy with whom I have been so
> long and so happily connected could not fail of being highly
> pleasing to me; but the assurance from them of their favourable
> acceptance of my conduct as their diocesan has afforded me a
> gratification which no words can express. On my part I should
> not do justice to my feelings, if I neglected this opportunity
> of avowing my own obligations to them for their cordial and
> affectionate co-operation with me in whatever I found occasion,
> at any time, to recommend to them as conducive to the great
> object we mutually had in view, the Glory of God and the
> advancement of true religion.

He reminded them that, as their Metropolitan, he would continue to
watch over and promote their interests and thanked them again for the
way in which they had communicated their sentiments.[4]

On 27 May 1808, the Archbishop once more found himself opposing
Lord Grenville in the House of Lords. Grenville had put forward a motion
for greater toleration for Roman Catholics. The bishops were divided,
but Archbishop Vernon again objected to offering political power to
Catholics and stated he was not acting out of any motives of bigotry nor
was he at all averse to the most liberal principles of toleration: "While
the spirit of the Constitution allowed the Catholics the fullest and purest
principles of toleration, it forbade that they enjoyed political power." He

---

[3]   *York Herald*, 6 February 1808.
[4]   The Archbishop to the Rural Dean of Westmoreland, undated, *Harcourt Papers* (HP), Vol. XII, p. 148.

opposed the motion, which was defeated. Grenville obtained 74 votes for his motion and his opponents 161.[5]

Entry to York diocese

Archbishop Vernon arrived in York on 23 June 1808. His arrival had been delayed by the unexpected death of his sister Martha, who was buried in Sudbury churchyard on 18 June. His sister Catherine had died in 1775 and his mother in 1794. As a mark of respect for Martha's death, the Archbishop entered York quietly and went directly to Bishopthorpe Palace. "The compliment intended to have been paid by the respectable inhabitants of the City in meeting his Grace upon the road and, in procession, ushering him to his residence, did not take place." Celebrations were postponed till the following day, when he made his formal public entry to York Minster and met for the first time the senior clergy of the diocese and the cathedral.[6]

The bells of York Minster rang out to welcome the first new archbishop for 31 years. A procession formed outside the west door. The Archbishop was accompanied by his chaplain and "a retinue of officers and servants". As he entered the nave, the organ struck up. The dean and chapter took the Archbishop to the vestry where he put on his robes. He was then escorted to his throne, and the service began. The music was conducted by the organist, Matthew Camidge: "The number of voices in our choir must be admitted to be inadequate to the immense space which the sound has to fill, especially in full choruses and when the church, as on this occasion, is unusually crowded: we may add however, that, at present we know of no cathedral where the lays sing in a better style or evince greater facility and correctness in reading music."[7] There were only seven lay choristers and eight "singing boys".

---

[5]   *Hansard: House of Lords* (27 May 1809), vol. 11, col. 681, accessed 31 July 2023.

[6]   *York Herald*, 25 June 1808.

[7]   *York Herald*, 2 July 1808.

Archbishop Vernon preached his first sermon as archbishop on the text from Matthew 13:12: "For whosever hath, to him shall be given, and he shall have more abundance: but whosoever hath not, from him shall be taken away even that he hath." After the sermon, the Archbishop and the clergy processed to the high altar, where communion was administered. The following day he entertained all the senior clergy to lunch at Etridges Hotel. Two days later the mayor and magistrates called at Bishopthorpe and "partook of an elegant cold collation". The Corporation of York presented the new archbishop with a silver cup worth £40.

The most senior clergyman present at York Minster was the Very Revd George Markham, who had been dean since 1802 and was also rector of Stokesley. He was accompanied by the Hon. & Revd Edward Rice, the precentor, and the Revd Robert Markham, who was the canon in residence, vicar of Bishopthorpe, rector of Bolton Percy, and archdeacon of York. Two of the other archdeacons were also present—the Revd Robert Waddilove, archdeacon of the East Riding, and the Revd Charles Baillie-Hamilton, archdeacon of Cleveland. Sir Richard Kaye, the archdeacon of Nottingham, was absent. Kaye was also Dean of Lincoln, where he lived, as well as rector of Kirkby-in-Ashfield and rector of Clayworth; he died in 1809.

George and Robert Markham were sons of the Archbishop's predecessor, William Markham. Both George and Robert had been up at Christ Church when Archbishop Vernon was a canon there. George's appointment as dean was a Crown appointment, but his rectory of Stokesley was in the gift of his father as Archbishop of York. When George died in 1822, his successor as rector of Stokesley was Archbishop Vernon's son, Leveson Venables Vernon. When Robert decided to give up the post of vicar of Bishopthorpe in 1814, he was succeeded by William Venables Vernon. A third Markham brother, Osborne, a lawyer, held the post of chancellor of the diocese until 1818, when he was succeeded by the new Archbishop's son Granville Venables Vernon, likewise a lawyer. Archbishop Vernon followed an accepted practice by placing three of his sons in posts in his gift.

During his first summer in York, Archbishop Vernon continued his previous practice of holding public days at his palace. The first took place at Bishopthorpe on Thursday 7 July and "continued every Thursday till the races". Race Week in 1808 was from 20 to 26 August. Archbishop Vernon also arranged an ordination, which took place on Sunday 14 August, when 15 priests and nine deacons were ordained. Papers had to be submitted to the Archbishop by 23 July, and candidates then presented themselves for examination on Thursday 11 August at 10 a.m. at Bishopthorpe Palace.

Accommodating his family

The Harcourt papers suggest that Archbishop Vernon built on to Bishopthorpe Palace on his arrival: "On first taking possession of the Palace at Bishopthorpe, the new Archbishop built various additional rooms, which greatly increased the amount of convenient accommodation."[8] Six small rooms were built above the chapel and a large block was added to the north side of the north range towards the garden during the Archbishop's time. However, the limited records available suggest these additions were not made until about 1835 by the architect Robert Smirke, who had been involved with restoring York Minster in 1829 and the Harcourt house at Nuneham in 1834.[9]

Irrespective of when the additions were made, the Archbishop must have had to fit his large family into whatever accommodation was available in June 1808, as he had no other country house. Of the 14 surviving children, he had to find rooms immediately for the seven younger ones. George at 22 was an MP and independent. Leveson (20) and William (19) were at Christ Church. Frederick (18) and Octavius (14) were at sea, Henry (16) at Sandhurst. Granville (15) was at Westminster, where he was to follow his two oldest brothers and become Captain of School in 1809. Those at home full time were Caroline (13), Anne (11), Charles (nine), Francis (seven), Egerton (five), Louisa (three) and Georgiana (one).

---

[8]   HP, Vol. XII, p. 149.

[9]   Eric Gee, *Bishopthorpe Palace: An Architectural History* (York: Ebor Press, 1983), p. 3.

BISHOPTHORPE PALACE,
YORKSHIRE
The Seat of the Archbishop of York

London Published by Jones & Co Jan.ʳ 10, 1829

Bishopthorpe Palace, the home of the Archbishop of York, in 1829

London, 1809

Archbishop Vernon's time in London in the winter of 1808–9 followed a familiar pattern. He was present in the House of Lords and attended functions at Court, including the celebrations for both the king's and the queen's birthdays. He acted as steward at the Westminster School annual dinner. He conducted christenings and marriages for friends and attended charity fundraising events. He was a steward at the service in St Paul's Cathedral for the Sons of Clergy charity and attended the dinner afterwards at the Merchant Taylors' Hall. He preached the Easter sermon at the Chapel Royal.

Death of the Second Earl Harcourt

The most significant event for Archbishop Vernon and his family in the spring of 1809 was the death of his brother-in-law, George Simon, Second Earl Harcourt. Lord Harcourt died at the age of 73 on 20 April at his house in Cavendish Square. His will left to his brother, General Harcourt, all his property for the general's life, with reserve to his widow Elizabeth, Countess Harcourt, and after her death to Edward, Archbishop of York, and to the heirs male of his body. The second earl had always taken a special interest in Archbishop Vernon's eldest son, George, whom he expected to be the future occupant of the Harcourt estates at Nuneham and Stanton Harcourt. The Archbishop's inheritance was now secure.

Archbishop Vernon and his family's succession to the Harcourt estates had not always been clear cut. Neither the second earl nor his brother, the third earl, had any children. However, the brothers had a sister Elisabeth, who married Sir William Lee and had two sons, William and George. The second earl could have left his property to his brother outright or entailed the estates to his sister Elisabeth Lee and her children. It is said he did not do so because, when offered the estates, Sir William Lee refused to take the name Harcourt.[10] The Archbishop, whose claim

---

[10]   William Henry Smyth, *Aedes Hartwellianae*, Vol. 2 (London: for private circulation, 1864), addenda p. 154.

came through his mother, the earl's aunt, agreed to change his name to Harcourt when he inherited the estates. He was no doubt helped by the fact that the second earl was married to his sister; however, Elisabeth Countess Harcourt always maintained she had no involvement in the drafting of her husband's will and that he would never have allowed her to interfere.[11]

The death of Lord Harcourt was a loss not only to Archbishop Vernon and his family but also to King George and Queen Charlotte, who had been close friends of Lord and Lady Harcourt and often stayed at Nuneham. Princess Elisabeth wrote to the Archbishop on behalf of the queen on the day of Lord Harcourt's death:

> The Queen has commanded me to say that she is so shocked at receiving the account of Lord Harcourt's death that it is impossible for her, at this moment, to answer you, and greatly distressed at her servant being already gone with an enquiry to you concerning him. We are fully sensible of the loss Lord Harcourt will ever be to *us,* and though we sincerely thank God he did not suffer in his last moments, we must ever regret him, for the King and Queen are both so thoroughly attached to those who they have known as long as Lord and Lady Harcourt, that they feel they have lost a sincere and faithful friend. For our dear and valuable Lady Harcourt our hearts bleed, yet we feel assured that her excellent principles and her faith in a just and merciful God will support her under so severe and heavy an affliction.

The princess concluded by adding her sisters and herself to those who had lost a kind and sincere friend.[12]

Archbishop Vernon left London in early June 1809 to undertake an extensive programme of visits to all parts of his diocese. These visits would supplement the knowledge he had already obtained when conducting

---

[11]   Elisabeth Dowager Countess Harcourt to William 3rd Earl Harcourt, undated, HP, Vol. XI, p. 119.

[12]   Princess Elisabeth to the Hon. E. Vernon Archbishop of York, 20 April 1809, HP, Vol. XII, p. 150.

confirmations throughout the diocese on behalf of his predecessor in 1801 and 1807. He was also familiar with part of his diocese as a result of family visits to Castle Howard, the home of his sister-in-law and her husband, the Earl and Countess of Carlisle.

Changing the family surname

Although Archbishop Vernon agreed to take the name of Harcourt when he inherited the Harcourt estates under the terms of the will of the second earl, this change of name did not take place till the death of the third earl in 1830. Only then did the Archbishop take possession of the estates at Nuneham and Stanton Harcourt. However, since subsequent chapters of this book encompass the periods before and after the name change, the Archbishop will in future be referred to as Archbishop Harcourt. His children also changed their surnames. All but two of his sons used the surname "Vernon-Harcourt". The exceptions were his eldest son, George, who used only the surname "Harcourt", and his seventh son, Granville, who used "Harcourt-Vernon".

4

The Archbishop in his diocese

At the start of the nineteenth century, the Diocese of York was one of the three largest in England, covering an area of about 5,300 square miles. Only Lincoln was larger, with 5,500 square miles. Although Lincoln and Norwich had over 1,000 benefices, York followed close behind, with 891. The population of some parts of the Archbishop's diocese was growing fast: many of the major towns had several chapels attached to their parish churches. With a population of about 1.4 million, only the Dioceses of Chester and London had greater populations, 1.9 million and 1.7 million respectively.[1]

Archbishop Harcourt could never hope to know all the clergy in York diocese, as he had been able to know those in Carlisle. Writing in the journal of the Ecclesiastical History Society in 1967, Dr Alan Stephenson criticized the Archbishop for his apparent ignorance of his diocese:

> It is doubtful Harcourt ever visited many parts of his Diocese. He was away from Yorkshire for the greater part of the year. Harcourt's ignorance of his Diocese is illustrated by the story of the institution of Archdeacon Boyd, who, when a young don, accepted in the year 1835 the living of Arncliffe in Craven. When he presented himself for institution at Bishopthorpe, the

---

[1] The figures for area, benefices and population are taken from G. F. A. Best, *Temporal Pillars: Queen Anne's Bounty, the Ecclesiastical Commissioners, and the Church of England* (Cambridge: Cambridge University Press, 1964), p. 545. The figures relate to the year 1835 and are derived mainly from the first report of the *Ecclesiastical Duties and Revenues Commission*. The population in 1808 will have been smaller, but the relative size of the diocese is likely to be about right.

Archbishop said sharply "Arncliffe, Arncliffe! I have no such living in my diocese". He rang for the registrar, who, on referring to his books, found that it was in his diocese.[2]

Dr Stephenson's assessment of Archbishop Harcourt's knowledge of his diocese was inaccurate. Harcourt conducted three formal visitations across the whole of his diocese in 1809, 1817 and 1825. In other years, he travelled widely to conduct confirmations and consecrate churches and burial grounds. During these tours, he stayed the night with the local rector or vicar or with the local landowner. On many evenings after the confirmation service had ended, he dined with the local clergy at a hotel or inn. He continued to visit parts of his diocese to consecrate churches or burial grounds and to conduct confirmations until the summer of 1843, when he was 85.

Visitations and confirmations

In the summer of 1809, the new archbishop set about his primary visitation. A printed leaflet was sent out to all clergy and churchwardens explaining when and where the Archbishop would conduct his visitation. There were 16 locations ranging from Nottingham in the south to Whitby in the north. Each visitation would take place between 8 a.m. and noon and be followed in the afternoon with a confirmation service. In addition, he conducted confirmation services at another 15 locations. In total, the Archbishop visited 31 churches and heard sermons from 31 or more clergy. Those selected to preach came from a church other than the one where the visitation took place. The Archbishop regularly met all the local clergy for a dinner following the services.

Archbishop Harcourt expected his clergy and churchwardens to treat the visitation seriously. "The parson, vicar or curate of every parish and

---

[2]   A. M. G. Stephenson, *Studies in Church History IV* (London: Ecclesiastical History Society, 1967), p. 148. The story about Arncliffe and Archdeacon Boyd was quoted from W. Boyd and W. A. Shuffrey, *Littondale Past and Present* (Leeds: Richard Jackson, 1893).

churchwardens are desired not to consider this a matter of mere form only, but are to meet together and read over these articles divers times, to deliberate and confer about them and the answering of them." The churchwardens were to write their answers according to their consciences and to bring them to the visitation. If churchwardens failed to write answers, the minister had to present the answers.

The Archbishop's questions for his primary visitation covered eight areas. These included the condition of the church or chapel—was it in good repair, did it have a decent reading desk, were the church rates made up? Similarly details of the living and house were recorded—was there a terrier of the glebe lands, and did the minister have a house in good repair? Archbishop Harcourt also wanted to know if the minister resided in the living "as he is required by law to do", and whether he preached regularly in the parish church. There were also questions about hospitals, schools and physicians in the parish and about the officers of the church: the form in which the terriers were to be provided was laid down and all the clergy had to bring their institutions, orders or licences as appropriate.[3] All documents had to be handed to the registrar early in the day. The clergy appeared before the Archbishop and the laity before Chancellor Osborne Markham or his surrogate.[4]

As the table below indicates, it was an arduous programme of visits. The Archbishop and his officers worked six days a week for most of the period from 10 June to 8 August, with a three-week break in July. Travel by coach was never comfortable, and almost every night the Archbishop and his officers would be staying with a different minister or landowner. In all, 40,181 candidates were confirmed.[5]

---

[3]   A terrier is a document, usually a survey, of the land and other temporal possessions of the parish church. It would typically include the quantity of acres and the names of tenants.

[4]   Visitation records for Archbishop Harcourt, Borthwick Institute for Archives, University of York, ref. V/1809/C.

[5]   Information on the dates of confirmations and numbers confirmed are taken from local newspapers. Visitation dates are also available in Archbishop Harcourt's visitation records and the newspapers.

1809 visitation and confirmations

Date	Location	Activity and nos. confirmed where available
Saturday 10 June	Southwell	Confirmation
Sunday 11 June		
Monday 12 June	Newark	Visitation and Confirmation (1,046)
Tuesday 13 June	Nottingham	Nottingham Deanery Confirmation (2,100) and consecration of new church of St James, Stannard Hill
Wednesday 14 June	Nottingham	Bingham Deanery Confirmation and Visitation
Thursday 15 June	Mansfield	Confirmation
Friday 16 June	Retford	Visitation and Confirmation
Saturday 17 June	Worksop	Confirmation
Sunday 18 June		
Monday 19 June	Doncaster	Visitation and Confirmation (1,948)
Tuesday 20 June	Rotherham	Confirmation (1,503)
Wednesday 21 June	Sheffield	Visitation and Confirmation (1,073)
Thursday 22 June	Barnsley	Confirmation (972)
Friday 23 June	Wakefield	Visitation and Confirmation (2,738)
Saturday 24 June	Pontefract	Confirmation (1,884)
Sunday 25 June		
Monday 26 June	Ripon	Visitation and Confirmation (2,258)
Tuesday 27 June	Otley	Confirmation (1,158)
Wednesday 28 June	Skipton	Visitation and Confirmation
Thursday 29 June	Huddersfield	Confirmation (1,337)
Friday 30 June	Halifax	Confirmation (1,590)

Date	Location	Activity and nos. confirmed where available
Saturday 1 July	Bradford	Confirmation (1,501) and consecration of St John's Great Horton
Sunday 2 July	Leeds	Town Confirmation (2,852)
Monday 3 July	Leeds	Visitation and Country Confirmation (3,285)
Break 4–24 July		
Tuesday 25 July	Hull	Visitation and Confirmation
Wednesday 26 July	Beverley	Visitation and Confirmation (874)
Thursday 27 July	Bridlington	Confirmation (364)
Friday 28 July	Scarborough	Visitation and Confirmation (382)
Saturday 29 July	Whitby	Confirmation (485)
Sunday 30 July		
Monday 31 July	Stokesley	Visitation and Confirmation (512)
Tuesday 1 August	Thirsk	Visitation and Confirmation
Wednesday 2 August		
Thursday 3 August	Malton	Visitation and Confirmation (811)
Friday 4 August		
Saturday 5 August		
Sunday 6 August		
Monday 7 August	York	Visitation and Confirmation (1,593)
Tuesday 8 August	Tadcaster	Confirmation (1,225)

These visitations attracted interest from the press. Following his visit to Newark, the *Hull Packet* wrote: "His Grace gave a most interesting and affectionate charge to the clergy, addressing them in the most conciliatory terms which impressed their minds with confidence that he would take the kindest interest in their welfare. His Grace concluded his charge with an affecting tribute to his predecessor Dr Markham."[6] The same newspaper, following his visits to Hull and Beverley, noted that, in his charge to the clergy, he had commented on the need for "better provision for the inferior classes". The Archbishop had also expressed concern that the way confirmation was conducted destroyed its intended beneficial effect.

The *Leeds Mercury* noted the Archbishop had arrived from Bradford on the Saturday evening, "having on his way visited and received much gratification from an inspection of the extensive woollen manufacturers Wormald, Gott & Wormald. His Grace held his confirmations in the morning at the parish church and in the evening at St John's." Having noted the numbers confirmed at various locations, the reporter praised the Archbishop: "It gives us pleasure to speak of men whose praiseworthy example from their elevated station is likely to give a tone and direction to the manner of their inferiors. With their view we mention that, as a pious, faithful and liberal minded divine, the Archbishop of York presents a bright example to all his clergy; and in his domestic circle his conduct is worthy of imitation, and his liberality to his servants has seldom been excelled."

The report commends the Archbishop for the way he treated his servants when leaving Carlisle and suggests no clergyman need shrink from the conscientious discharge of his duties under his governance. The reporter quotes a story of a curate in Carlisle diocese, who displeased the squire by his sermon. The squire complained to the bishop, who asked for a copy of the "noxious discourse". The sermon was duly sent; shortly afterwards the vicarage became vacant, and the bishop appointed the offending curate to the vicarage.[7] The story can have done the Archbishop's image no harm amongst the local population and the clergy.

The Archbishop organized a second visitation in 1817 and a third in 1825. Both visitations involved an arduous programme similar to the 1809 visitation. In the 1817 one, he had some assistance from his son Granville, although Osborne Markham remained chancellor. By the 1825

---

6   *Hull Packet*, 20 June 1809. The archbishop's charges were not published; information on his charges has been drawn from newspaper reports.

7   *Leeds Mercury*, 8 July 1809.

visitation, Granville had replaced Markham as chancellor and was again present for the majority of visits.

The energy of the 67-year-old Archbishop at the time of the 1825 visitation is illustrated by his visit to Leeds on Monday 1 August. He had spent the weekend at Harewood House, the home of Edward Lascelles, first Earl of Harewood. He travelled the nine miles to Leeds early on Monday morning and arrived in time to call at the vicarage before the first confirmation service began at 10 a.m. in Leeds parish church. The male and female candidates sat separately, and the Archbishop sat facing them from the altar. At 12.30 p.m., he moved to the vicar's pew and listened to a sermon from Revd Charles Musgrave, vicar of Whitkirk. Following a few minutes' rest in the vestry, the Archbishop returned to a seat behind the communion rail and, after the churchwardens from the local churches had been sent off to St James's Church, he gave his charge to the 50 clergy. He then withdrew again to the vestry for a cold collation: "His Grace appeared flushed and fatigued and partook lightly of the refreshments." He returned to the church to confirm another 90 candidates before dining at 4 p.m. with the clergy at a local hotel.[8]

In his 1825 charge, the Archbishop recalled that on his previous visitations he had spoken of the work of Queen Anne's Bounty, which provided funds to support poor livings, the need for more space in church for those of limited means, the Clergy Residency Act and the system of National Schools. He noted that Queen Anne's Bounty now had more funds to spend as a result of the increase in value of its investments. The £1.5m granted by Parliament was making it possible for more churches and chapels to be built in highly populated areas. He therefore intended to use "this opportunity to suggest, for [the clergy's] consideration, some plain and simple truths on which he had always considered that religious knowledge, to give it either truth or consistency, must rest". He made clear he did not intend to impose his conception of the truth on others. He emphasized that

> we must take account of the whole of scripture, if we hope to have
> a clear conception of the truth, of God's will and of our own duty.

---

[8]   *Leeds Intelligencer*, 4 August 1825.

> We must receive God's promises in such wise as they be generally
> set forth to us in Holy Scripture. We must not give more weight
> to one doctrine to the exclusion of others. This tendency was
> the more dangerous when the bias had in it a portion of reason
> or truth.

He mentioned specifically the doctrine of predestination in Article XVII
of the Church's Articles of Religion. The gospel presented not only a
covenant of grace but also a covenant of works. He concluded by saying
he was sure that, if anything he had said met their own minds, the clergy
would give it all the weight it deserved. He asked that what had been
spoken of in love should not be made a subject of contention.

The *Yorkshire Gazette*, which provided a comprehensive summary
of the charge, said:

> This excellent charge was delivered in a tone of affectionate
> earnestness—the most remote that can possibly be conceived
> from that of dictation or authority; and we hope it will receive all
> that deference to which its plain and simple elucidation of divine
> truth and the character of the distinguished prelate entitle it.[9]

The *Leeds Intelligencer* stated that the Archbishop "delivered a long and
impressive charge inculcating that the clergy should preach the whole
of the Gospel—works as well as faith" and noted the favourable manner
in which it had been received.[10] The only recorded problem in the 1825
visitation was on the visit to Skipton. The Archbishop, when drawing
his papers from his robes, found he had brought a sermon rather than
his charge, which had been left at Harewood House. Unfortunately, this
mistake received almost as much press attention as the favourable reports
on his visits elsewhere.

---

[9]   *Yorkshire Gazette*, 9 July 1825—the summary of the Archbishop's charge in
      the previous paragraph is also derived from this paper. There are no copies
      of the archbishop's charges in the visitation records in York.

[10] *Leeds Intelligencer*, 14 July 1825.

Increasing church accommodation

The need for more Church of England places of worship was increasingly recognized during the early years of Harcourt's archiepiscopate. The established Church was conscious that the absence of church accommodation in most of its churches in growing industrial towns was driving worshippers to attend non-conformist churches. In 1818, for example, it was estimated that Sheffield's Anglican churches had space for 6,280 out of a population of 55,000.[11] Even where space was available, the majority of pews were reserved by those who could afford to pay for them.

It was often difficult to get agreement to supply more room in Anglican churches. Where much of a church's income came from pew rents, an existing church might be hostile to the idea of another church in its neighbourhood. The patrons and incumbents of existing churches also wanted to protect their interests. The system for permitting collections to raise funds to rebuild or extend churches was complex and inadequate for contemporary needs. Opening a non-conformist chapel only required a licence, which could be obtained without difficulty. Often the only way to enable a new Anglican church to be built or to divide a parish was to obtain an Act of Parliament.

Amongst those who called attention to this situation in the House of Lords in 1810 was the Earl of Harrowby. Harrowby was married to one of the Archbishop's sisters-in-law, Lady Susan Leveson Gower. When in London, Lord and Lady Harrowby lived next door to the Archbishop and Lady Anne at 44 Grosvenor Square. In subsequent years, Harrowby and the Archbishop often sat on committees and commissions concerned with Church reform. Harrowby was one of the first to suggest that Parliament might get involved in providing funds for the building of new churches, as had happened in the time of Queen Anne. He was keen to see proposals brought forward, but recognized that funds might not be available until the conclusion of the war with France. Harrowby was one of the Archbishop's closest friends.

---

[11]   M. H. Port, *Six Hundred New Churches: The Church Building Commission 1818–1856* (London: SPCK, 1961), pp. 5–6.

A further driver for the increase in church accommodation was the growth in schools for children from poor families. If there were insufficient places of public worship, the benefits arising from teaching children the main elements of the Christian faith in school would be lost. A Quaker, Joseph Lancaster, had set up a system which enabled some 200–300 children to be taught by one master. The system involved older pupils teaching the younger ones. Originally developed for India, Lancaster set up his first school in the United Kingdom in London in 1798. As the number of schools increased, the British & Foreign Schools Society was established to develop and coordinate the work of schools established under the Lancasterian system. These schools offered non-denominational religious education.

A number of Anglicans including a layman, Joshua Watson, and a chaplain to the Archbishop of Canterbury, Christopher Wordsworth, were concerned that children were not being encouraged to worship in Anglican churches. Watson and Wordsworth set up a society to promote schools linked to the Church of England and Wales. The National Society for Promoting the Education of the Poor in the Principles of the Established Church of England and Wales was formed on 21 October 1811. Known as the "National Society", the Prince Regent was the patron and all the bishops were members of the General Committee. The Archbishop of Canterbury was the chairman, and, in his absence, the Archbishop of York took the chair. Archbishop Harcourt regularly attended National Society committee meetings and the annual examinations in reading, writing and arithmetic, which took place in London every May.

There was a widespread belief amongst both Tory and Whig parliamentarians that morals could only be inculcated by religious principles. Building more churches "would promote greater docility and more orderly habits among the lower orders".[12] Once the war with Napoleon ended in 1815, pressure mounted on Parliament for the provision of funds to build more Anglican churches. The pressure came from laymen led by Joshua Watson, who had played a leading role in establishing the National Society. He and John Bowdler, a lawyer, sent a memorandum signed by 120 others to the Tory Prime Minister, Lord

---

[12]   Port, *Six Hundred New Churches*, p. 27.

Liverpool, emphasizing the need for more churches.[13] A meeting in 1817 in the City of London Tavern speculated that, with the growth of Methodism and other non-conformist groups, the majority of the population might no longer adhere to the Church of England. Its privileged position as the established Church in England and Wales could be threatened.

In parallel with the pressure on Parliament to provide funds, the same laymen were looking to found a society to promote the provision of more church accommodation. The proposed society was criticized by the Lord Chancellor, Lord Eldon, for fear it might infringe the rights of patrons and incumbents. The supporters of the proposed society made plain that they intended to work with the church authorities and that the proposal had the support of the prime minister and the bishops, including the Archbishops of Canterbury and York. Eventually, on 6 February 1818, the Archbishop of Canterbury chaired a meeting in the Freemasons' Hall in Drury Lane at which the Society for Promoting the Enlargement and Building of Churches and Chapels was formed. "The want of church room, especially for the lower classes, in all populous parishes which surround the City of London and in many other parts of the Kingdom has long been deplored." Lord Harrowby, the Archbishop of Canterbury, and the Archbishop of York gave 200 guineas each. By 25 May 1818, funds to the value of £39,123 7s 9d had been collected. The Society subsequently became known as the Incorporated Church Building Society.

Early in 1818 the Prince Regent, in his speech from the throne, had referred to the need for new churches. After much parliamentary debate and with the support of the prime minister, Lord Liverpool, a bill was brought forward to establish a commission to build them. Lord Harrowby emphasized the measure was for the advantage not just of the clergy but of religion in general and for the community at large. The first Church Building Act 1818 was passed in some haste and was soon amended by subsequent Church Building Acts.[14] The commissioners were provided

---

[13]   Gill Hedley, *Free Seats for All: The Boom in Church Building after Waterloo* (London: Umbria Press, 2018, for the National Churches Trust), p. 19.

[14]   Act for Building and Promoting the Building of Additional Churches in Populous Parishes 1818 (58 Geo III c.45).

with £1m, equivalent to about £75m today, and a further £500,000 was added in 1824. The hope was that the initial funds would lead to the building of 100 churches. It was up to the 34 commissioners to expend the funds as economically as possible. The churches, often referred to as "Waterloo churches", had to be functional with limited ornamentation. The Archbishop of Canterbury chaired the commission. Inevitably the Archbishop of York was also a member. Lord Harrowby and Joshua Watson, who had both played a key role in forming the Incorporated Church Building Society, were amongst the lay members.

Archbishop Harcourt, along with all diocesan bishops, received a letter from the Archbishop of Canterbury in August 1818 outlining the key features of the act and asking him to assess the needs in York diocese. Dr Harcourt immediately wrote to his four archdeacons asking them to look at their more populous areas and provide him with population figures, number of church places and information on whether the incumbents or parishes were in a position to contribute wholly or in part to new church buildings. The archdeacons were to establish local committees and appoint such clergymen to them as would be most competent to collect the required information. The committees would report to the Archbishop, and he would be the channel of communication with the commission.[15]

By early September, Archbishop Harcourt had received information from all parts of his diocese. Barnsley, Bradford, Doncaster, Halifax, Huddersfield, Sheffield and Wakefield had all set out their requirements. The archdeacon for the East Riding, the Revd Darley Waddilove, wrote to him outlining the need for more church places in Scarborough, Hull and Ferriby; the archdeacon thought the inhabitants of Ferriby could probably find the funds for a new church if they could work together.[16]

The new act created considerable work for the Archbishop and his staff. The main bulk of the administration fell to Joseph Buckle, the deputy registrar of York diocese. The Archbishop himself liked to get involved

---

[15]   Church Building Commission minutes, MB.1, 2 September 1818, Lambeth Palace Library.

[16]   New Churches file—Archbishop Harcourt's papers, Borthwick Institute, University of York.

with submissions to the secretary of the commission, George Jenner.
Archbishop Harcourt regularly attended meetings of the commission
when in London. [17] "The Commissioners usually awaited his opinion
before deciding matters of any importance to his diocese." Although he
had already entered his seventh decade, he was alert to its needs.[18]

Archbishop Harcourt had clear views on the design and size of new
churches. The commissioners did not like the pulpit to be placed in the
centre of the church since it blocked the view of the altar. However, by
placing the pulpit and reading desk either side of the altar, it was more
difficult for the minister to make himself heard. Many churches therefore
still favoured a central pulpit. Archbishop Harcourt was the diocesan who
most frequently supported a request for a central pulpit. After a circuit
of the West Riding in 1827, he declared himself in favour of smaller
churches: "In very few of the larger [churches], from the situation of
the reading desk and pulpit, can the minister, unless gifted with a very
powerful voice, make himself heard, and consequently the congregations
are very thin." When, on a subsequent occasion, the commission wanted
to reduce the size of a church from 1,500 to 1,200, Archbishop Harcourt
favoured a further reduction to 1,000.[19]

The Archbishop had made clear to his clergy in his first charge that
he was concerned at the limited space available in Anglican churches
for those who could not afford to rent a pew. It was a requirement for a
grant from the commission that a significant proportion of the seats in
new churches should be free. It was, however, necessary for some pews to
be available to rent to provide an income for the minister, who typically
received £150 a year.

Archbishop Harcourt obtained funds for 16 new churches in the West
Riding and for one in Nottinghamshire from the first parliamentary
grant. Most were completed between 1822 and 1827 with the whole cost
met by the commission. Seven were very large churches seating around
2,000 or more. The first commissioners' church to be consecrated by

---

[17]   Port, *Six Hundred New Churches*, p. 37.

[18]   Port, *Six Hundred New Churches*, p. 32.

[19]   Church Building Commission minutes, MB.6, pp. 210–211, and Port, *Six Hundred New Churches*, p. 100.

Archbishop Harcourt was St George's Barnsley in October 1822; with 861 free seats and 389 to rent, it cost £5,963. This was followed in August 1824 by St Lawrence's Pudsey, a vast church seating 2,000 and costing £13,475. The last of the 16 churches to be consecrated was St Philip's Sheffield in July 1828, another church with 2,000 seats; it cost £13,116.

By the time of the second parliamentary grant of £500,000 in 1824, the commissioners had come to realize that acceptable churches could be built for more modest sums than they had first thought. They had also come to realize that smaller churches might be more successful for the reasons Dr Harcourt had indicated. In the second phase the commissioners rarely paid the full cost of a new church and few churches had seats for 1,000 or more. Churches with 600 to 700 seats were more typical. One of the few exceptions was St John's Golcar, which the Archbishop consecrated with a further nine new churches in the summer of 1830; it had seats for 950 and cost £3,133. The full cost was met by the commissioners. In total the Diocese of York received grants for 31 churches from the second parliamentary grant.

A total of 111 new churches were consecrated in the Diocese of York during Archbishop Harcourt's archiepiscopate, plus 76 new or extended burial grounds.[20] Of the new churches, 79 were consecrated in the years from 1809 to 1835. The number decreased from 1836, when most of the fast-growing West Riding was transferred to the new Diocese of Ripon, and Nottinghamshire was added to the Diocese of Lincoln. Between 1836 and his death in 1847 a further 32 churches were consecrated by Archbishop Harcourt or, in his later years, by other bishops on his behalf. He consecrated his final two churches at Elsecar and Kimberworth in June 1843, when he was 85. He stayed the intervening night at Wentworth House with Earl Fitzwilliam, who had paid for both churches. He returned to Bishopthorpe from Kimberworth by train with his chaplain,

---

[20]   A list of churches and burial grounds consecrated in the diocese of York during Dr Harcourt's archiepiscopate is attached at Appendix 2. The information has been compiled from the archbishop's registers at the Borthwick Institute, newspaper reports and church websites.

the Revd William Henry Dixon, his son Egerton, who was now registrar for the diocese, and Joseph Buckle, the deputy registrar.[21]

The consecration of new churches and burial grounds ensured that the Archbishop kept in close touch with the growing areas of his diocese. He used the opportunity of consecration visits to conduct confirmation services. By holding confirmations more frequently, the numbers at each service were reduced and the services could be more orderly. Every year he visited around a dozen locations in his diocese to consecrate churches or burial grounds, typically in January or during the months of August to October. Even in 1841, when he was rising 84, he still conducted seven consecrations. With commitments in both London and the diocese, he and Lady Anne had to travel frequently between London and York, no easy journey before the arrival of the railway in 1840. The Archbishop made sure he kept in touch with his diocese as far as his commitments in London allowed. By encouraging wealthy individuals to donate land and funds to build new churches and by tapping into the resources of the commissioners, Archbishop Harcourt went a long way to achieving the objective he set out in his 1809 visitation to provide more free seats in Anglican churches.

---

[21]   *Sheffield Independent*, 10 June 1843.

5

Patronage and pluralities, nepotism and non-residence

As in all dioceses, Archbishop Harcourt's freedom to appoint clergy in his parishes was limited by the patronage system and the right of all incumbents to remain in their livings till death. He could, however, examine candidates for ordination and did influence how they were trained. He had the right to review all candidates for appointment as incumbents or curates but would seldom be able to choose who was selected. The right to appoint was held by a diverse range of patrons including the Crown, the Lord Chancellor, the dean and chapter of the cathedral, local corporations and laymen. Although all appointments in York diocese required a licence from the Archbishop to exercise ministry and to preach, his powers to object were limited. He could, however, use his influence to ensure patrons did not abuse their rights and could offer advice if consulted.

In his Diocese of York, the Archbishop could appoint up to 57 livings. He also had the right to appoint the four residentiary canons, as well as the 24 prebends, sub-dean, chancellor, precentor and succentor at York Minster. He could appoint the 16 prebends at Southwell and the eight prebends and sub-dean at Ripon, as well as his four archdeacons. When making appointments in his gift, the Archbishop had to balance the need to fill posts with worthy and effective candidates with what would then be seen as a prime duty—to secure suitable posts for his family members, friends and political allies.

During Archbishop Harcourt's 40 years in the Diocese of York, the appointment of clergy to parishes was influenced not only by the patronage system but also by three other inter-connected issues: the diverse value of clergy livings, pluralism and non-residence. The large number of poorly rewarded livings encouraged clergy to become pluralists. As a consequence of pluralism, the incumbent must be non-resident in all but one of his parishes. Residence was also made difficult if the incumbent was not provided with a house. However, pluralities were not always harmful. If an incumbent had two adjoining parishes with low incomes and small populations, the provision of a single priest for both made sense. If the incumbent could find a suitable house a mile or so outside his parish, he could serve his people well, but would still be classified as non-resident. Even if the incumbent lived some distance away from one of his parishes, he might make provision for his people by employing a resident curate. Sometimes the curate might be the incumbent of an adjacent small parish, who needed additional income to live to the standard expected of a clergyman in the early nineteenth century.

Clergy incomes in the Diocese of York

Archbishop Harcourt's task in the Diocese of York was made more difficult by the generally lower levels of clergy income in his diocese than in the Church of England and Wales as a whole. The figures in the table below are taken from returns made to the Ecclesiastical Commission in 1835. Information on incomes was available for 879 benefices in York diocese. The first column shows the income of the 62 livings in the gift of Archbishop Harcourt, of which 57 were in York diocese.

Incumbent incomes 1835

Income range	Archbishop of York benefices		York Diocese benefices		Church of England & Wales benefices	
	no.	%	no.	%	no.	%
Under £50	4	6.4	49	5.6	297	2.8
£50–£99	11	17.7	191	21.7	1,629	15.5
£100–£149	13	20.9	181	20.6	1,602	15.3
£150–£199	11	17.7	109	12.4	1,355	12.9
£200–£299	8	12.9	136	15.5	1,978	18.9
£300–£399	6	9.7	77	8.8	1,326	12.7
£400–£499	2	3.2	44	5.0	830	7.9
£500–£749	3	4.8	49	5.6	954	9.0
£750 or more	4	6.5	43	4.9	507	4.8
Totals	62		879		10,478	

The figures prepared for the Ecclesiastical Commissioners in 1835 were inevitably estimates and were affected by the quality of an incumbent's bookkeeping due to the large number of sources of income.[1] Much depended on the extent to which the incumbent was able to collect his tithes and, where he farmed his own glebe, his skills as a farmer. At the lower end of the range, an incumbent might seek to minimize his income in the hope of receiving an augmentation from Queen Anne's Bounty. Such augmentations were in the form of a grant to purchase land rather than an addition to income.

The table demonstrates that Archbishop Harcourt was at a disadvantage when wishing to attract clergy to his diocese. The average incumbent income in York diocese was £250 as opposed to the national average of £285. Such average figures can be distorted by a small number of high

---

[1]   The figures are taken from the *Commission to inquire into the Revenues and Patronage of the Established Church of England and Wales*, 16 June 1835, as reproduced in *Clerical Guide 1836*, pp. i–xxxviii.

incomes. In the Diocese of York in 1835, 48 per cent of incumbents had an income of under £150 a year. Nationally around a third, or 34 per cent, received less than £150. York was also less attractive to curates. The average income in York diocese was £75 as opposed to a national figure of £81. Amongst English dioceses, only Norwich diocese had a lower average income for curates.

Training of literates

To overcome the problem of low incomes, Archbishop Harcourt had to look more widely for his clergy than graduates of the two old English universities. The majority of clergy at this time were graduates of Oxford and Cambridge, around two-thirds of whom were ordained. Moving to a fast-growing West Riding industrial town or to a remote moorland parish might not be attractive to a man accustomed to the cultural delights and educated communities of Oxford and Cambridge. As had been the case in Carlisle diocese, many posts in York diocese were filled by clergy who had not been to university. The proper education of literates, as non-graduate clergy were then known, was an area to which Archbishop Harcourt devoted considerable attention.

The need to accept literates was driven by the increasing demand for more clergy. The 111 new churches consecrated by the Archbishop would all have needed their own clergyman. The output of graduates from Oxford and Cambridge did not keep pace with population growth. The increasing recognition that every parish should have a resident minister put pressure on non-resident incumbents to provide a resident curate. Circumstances were such in York diocese that it would have been impossible to provide sufficient clergy without accepting literates. For almost the first 20 years of Archbishop Harcourt's time at York, around half of those ordained were not graduates. The number of literates started to fall from about 1830, but it was not until about 1840 that the number of literates ordained for York diocese fell to 10 per cent or less of all ordinands.[2] By this time, large parts of the West Riding had passed into the new Diocese of Ripon. It was still, however, something of an achievement that in his final years Archbishop Harcourt managed to secure so many graduate ordinands.

The Archbishop has been accused of not taking the training and examination of ordinands sufficiently seriously. Sabine Baring-Gould, in *Church Revival*, stated that when John Sharp went for ordination in 1833, the Archbishop interviewed the candidate briefly: "Well Mr Sharp, so you are going to be curate to your father. Make my compliments to him when you go home. My secretary has your testimonials; he will give you full instructions. Be sure to be at the Minster in good time." Sharp's father was Samuel Sharp, vicar of Wakefield from 1810 and someone Dr Harcourt will have known well through his visitations and regular confirmations in Wakefield parish church. The young John Sharp was subsequently incumbent of Horbury, a living in his father's gift.[3] Clerical fathers often tutored their sons and could seldom afford the cost of three years at Oxford or Cambridge. The vicar of Wakefield earned £537 in 1835.

Although it was widely considered desirable for a clergyman to have an Oxford or Cambridge degree, it was clear to the Archbishop and his staff that a policy of only accepting graduates for ordination was impractical in the Diocese of York. "Harcourt's base line for fitness was quite simply

---

[2]   The most comprehensive analysis of recruitment patterns in the established church is provided by Dr Sara Slinn, *The Education of the Anglican Clergy 1780–1839* (Woodbridge: Boydell Press, 2017). Her articles in the *Yorkshire Archaeological Journal* 80 (2008), pp. 167–87 and 81 (2009), pp. 279–309 review more specifically "Archbishop Harcourt's Recruitment of Literate Clergymen and his Seminaries for Literates in the Diocese of York".

[3]   The comment is quoted in F. W. B. Bullock, *A History of Training for the Ministry of the Church of England 1800–1874* (St Leonards-on-Sea: Budd and Gillatt, 1955) p. 73. Bullock also states that the Archbishop and other bishops had been praised for the quality of the examinations held for deacons' orders (p. 38). Bullock reproduces the story told by Harold Anson of the Archbishop ordaining his nephew John Anson: "I think it will save both you and me some trouble if I shoot through both barrels; so I will ordain you both deacon and priest this afternoon." (p. 73)

those qualifications laid down in Canon 34: character testimonials and proof of learning sufficient to fulfil priestly duties, judged by examination in the period leading up to ordination."[4] He was content to ordain men of humble origin as long as they filled the requirements of the canon. St Bees theological college in Cumbria provided several candidates from humbler backgrounds, who could often be more appropriate for remote communities in the Dales. Literates would be more willing to accept a poor living or an appointment to a district church in an industrial town, where the curate's stipend would not keep a "gentleman" clergyman in the manner he might think appropriate.

St Bees had been founded in 1816 by the Bishop of Chester with funds provided by the Lowther family, whose riches from coal mining had continued to grow. However, with 30 to 40 students at any one time, St Bees produced insufficient ordinands to meet the needs of the established Church. In 1825, the bishops of the northern dioceses met and resolved to improve clergy standards by taking only graduates or candidates from St Bees. Such a strategy was, however, unachievable in the short term. Demand for clergy exceeded output. There was no northern university to supplement graduates from Oxford and Cambridge till Durham was founded in 1832. St David's theological college, Lampeter, opened in 1827, but its initial output of candidates for ordination was small. Archbishop Harcourt had to find another way to ensure his new clergy were adequately educated.

As an interim measure, Archbishop Harcourt introduced new regulations in 1827. Literates would only be accepted for ordination in the Diocese of York if they had either studied for two years with a clerical tutor approved by the Archbishop or attended St Bees. Research by Dr Sara Slinn suggests that the number ordained in the manner approved by the Archbishop rose from about 20 per cent of literates in Dr Harcourt's early years to around half of all literates in 1826–7 and peaked at about 67 per cent in the following year. Thereafter, numbers following the Archbishop's regulations remained around 50 per cent of literates ordained in York diocese.[5]

---

4   Slinn, "Recruitment of Literate Clergymen" (2009), p. 279.

5   Slinn, "Recruitment of Literate Clergymen" (2009), p. 305.

It was inevitable that there would be exceptions, particularly where the candidate was put forward by an experienced incumbent who was known to the Archbishop. As the case of John Sharp quoted above illustrates, Archbishop Harcourt was unlikely to reject the son of the vicar of Wakefield. Another example is Charles Fletcher, who was over the age limit of 30. Fletcher was ordained deacon in 1827 to serve for £50 a year at Sneinton, a suburb of Nottingham. He was recommended by Archdeacon Eyre, a good friend of the Archbishop.[6] Fletcher was to be curate to George Wilkins, who was perpetual curate of Sneinton and incumbent of St Mary's, Nottingham. Harcourt would have known Wilkins from his many visits to Nottingham and must have thought highly of him, as he appointed Wilkins Archdeacon of Nottingham in 1832 following Eyre's death. Archbishop Harcourt's visitations and confirmation tours had enabled him to get to know the leading clergy in major towns in the diocese. His archdeacons could supplement his knowledge when deciding who to approve as tutors for his new policy and who to accept for ordination when the candidate had not been to an approved tutor.

Archbishop Harcourt does not seem to have laid down a reading list, and there is no surviving list of officially approved tutors. Amongst the tutors who provided the most candidates were Thomas Rogers of Wakefield, James Knight of Halifax, James Barber of Wilsden, and William Snowden of Bawtry and Swillington. These and others were the men who helped the Archbishop improve the standard of clergy in York diocese. A letter in the *Gentleman's Magazine* of May 1819 stated: "His grace of York has oftener than once been pleased to say that, generally speaking, he has found the non-graduated [sic] clergy to make the most exemplary parish priests."[7] The clergy who became tutors were often spurred on by the need to make a reasonable living. Providing clerical training could be remunerative, particularly if the incumbent had a large house with room to accommodate the students. Students studying in an incumbent's home were able to participate in the life of the parish and

---

6   Archdeacon Eyre regularly dined at Bishopthorpe. His niece Julia married the Archbishop's seventh son, Granville Harcourt-Vernon.

7   *Gentleman's Magazine*, May 1819, p. 420, quoted in Slinn, "Recruitment of Literate Clergymen".

undertake duties such as home visits and teaching at Sunday school. Training with a clerical tutor combined academic learning with practical parish experience.

Thomas Rogers taught many of the first candidates under the Archbishop's scheme. Rogers was headmaster of Wakefield Grammar School, evening lecturer at St John's Chapel, where he drew large crowds, and chaplain to the West Riding House of Correction. He was author of a book on the liturgy of the Church of England. Many grammar schools provided some form of post-school education, and Rogers was following an established practice. His fees seem to have been modest at £30 per year.

James Knight was another tutor who trained several candidates under the Archbishop's scheme. He was the son of Samuel Knight, the vicar of Halifax, and a noted evangelical. James Knight served as curate in one of his father's district churches until 1824, when he was appointed perpetual curate of St Paul's Sheffield, a living worth £136 a year in 1835. Records show he was paid £60 a year by the Elland Society to train ordinands, a useful supplement to his income.[8] The choice of men like Knight demonstrates that Archbishop Harcourt was happy to have his literate ordinands trained by evangelical clergymen.

John Barber had even more need to supplement his income with the training of ordinands than Knight. Barber received £46 a year as the first incumbent of St Matthew's Wilsden, a church in Bradford parish. The Archbishop heard Barber preach when he consecrated the new church on 1 November 1826.[9] Barber made good use of his connection to the Archbishop when promoting his "Clerical Institution at Wilsden". "His Grace the Archbishop of York has been pleased to confer on the Rev John Barber of St John's College, Cambridge, and incumbent of St Matthew's Wilsden, the privilege of educating candidates for Holy Orders in the

---

8   The Elland Society was founded in 1767 by a group of evangelical clergy and from 1777 supported the training of evangelical clergy in the Diocese of York. <https://www.ellandsociety.org/>, accessed 16 June 2023. Cf. Slinn, "Recruitment of Literate Clergymen" (2009), p. 305.

9   *Leeds Intelligencer*, 9 November 1826.

Diocese of York in conformity with his Grace's present regulations."[10] Barber could accommodate two candidates in his house, with others living in the village. The Archbishop's endorsement meant he had the opportunity to educate candidates for the Diocese of Chester.[11] Barber also prepared graduates for ordination. One such was Thomas Baker, a graduate of St Edmund Hall, Oxford and "the Clerical establishment at Wilsden". He was ordained on 22 November 1829, when the Archbishop complimented him on "having passed a most excellent examination".[12]

William Snowden's situation was somewhat different. He was incumbent of Horbury, a living in the gift of the Lord Chancellor and worth £225 a year. Snowden's family had health problems, and he decided to move to Bawtry in Nottinghamshire. To supplement his income after employing a curate at Horbury, he took in pupils for entry to public schools and universities as well as candidates for ordination. His advertisements emphasized his connections with the Archbishop: "He is authorised by his diocesan to prepare for Holy Orders within the limits of his Grace's jurisdiction such persons as may be desirous to qualify themselves for the Church without previously graduating at one of the universities."[13] In 1837, Snowden became rector of Swillington near Leeds, a valuable living in the gift of Sir James Lowther, a friend of the Archbishop from his time at Carlisle. Although Swillington was worth £510, Snowden continued to prepare ordinands, including graduates. Snowden was himself a literate and wrote a pamphlet defending literates.[14] He was awarded a Lambeth degree by the Archbishop of Canterbury in May 1829.[15]

As time went on, the number of graduates increased with the additional output from Durham and London and an increase in numbers from the

---

[10]   Slinn, "Recruitment of Literate Clergymen" (2009), p. 296; *Derby Mercury* advertisement, 9 April 1828.

[11]   William Cudworth, *Round About Bradford* (Bradford: T. Brear, 1876) p. 231.

[12]   *Staffordshire Advertiser*, 28 November 1829.

[13]   *Stamford Mercury*, 10 December 1830.

[14]   A Yorkshire Incumbent, *The case for Non-Graduate Clergy, usually called Literates* (London: Sherwood, Gilbert & Piper, 1830). The pamphlet was addressed to the Archbishop of Canterbury.

[15]   Clergy of the Church of England Database.

old universities. York diocese was able to attract a greater share of those graduates, and the need for Archbishop Harcourt's scheme fell away. Some tutors adapted to prepare graduates for ordination. The scheme, however, had a profound effect on the nature of the clergy in Yorkshire. Most of the tutors were of an evangelical persuasion, and for many years to come, the church in parts of Yorkshire was dominated by evangelicals. Writing to Lord Liverpool in 1817, Archbishop Harcourt stated he found that those "nicknamed evangelical" were most useful.[16] The Archbishop seems to have been happy with the predominance of evangelicals.

Non-residence and pluralism

"At the beginning of the nineteenth century feeling ran high against non-residence and pluralism ... and there were threats of prosecution of clergy for non-residence."[17] The Clergy Residence Act of 1803 was designed to regulate the situation rather than abolish non-residence. Heads of Oxford and Cambridge colleges, for example, were exempt from the requirement to reside, as well as holders of a second benefice. Bishops could issue exemption certificates to those of ill health and without suitable accommodation. Bishops had to submit annual returns to the Privy Council and had to satisfy themselves that adequate duty was being offered in parishes where the incumbent was non-resident.

Archbishop Harcourt had a challenging task if he was to reduce the incidence of non-residence. He had an above average number of parishes with very low incomes, which encouraged pluralities, and an above average proportion of parishes without a suitable glebe house. Yet when he was appointed, the diocese already had a greater proportion of parishes served by resident clergy than the Church of England and Wales as a whole. In spite of these disadvantages, he managed to continue to reduce the number of incumbents who did not do duty in their parishes,

---

[16] Archbishop of York to the 2nd Earl of Liverpool, 23 December 1817, British Library, Add. MS 3863, f. 132.

[17] W. M. Jacob, *The Clerical Profession in the Long Eighteenth Century 1680–1840* (Oxford: Oxford University Press, 2007), p. 110.

but at a slower rate than in the Church as a whole. By his death, three-quarters of the parishes remaining in the Diocese of York were served by their incumbent and almost two-thirds were resident.

The table below shows that in 1835 half the parishes in York diocese did not have a glebe house fit for the incumbent. Although loans were available from Queen Anne's Bounty to construct a house, it was a major undertaking for a clergyman to build and finance a house out of his income. When he left the living, the house would remain for the next incumbent. His only alternative was to rent somewhere suitable—not always easy in a rural parish.

Glebe house availability 1835[18]

	York diocese	National Church
House fit for use	429 (48.0%)	5,947 (56.4%)
House unfit	167 (18.7%)	1,728 (16.4%)
No house	298 (33.3%)	2,878 (27.3%)
Totals	894	10,553

The tables below show the pattern of non-residence in the Diocese of York during Harcourt's archiepiscopate. The number of resident incumbents appears to fall between 1810 and 1827. The 1810 return was inaccurate with some non-residents doing duty categorized as resident. However the total figure of residents and non-residents doing duty of 61 per cent in 1810 is probably accurate and higher than the national figure of 49 per cent. In subsequent years, the number of resident clergy in York diocese improves more slowly than the overall national figure. The total combined figure for residents and non-residents doing duty in York diocese are better than the national average throughout the period. However, the figures for the Church as a whole improved faster

---

[18]   The figures are taken from the *Commission to inquire into the Revenues and Patronage of the Established Church of England and Wales*, 16 June 1835, as reproduced in *Clerical Guide 1836*, p. 21.

than those for the Diocese of York. Once York was reduced to only 522 benefices in 1836.

Trends in non-residence in the Diocese of York,
1810–46: parishes with resident incumbent[19]

Year	No. of parishes	York per cent	National per cent
1810	461	53.0	43.1
1827	364	44.0	41.9
1831	364	43.9	44.0
1835	410	49.1	48.7
1846	351	67.2	65.4

Trends in non-residence in the Diocese of York,
1810–46: parishes with non-resident doing duty

Year	No. of parishes	York per cent	National per cent
1810	72	8.3	6.1
1827	171	20.7	15.1
1831	179	21.6	16.0
1835	168	20.1	15.6
1846	62	11.9	10.3

---

[19]   The figures are based on returns to Parliament as quoted in Peter Virgin, *The Church in an Age of Negligence: Ecclesiastical Structure and Problems of Church Reform 1700–1840* (Cambridge: James Clarke & Co., 1989), p. 290 and p. 293.

Trends in non-residence in the Diocese of York, 1810–46:
parishes with non-resident not doing duty

Year	No. of parishes	York per cent	National per cent
1810	337	38.7	50.8
1827	293	35.4	43.0
1831	286	34.5	40.0
1835	256	30.7	35.7
1846	109	20.9	24.3

The case of Sydney Smith

Archbishop Harcourt's ambivalent attitude to non-residence and his acceptance of pluralities is well illustrated by the case of Sydney Smith. As founding editor of the *Edinburgh Review*, author of the *Letters of Peter Plymley*, a noted preacher with an acerbic wit and a brilliant conversationalist, Smith was a well-known public figure and Whig commentator. Harcourt could hardly ignore the fact that Smith lived in London and left his parish of Foston, some 12 miles from York, in the care of a curate. Writing to Francis Jeffrey in November 1807, Smith was awaiting the appointment of his "new master at York. I care very little whether he makes me reside or not, and shall take to grazing as quietly as Nebuchadnezzar."[20] When, however, the Archbishop did suggest he should reside at Foston, he was not so keen to move. Writing to his friend Lady Holland, Smith said: "I have no doubt from what you say the Archbishop acted conscientiously. I will do human nature justice to say we are all prone to make other people do their duty." He continued

---

[20] Sydney Smith to Francis Jeffrey, 18 November 1807, Nowell C. Smith (ed.), *Letters of Sydney Smith* (Oxford: Clarendon Press, 1953), letter 120.

by saying he "deprecates Yorkshire as a great evil and if I can procure any tolerable situation in the south, I will do so".[21]

Foston was a good living with an income of about £800 at the time, but it had no suitable house. Smith could not find a living in the south to replace Foston and in June 1809 made the move to Yorkshire. He took a lease on a house at Heslington, some 12 miles from Foston and two miles from York. He drove over to Foston every Sunday to take two services. The Archbishop allowed him to remain non-resident for another four years, whilst Smith continued to hope to find a living in the south. Eventually he started building a parsonage in the parish in June 1813 and moved into the new house with his family in March 1814; he was the first resident rector of Foston since Charles II's time.

In 1823, Sydney Smith was invited to be rector of Londesborough, a living in the gift of the Duke of Devonshire. This was to be in addition to his living of Foston. Londesborough is about 20 miles from Foston and was also worth about £800 a year. The living was destined for William Howard, grandson of the Earl and Countess of Carlisle (the latter being Lady Anne's sister) and nephew of the Duke of Devonshire. The duke's sister, Georgiana, was married to Lord Morpeth, the Earl of Carlisle's eldest son; William Howard would not be old enough to take the living for another nine years. To secure the arrangement, Smith had to sign a resignation bond and agree to leave the living when William reached the required age. Such bonds were made illegal five years later and were not generally favoured by bishops. We must assume that the Archbishop had little choice but to accept the arrangements, bearing in mind his family connections. With an income of £1,600 a year, Smith was able to afford a curate for Londesborough.

Sydney Smith was a Whig and a proponent of Catholic emancipation amongst predominantly Tory clergy and gentry who had little time for concessions to Catholics. An altercation with a local clergyman led to the involvement of the Earl of Carlisle as mediator. The earl wrote to Smith suggesting he avoided attacking all aspects of society: "When you are so capable of giving us both instruction and pleasure, why run amuck

---

[21]   Sydney Smith to Lady Holland, undated, Smith (ed.), *Letters of Sydney Smith*, letter 129.

at every component part of society: Order, Class, Profession, the Bar, the Bench, rural residents, West Indian proprietors, youthful sportsmen, brother magistrates?"[22] Smith did not want to fall out with the leading local aristocrat and wrote a conciliatory reply. He had, however, already sent a controversial article on America to the *Edinburgh Review*. The earl was furious, refused to see Smith and complained to the Archbishop. Smith's interview at Bishopthorpe was embarrassing and, on returning home, he wrote a long letter to the Earl of Carlisle. Smith was not prepared to make an abject apology. He defended his position and accused the earl of suggesting to the Archbishop that Smith's opinions were unlawful. Letters continued to pass back and forth between Foston and Castle Howard. The earl and Smith never spoke again; the earl died in September 1825. Fortunately for Smith, the dispute with the old earl did not harm his relations with the new Earl of Carlisle and Lady Georgiana.[23]

Smith held the living of Foston till 1829, when he became incumbent of Coombe Florey in Somerset. In spite of the awkward dispute with Lord Carlisle, his friendship with the Archbishop and his son William Vernon-Harcourt continued to thrive. Smith also corresponded regularly with the Archbishop's daughter Georgiana. The Archbishop entertained Smith and his family at Bishopthorpe and at Nuneham in Oxfordshire long after Smith had left Foston. Smith wrote to the Archbishop's chaplain in 1816: "I have a most commendable gilt frame for a certain print the Archbishop promised to give me. Pray say for me that I must either hang up the empty frame in token of his Grace's forgetfulness or a full one in token of my respect and thankfulness for his uniform kindness to me."[24]

---

[22] Earl of Carlisle to Sydney Smith, October 1824, Castle Howard Archives, J14/1/496.

[23] The story of the dispute with the Earl of Carlisle is set out in full in Peter Virgin, *Sydney Smith* (London: HarperCollins, 1994) pp. 211–16 and draws on letters in the Castle Howard Archives, J14/1/483–498.

[24] Sydney Smith to the Archbishop's chaplain, 19 August 1816, *Harcourt Papers* (HP), Vol. XII, p. 202.

Patronage and nepotism

Writing immediately following his death, *The Times* stated that the Archbishop "dispensed the great patronage with which a long episcopal life furnished him in a manner which, if it calls for no very extraordinary applause, ought certainly to escape from any kind of censure beyond that which attaches to a little more nepotism than in modern times is sanctioned by the practice of men in high places".[25] Archbishop Harcourt struck a fine balance between the need, as perceived at the time, to provide for his family and for those who had favoured him with the need to ensure his parishes had the services of a competent priest. He also had to ensure, as far as he could, that the diocese was administered by able archdeacons and lay officers.[26]

Appointments to archdeaconries

The four posts which were most critical to the efficient running of the diocese were the four archdeaconries of York, East Riding, Cleveland and Nottingham. Anthony Trollope wrote in 1866:

> An archdeacon has a great deal to do and very little to get. For this reason, an archdeacon must have at least one good living. He is

[25] *The Times*, 8 November 1847, p. 5.

[26] The information throughout this chapter on clergy appointments was obtained from the *Clergy of the Church of England Database* (CCEd) over several months between January and December 2022. The CCEd provides information on clergy for the period up to 1835. The CCEd information was checked against the *Clerical Guides* of 1817 and 1836 (London: FC & J Rivington 1817, 1822, 1829 and 1836)) and the *Clergy List* of 1841 (London: C Cox 1841–1867) and individual church websites. The information on clergy incomes has been taken from the 16 June 1835 report of the *Commission to Inquire into the Revenues and Patronage of the Established Church of England and Wales*. The income figures are estimates averaged over three years to December 1831.

not infrequently a man of means . . . He has to be able to keep a
curate or two, give a dinner and keep at least a one-horse chaise.
He must be able to take his place in county society. He must know
his brother rectors and vicars and have an eye on their welfare.[27]

Fees paid by clergy and churchwardens at visitations and in their courts
were the only source of income for archdeacons. Out of these fees an
archdeacon had to meet the costs of travel, entertainment and payments
to clerks. In 1835, the gross income of the archdeacon of York was £97,
but the net only £59 after expenses. The other three archdeaconries had
net incomes of East Riding £51, Cleveland £30 and Nottingham £15.[28]
The archbishop would need to ensure his archdeacons had at least one
valuable incumbency or a large private income before appointment.

Archbishop Harcourt's first appointment was to the archdeaconry of
Nottingham following Sir Richard Kaye's death in 1809. The Archbishop
chose John Eyre. Eyre had been a chaplain to the Duke of Portland and
had been made a prebend of both York and Southwell by Archbishop
Markham. He held three livings. He was rector of Babworth (£850),
vicar of Headon (£200), and rector of Barton-in-Fabis (£360), which he
exchanged for Beelsby (£450), a Southwell Chapter living, in 1826. He
was also sinecure rector of Headon (£178). Headon was a living in the gift
of the Eyre family, who had extensive estates in north Nottinghamshire.
Eyre fulfilled all of Trollope's criteria and served as archdeacon till his
death in 1830.

The Archbishop's subsequent appointments to the archdeaconry of
Nottingham were men of more modest background. William Barrow
had been running an academy in Sedbergh and may have been known to
Archbishop Harcourt when he was Bishop of Carlisle. He was incumbent
of Waltham in Lincolnshire (£331) and appointed by Harcourt as a
Southwell prebend in 1815. He exchanged Waltham for Beelsby, now
vacant following Eyre's death. Barrow resigned after two years due to ill
health and was replaced by George Wilkins, who was incumbent of St

---

[27] Anthony Trollope, *Clergymen of the Church of England* (London: Chapman
     and Hall,1866), pp. 42–4.

[28] *Commission on Revenues and Patronage in the Established Church*, 1835.

Mary's Nottingham (£699). The Archbishop, who had made Wilkins a prebend of Southwell in 1823, will have known him through his several visits to St Mary's for visitations and confirmations.[29]

The archdeaconry of York was held by Archbishop Markham's son Robert till 1837. Markham also held the living of Bolton Percy (£1,540), the most valuable living in the gift of the Archbishop of York. When he eventually could appoint to the York archdeaconry, Harcourt chose Stuart Corbett, who held the valuable livings of Kirk Bramwith (£517) and Scrayingham (£662).[30] He was succeeded on his death in 1845 by Stephen Creyke, who had been a successful headmaster of St Peter's School in York and for many years chaplain to Harcourt. Creyke was rector of Beeford (£779) and Farlington with Marston (£130). He had been appointed to both incumbencies by Archbishop Harcourt and was clearly chosen for the archdeaconry on the basis of merit.

Francis Wrangham was another archdeacon who had progressed on the basis of his own abilities. Wrangham was the son of a Malton farmer. He had been a tutor to the Duke of Manchester and was examining chaplain to Archbishop Harcourt from 1814 to 1834. The Archbishop told Sydney Smith he considered Wrangham to be an ornament to his diocese.[31] Wrangham was a noted author, translator and editor as well as a competent incumbent of Hunmanby (£350), the East Riding parish he served from 1795 till his death. He was appointed archdeacon of Cleveland in 1820 and in 1828 exchanged Cleveland for the archdeaconry of the East Riding. He was a supporter of Catholic emancipation. He was succeeded as archdeacon of East Riding in 1842 by his son-in-law, Robert Wilberforce, a supporter of the Oxford Movement and son of William Wilberforce, the anti-slavery campaigner.[32]

---

[29] Wilkins' father had been architect to Earl Manvers, who was patron of St Mary's.

[30] Corbett probably had family money as he was a nephew of the Marquis of Bute and cousin of the Earl of Wharncliffe.

[31] David Kaloustian, *Francis Wrangham* (Oxford: Oxford Dictionary of National Biography entry, 23 September 2004), accessed July 2020.

[32] Robert Wilberforce was rector of Burton Agnes and was received into the Roman Catholic Church in 1854.

Francis Wrangham's move to the East Riding archdeaconry enabled the Archbishop to appoint his third son Leveson to the vacant archdeaconry of Cleveland. At the time, Leveson was rector of Stokesley (£1,026) and of Stainton (£323), two livings in his father's gift. He was also a prebend of York and chancellor of York Minster. Leveson resigned the archdeaconry in 1832.[33] He was succeeded by Henry Todd, who was rector of Settrington (£1,045) from 1820.[34] Todd died in 1845, and for the final two years of his life the Archbishop was served as archdeacon of Cleveland by Edward Churton, a Christ Church graduate and high churchman. He had been appointed incumbent of Craike (£672) by the Bishop of Durham and had been a prebendary of York since 1841.

Providing for the Archbishop's immediate family

As already noted, the Archbishop provided his second surviving son, Leveson, with the archdeaconry of Cleveland and with a succession of valuable livings. In 1835, Leveson decided to move south and was appointed incumbent of Beckenham in Kent (£900). Beckenham was a living in the gift of Joseph Cator, who had two clergyman sons, Charles and Thomas. Thomas was already provided with a Yorkshire living.[35] Charles Cator, who had been rector of Beckenham, was appointed as Leveson's replacement at Stokesley (£1,026), a satisfactory exchange

---

[33] Leveson had been ordained in 1812 and immediately appointed incumbent of Sutton in the Forest (£395) by his father. He moved to be incumbent of Rothbury (£1,106) in Northumberland in 1813 and remained there till 1822, when he was moved to Stokesley (£1,026). He was succeeded at Rothbury by his brother Charles, the Archbishop's ninth son. Leveson was also sinecure rector of Kirkby-in-Cleveland (£359) from 1819–23.

[34] Settrington was a living in the gift of the Earl of Bridgewater, a cousin of the archbishop's wife. Todd was librarian at Lambeth Palace, a prebendary of York and a crown chaplain.

[35] Thomas Cator was rector of Kirk Smeaton and Womersley and lived at Skelbrooke Park near Doncaster.

for both families. Leveson resigned his archdeaconry but retained the chancellorship of York Minster when he moved to Beckenham.

Archbishop Harcourt also used his patronage to provide for a further four sons: William, Granville, Charles and Egerton. William and Charles were ordained and would have expected similar treatment to Leveson. Harcourt had only allowed William to leave the navy and seek ordination after the death of his second son Edward, who had been destined for the Church. Granville and Egerton were lawyers and were also able to benefit from their father's patronage when suitable appointments became available.

William Vernon-Harcourt was ordained deacon in August 1813 and priest a month later. He took up his duties as vicar of Bishopthorpe (£134) in February 1814; however, the modest income it supplied was scarcely adequate for his needs, particularly after his marriage in 1824. In 1816, his father increased his responsibilities and income by appointing him incumbent of Etton (£853); he also gave him the sinecure rectory of Kirkby-in-Cleveland in 1823, which added a further £359.

William left Bishopthorpe parish in 1824 and was appointed to the parish of Wheldrake (£450), obtaining a dispensation from the Archbishop of Canterbury to hold Etton and Wheldrake in plurality. Since Kirkby-in-Cleveland involved no cure of souls, a dispensation for this appointment was not required. In 1834, he left Wheldrake and returned to Bishopthorpe for three years, but in 1837 he gave up both Etton and Bishopthorpe on appointment as rector of Bolton Percy (£1,540). This was the most valuable living in the Archbishop's gift and, as previously noted, had been held by Archbishop Markham's son Robert.

William combined his parish duties with the responsibilities of a residentiary canon of York Minster, a role where he could be of considerable help to his father and from which he could also receive additional income. William was at heart a scientist. He was involved with the founding of the Yorkshire Philosophical Society and the British Association for the Advancement of Science and was a Fellow of the Royal Society.[36]

---

[36] William had served five years in the Royal Navy in the West Indies before going to Christ Church Oxford in 1807. The CCEd indicates he served as

The clerical career of William's younger brother Charles was less complex. Born in 1798, he was ordained deacon by his father in October 1823 and raised to the priesthood a month later on 17 November. He succeeded his older brother Leveson as rector of Rothbury (£1,106) in December 1822.[37] He remained at Rothbury, a town in Northumberland with about 3,000 inhabitants, till his death in 1870. He was unmarried and struggled to live within his income. In July 1823, only six months after his appointment, his father wrote to Charles, enclosing a cheque for £100. "I am well aware that you have not the character requisite for forming a good economist, I mean activity and method, but I earnestly exhort you to endeavour to acquire them for your own comfort and credit's sake." His father went on to explain how he had had to manage his funds very carefully when rector of Sudbury. He concluded: "You have my secret on this most important subject; whether you will profit by it remains to be seen."[38] Charles's income was enhanced by £178 in 1830, when he was made sinecure rector of Headon in Nottinghamshire, an Eyre family living.[39] In 1837, he was appointed a canon of Carlisle, a further improvement to his income. Charles seems to have benefited less from his father's patronage than his two older clerical brothers.

---

incumbent of the parish of Nunburnholme, another of the Archbishop's livings, for six months from March to October 1816. He was rector of Bolton Percy till 1865. He married Matilda Gooch in 1824 and they had seven children. He inherited the Harcourt estates from his eldest brother George in 1861 and lived at Nuneham Park for the last ten years of his life.

[37] The right to appoint the rector of Rothbury alternated between the Bishop of Carlisle and the Archbishop of York. Leveson had been appointed by his father. It must be assumed that the archbishop had agreed the appointment of Charles with the Bishop of Carlisle before Leveson resigned.

[38] Archbishop to Charles Vernon-Harcourt, 31 July 1823, HP, Vol XII, pp. 213–15.

[39] In 1830, the sinecure rectory of Headon was in the gift of Anthony Hardolph Eyre, whose daughter Julia was married to Granville Harcourt-Vernon. Granville became Patron of Headon on succeeding to the Grove estate on Eyre's death.

The Archbishop also found appointments for his two lawyer sons. Granville Harcourt-Vernon trained as a barrister and was appointed chancellor of the Diocese of York in 1818. In 1820, as principal of the Chancery Court of York, Granville presided over the dispute between a group of parishioners of St Paul's Sheffield and their incumbent concerning the use of hymns in Book of Common Prayer services. As will be seen, the dispute was resolved by the Archbishop. Although the chancellorship was generally reckoned to be a sinecure, with the bulk of the work undertaken by a deputy, Granville accompanied his father on two visitations. The role was worth about £1,000 a year out of which Granville would have had to find around £200 to pay a deputy.[40]

Egerton Vernon-Harcourt was the Archbishop's youngest son. Born in 1803, he qualified as a barrister in 1830 and was appointed registrar of the Diocese of York by his father.[41] Egerton and his wife, Laura Milner, lived at Whitwell Hall, Whitwell-on-the-Hill, some 14 miles from York. He gave extensive support to his father during his last years, when he accompanied him on his journeys around the diocese and acted for him on many legal issues.

Helping the wider family

Having given priority to five of his sons, the Archbishop was expected to give help to his and his wife's wider families. He ordained his nephew, John Sedley Venables Vernon, as deacon in December 1821.[42] The family living of Sudbury was not available, as it was occupied by Frederick

---

[40] The income figures are quoted in *The History of Parliament* members' biographies and obtained from the Black Book of 1832, and are unlikely to be accurate. Granville was MP for Aldborough 1815–20 and for East Retford 1831–47.

[41] The date of his appointment is uncertain. He was in post by 1835 at the latest. Egerton was a deputy lord lieutenant, JP and a member of the Council of King's College, London from 1856–68.

[42] John Sedley Venables Vernon was the third son of the archbishop's brother Henry, who lived at Nuthall Temple in Nottinghamshire. Henry succeeded

Anson, another of the Archbishop's nephews.[43] Fortunately for John Vernon, his uncle was able to present him to the rectory of Molesworth, Huntingdonshire (£228) on 22 March 1822, the day he was ordained priest. Following Archdeacon John Eyre's death in 1826, the Archbishop offered John Vernon the rectory of Barton-in-Fabis (£360) in place of Molesworth. He also made the young priest a prebendary of Southwell in the same year. John Vernon only stayed at Barton-in-Fabis for three years, when he was presented with the incumbency of Kirkby-in-Ashfield (£730) by the Duke of Portland. John Vernon added the rectory of Nuthall, a family living (£430), in 1837.

Archbishop Harcourt was also able to help his wife's nephew, the Hon. Henry Howard. Ordained deacon on the 2 July and priested three weeks later, Howard was appointed to the Archbishop's living of Stainton-in-Cleveland (£323). After two years, Harcourt appointed him a prebendary of York Minster. His father, the Earl of Carlisle, added the family living of Slingsby (£557) in 1823. In 1824, Archbishop Harcourt offered Howard Sutton-on-the-Forest (£395) in place of Stainton. Although not significantly more valuable, Sutton and Slingsby were only 14 miles apart, as opposed to about 33 between Stainton and Slingsby. Howard served Sutton and Slingsby till 1834, when he was made Dean of Lichfield and rector of Donnington (£673) in Shropshire, a living in the gift of his uncle, the Duke of Sutherland.[44]

The Archbishop also offered livings to more distant family connections. When the living of Carlton-in-Lindrick (£576) became available in 1826, he offered it to Charles Wasteneys Eyre. Charles was the son of Archdeacon Eyre and a cousin of the Archbishop's son Granville's wife Julia. Charles added Babworth (£800) when his father died.[45] In 1826 the

---

his half-brother George as the third Lord Vernon in 1813.

[43]   Frederick Anson was the son of George Anson and Mary Venables Vernon, Dr Harcourt's oldest half-sister. He was subsequently appointed Dean of Chester.

[44]   The archbishop's brother-in-law and friend from Oxford.

[45]   Granville inherited through his wife the Eyre estates of Grove and Headon in north Nottinghamshire, whilst Charles Wasteneys Eyre inherited the Eyre estates at Rampton.

Archbishop gave the living of Molesworth (£228) to Charles Eyre's first cousin George Hardolph Eyre. The living had just been vacated by John Vernon. George Eyre was also vicar of Headon (£200), where in 1830 Charles Vernon-Harcourt was to become sinecure rector.

In 1827, Archbishop Harcourt appointed Charles Vanden Bempde Johnstone to the valuable parish of Felixkirk (£450). Johnstone was brother-in-law to the Archbishop's daughter Louisa. He had been ordained by the Archbishop in 1825 and served about 18 months as a curate on £50 a year "plus surplice fees" in the East Riding parish of Skirpenbeck. Dr Harcourt offered similar help to his son William's brother-in-law William Gooch. Gooch held the family living of Benacre (£440) in Suffolk and the Archbishop added Stainton-in-Cleveland (£323) when it was vacated by Leveson Vernon-Harcourt in 1833. Gooch was appointed a prebendary of York in 1845. In 1846, Archbishop Harcourt appointed his great-nephew Henry Brooke Boothby to Nunburnholme (£302).

One further clergyman who benefited from his connections with the Eyre family was Robert Bryan Cooke. Cooke was the grandson of Mary Eyre, daughter of Anthony Eyre of Rampton. He was given the family living of Owston (£93) near Doncaster by his elder brother in 1833. The Archbishop added Wheldrake (£474) in 1834, when his son William returned to Bishopthorpe for three years.

Promoting the able and filling the poorly remunerated livings

Archbishop Harcourt did not use all his most valuable livings for his archdeacons and family members. Some would inevitably go to younger sons of distinguished county families and to friends and dependents of politicians and others who had favoured his family. However, he was also able to promote humbler clergy, who he had met during his travels on diocesan business. He was willing to promote literates and evangelicals where the opportunity arose, and the cleric seemed the most appropriate man for the role. He looked after those who served him well. He frequently promoted the sons of clergy and curates who had served in the parish for some years.

The Archbishop's appointments to the valuable parish of Beeford illustrate his approach. Beeford, a village of 1,000 inhabitants in the East Riding, became available in 1812 and was worth about £779. Archbishop Harcourt's first appointment to the parish was William Walbanke Childers, a younger son of Childers Walbanke Childers of Cantley Hall near Doncaster, a major landowner with 5,000 acres in Yorkshire and 7,000 in Norfolk. William already had the family living of Cantley, worth £233. When William died in 1833, the Archbishop gave the living to William Tiffin, a man of humbler origin, whom he had first met in 1796, when he appointed him master at Dalston Grammar School, a mile or so down the road from the Bishop of Carlisle's home, Rose Castle. Tiffin was a literate and was ordained by Harcourt at Rose Castle in 1800. He was appointed curate to Joseph Dacre Carlyle at Castle Sowerby on £30 a year. Tiffin's first step up the ladder was a chaplaincy with the Countess of Lonsdale in 1811. In 1812, Archbishop Harcourt secured for Tiffin the vicarage of Kirkby-in-Cleveland, where the Dean of Christchurch was sinecure rector, and in 1814 added Ormesby (£167). Tiffin relinquished Kirkby and Ormesby for two other livings in the Archbishop's gift in 1815, when he was made incumbent of Hayton (£152) in Nottinghamshire and Mattersey (£293). Nineteen years later he relinquished these two livings for Beeford (£779), where he remained till his death in December 1844.[46] Tiffin spent £800 on building a rectory at Beeford and was also made rural dean by the Archbishop.

Another clergyman who benefited from the Archbishop's patronage was the Revd William Henry Dixon. According to Dixon's obituary in the *Gentleman's Magazine*, "The admirable way in which [Dixon] performed the services of the Church and his great courtesy and elegant refinement of manners attracted the attention of the late Archbishop, who appointed him one of his domestic chaplains and was his zealous friend and patron."[47] Harcourt appointed Dixon vicar of Bishopthorpe in 1824, a post he held in plurality with the incumbency of Topcliffe from

---

[46] The CCEd is the source for Tiffin's appointments. Some obituaries make reference to Tiffin being a graduate of Cambridge, but this is another William Tiffin from Norfolk.

[47] *Gentleman's Magazine* 195 (1853), p. 428.

1828. In 1834, Dixon gave up both posts on appointment as vicar of Sutton-on-the-Forest (£395). In 1837, he resigned Sutton-on-the-Forest and returned to Bishopthorpe. At the same time, Dr Harcourt added the vicarage of Etton (£653), a post vacated by William Vernon-Harcourt. Dixon was also a prebendary of Ripon and a canon of York. He was the Archbishop's chaplain from 1828. He had a degree in music from Cambridge and played a leading role in the York music festivals.[48]

If Archbishop Harcourt was to fill the poorly remunerated livings, pluralism would have to be accepted. Acklam West (£44) was in the gift of the Archbishop. The neighbouring parish of Middlesbrough (£34) was in the gift of Thomas Hustler of Acklam Hall. William M. Preston was appointed to both livings in 1816 and was to remain till 1823. An income of £78 was hardly adequate, and Preston was offered the additional parish of Startforth (£150) by the Earl of Lonsdale. When Isaac Benson, a literate, was appointed to those same two small livings in 1824, he had to supplement his income by running a school.

The Archbishop liked to promote clergy already working in the parish. He was patron of the parish of Silkstone, which included the growing town of Barnsley. When the new church of St George at Barnsley (£123) was opened in 1833, Harcourt appointed as incumbent Matthew Mark, a literate who had been a curate in the parish. When Sir Robert Affleck left Doncaster (£125) for Silkstone in 1817, the Archbishop appointed the curate John Sharpe to the vicarage and added the neighbouring small parish of Brodsworth (£367) in 1827. On the death of William Margetson Heald at Birstall (£275) in 1835, Harcourt offered the living to his son William Heald Junior, who had been his father's curate. When Lamplugh Hird, perpetual curate of Keyingham (£92) and vicar of Paull (£160) died in 1842, Archbishop Harcourt promoted Joshua Smyth, a literate and curate at both Paull and Keyingham, to be perpetual curate of Keyingham and James Jones, another curate in the parish, to be vicar of Paull. To ensure Joshua Smyth had a reasonable income, the Archbishop

---

Additional information about Dixon is contained in *A memoir of WH Dixon*, printed for private distribution in 1860 and reproduced by the British Library in 2010. Dixon was independently wealthy from an inheritance from an uncle on his mother's side of the family.

appears to have asked the dean and chapter of York to add the vicarage of Burton Pidsea (£42). Smyth had been receiving £100 as curate. When Lythe (£123) became vacant in 1826, the Archbishop promoted the curate W. Long, who had served in the parish since 1812.

Not all the Archbishop's promotions were a success. James Dallin had been appointed vicar of Holy Trinity Goodramgate (£138) by Archbishop Harcourt's predecessor in 1803. Dallin was a vicar choral at York Minster and Harcourt added the parish of Rudston (£236) in 1823. Rudston is near Bridlington, and Dallin obtained a dispensation to hold both livings. When James Dallin died in 1833, Harcourt promoted the curate Edward John Raines to Holy Trinity Goodramgate. Raines was also a vicar choral at York Minster. Robert Dallin, who had been curate to his father at Rudston since 1824, took over Rudston. Robert's appointment was not a success. In 1846, he was suspended for two years for drunkenness, following a report by the vicar of Hunmanby.[49]

Promotion of a son to succeed his father was generally favoured by the Archbishop. When James Richardson, vicar of Crambe (£180) and perpetual curate of Huttons Ambo (£93), two villages some four miles apart, died, he was succeeded at both parishes by his son William Richardson. At Guisborough (£72), the Archbishop appointed William Williamson to succeed his father on the latter's death in 1835. William had been his father's curate. Unfortunately, like his father, he died of cholera some six months after his promotion.

Advising patrons

The extent to which patrons consulted the Archbishop is uncertain, since few letters on the subject appear to have survived. It must be expected that he would have been consulted on appointments to bishoprics, although such appointments would usually be influenced by political factors. When the Earl of Liverpool was appointing Dr Howley as Bishop of London in 1813, he expressed his gratitude to Archbishop Harcourt for approving

---

[49]   *Archbishop Thompson's Visitation Returns*, ed. Edward Royle, Ruth M. Larsen, Borthwick Institute, Texts and Studies 34 (2006), p. 36.

the appointment of Howley and wrote: "It is unnecessary for me to add that I have had no object whatever in this recommendation but to make the arrangement which appeared to me, under all the circumstances, to be most likely to promote the interests of the Established Church."[50] In 1836, when the Diocese of Ripon was carved out of the Diocese of York, the Harcourt Papers note that "Lord Melbourne had such confidence in the Archbishop's judgement that, under his advice, he nominated in 1836 Bishop Longley to the see of Ripon and in 1837 Bishop Denison to the see of Salisbury". It was also on the basis of Archbishop Harcourt's advice to Lord Melbourne that Samuel Wilberforce, the future Bishop of Oxford, was recommended to the Prince Consort as his chaplain.[51]

In April 1812, Prime Minister Spencer Perceval asked the Archbishop for his advice concerning the sinecure rectory of Gedney in Lincolnshire. Perceval did not want to make an appointment "if the exercise of it could, consistently with the advantage of the parish, be withholden till some measures might be taken with a view to the erection of a church and a residence for a clergyman".[52] Perceval had been poorly briefed. In addition to the sinecure rectory worth £783, Gedney had a vicarage worth £667 and a church for its 1,800 inhabitants. Both appointments were in the gift of the king. The Hon. Thomas Alfred Harris, second son of the Earl of Malmesbury, was appointed to the rectory in June 1812. He was also rector of Chilmark (£426) in Wiltshire and was married to a daughter of George Markham, Dean of York.

In December 1817, Dr Coulthurst, the vicar of Halifax, died and the prime minister, Lord Liverpool, on behalf of the Crown asked the Archbishop for his views on the appointment of Samuel Knight to the vacancy. Knight had been perpetual curate at Halifax Holy Trinity chapel since 1798. Lord Liverpool had received innumerable letters from parishioners supporting Knight. Liverpool wrote:

---

[50]   Lord Liverpool to Archbishop of York, 18 August 1813, HP, vol XII, p. 196. Howley was subsequently to be appointed Archbishop of Canterbury.

[51]   HP, Vol. XII, pp. 229–30.

[52]   S. Perceval to the Archbishop of York, 18 April 1812, HP, Vol. XII, pp. 192–3.

I am not in general disposed to pay attention to these kinds of representations for local preferment. They are obviously liable to great objections, but there are circumstances which may justify a departure from the general rule, and if I was to learn from you that Mr Knight was not only unexceptionable, but was eminently qualified for the situation, I might be disposed to attend to the representations which have been made to me and to recommend Mr Knight for the living.[53]

The Archbishop wrote back to Lord Liverpool: "Of Mr Knight I can with great confidence report to your Lordship most favourably. He is a pious, active intelligent man, firm in his principles, political as well as religious, and I understand very generally beloved and respected in Halifax and its chapelries. I can answer for his having been held in great estimation by poor Dr Coulthurst." Dr Harcourt mentioned he had met Knight on visits to Halifax and emphasized that it was his serious and deliberate opinion that Knight was sufficiently qualified for the role. He noted that Knight was what is termed an evangelical and that he had found such clergy most useful and respectable. Knight was installed as vicar of Halifax in February 1818.[54] At the time, Lord Liverpool understood the living was worth "five or six hundred a year". The 1841 *Clergy List* valued Halifax at £1,678. The perpetual curacy of Holy Trinity was worth £130.[55]

The extent to which Dr Harcourt's views were respected by patrons is further illustrated by the decision of Lord Brougham when Chancellor in 1830 to invite him to name clergymen for the Lord Chancellor's poor livings in the diocese. This was "a favour to the Archbishop which [the

---

[53]   Earl of Liverpool to the Archbishop of York, 20 December 1817, HP, Vol. XII, pp. 197–9.

[54]   The Archbishop to Lord Liverpool, 23 December 1817, and Lord Liverpool to the archbishop, 29 December 1817, HP, Vol. XII, pp. 199–201. Knight's father had been an independent minister. Knight was supported at Cambridge by the Elland Society and was also vicar of Humberston in Lincolnshire, a living he resigned on becoming vicar of Halifax.

[55]   *Clergy List* (London: G Cox 1841).

chancellor] did to no other Bishops".[56] The Lord Chancellor must have been satisfied that the Archbishop knew his diocese sufficiently well to perform this task.

The Archbishop could also become involved where there were disputes between a patron and the local inhabitants regarding the appointment of an incumbent. A dispute arose in May 1829 between the vicar of Almondbury, a growing suburb of Huddersfield, and the congregation of the chapel at Meltham, a district in Almondbury parish. A large group of inhabitants wanted to appoint a Mr Keen, who had been curate to the previous incumbent of Meltham Chapel. The right to appoint rested with the vicar of Almondbury, who had appointed himself to the role. The inhabitants, with the support of 50 constables sworn in by a local magistrate, a Mr Stocks, prevented the vicar of Almondbury entering the Meltham Chapel. For a period of three months, no services were held in the church or corpses buried in the churchyard. Lord Harewood, the chairman of the magistrates, became involved, as did the Archbishop, who in turn involved the prime minister, Robert Peel. Stocks eventually realized he was in the wrong. He returned to Meltham and tried to depose the 50 constables and secure the entry of the vicar to the chapel. Peace was ultimately restored. Stocks tried to justify his behaviour to the Archbishop, who would not accept Stocks' explanation. The Archbishop pointed out to Stocks that for three months he had supported illegal action by some inhabitants of Meltham.[57]

Sir Robert Peel took the Archbishop's advice during his two terms as prime minister. In 1835, Peel needed to find a new vicar of Dewsbury, a major and growing parish with several district churches. Peel stated he was "entirely confident in the advice" the Archbishop might give. Peel had been considering a candidate named Howgill, who had been minister at one of the district churches. The Archbishop replied that he was awaiting references for various candidates. The Archbishop then recommended Thomas Allbut, whom Peel appointed. Allbut had

---

[56]   HP, Vol. XII, p. 219.

[57]   Correspondence between the Archbishop and Sir Robert Peel and M. Stocks, July and August 1829, National Archives, HO 44/18, ff. 458, 460, 462, 466 and 468; *Leeds Intelligencer*, 23 July 1829; *York Herald*, 9 August 1829.

been curate at Dewsbury for three years and is another example of the Archbishop promoting existing parish clergy.[58]

Peel continued to consult Archbishop Harcourt during his second term of office from 1841 to 1846. It was the practice to appoint a minister for new district churches as soon as they were constituted and before the church was built. The Archbishop advised on appointments to two proposed churches in Hull, one in Stainton-in-Cleveland and one in Darnall, Sheffield in 1844–5. In 1846, when aged 89, the Archbishop consulted the clergy of Pontefract before recommending to Peel a candidate for Christ Church, East Knottingley.[59]

Archbishop Harcourt gained a wide knowledge of his clergy from visitations and from his tours to consecrate churches and burial grounds and to conduct confirmations. Dinners and informal gatherings held during his travels gave him the chance to get to know clergy of all ranks in his diocese. This knowledge enabled him to identify clergy worthy of promotion and to assist patrons. He consulted locally before recommending candidates for incumbencies. He drew on his small team of chaplains, secretary and registrar as well as his archdeacons to identify candidates worthy of promotion. Patrons who asked his advice found it worth taking.

---

[58]   The Archbishop of York to Sir Robert Peel, 10 April 1835 and undated, British Library, Peel letters, Add. MS 40419, f. 295, Add. MS 40420, f. 117 and f. 118.

[59]   The Archbishop of York to Sir Robert Peel, 8 November 1844, British Library, Peel letters, Add. MS 40457, ff. 362–3 and Add. MS 40553, ff. 256–256b; The Archbishop to Sir Robert Peel and Peel's replies, 7 January 1844, Add. MS 40557, ff. 244–57; 16 January 1846, Add. MS 40582, f. 331; 14 April 1846, Add. MS 40589, f. 383.

6

The Archbishop's contribution to music

Music was important to the Archbishop. Although there are no records of him receiving any musical education as a child or undergraduate, his invitation in 1810 to become a director of the Concerts of Ancient Music suggests he had a good knowledge of the subject.[1] This role required him to be able to compile concert programmes and select performers. He played a leading role in establishing the York Music Festivals, the first of which took place in York Minster in 1823. Prior to this date, he and Lady Anne had sponsored concerts in York as well as being involved with a music festival in Carlisle.

Organizing concerts programmes for the wealthy and aristocratic members of the community may have been important at the time, but Archbishop Harcourt's enduring contribution in the field of music was to hymn singing in Church of England services. Metrical psalms such as those of Sternhold and Hopkins and Tate and Brady had been sung in services since the sixteenth century. More modern hymnals were widely used in the early nineteenth century, particularly by evangelicals, but their use in Book of Common Prayer services was questionable. A case brought before the Consistory Court of York in 1820 gave the Archbishop the opportunity to establish the right to sing hymns in Prayerbook services.

---

[1]   The spellings "Antient" and "Ancient" are both used. The concert programmes use "Antient", but the press mostly "Ancient".

Concerts of Ancient Music

The Concerts of Ancient Music had been established by a committee of noblemen led by the Earl of Sandwich in 1776. The music played had to be at least 25 years old. There were usually eight directors, who each took responsibility for one or two concerts each season. The director selected the music to be played and chose the principal performers. By the time the Archbishop became a director in 1810, the concerts were held in the Hanover Square Rooms. There were 12 concerts a season, usually on a Wednesday evening, between February and May.[2]

The Archbishop directed his first concert on 20 February 1811 and a second on 13 March. His fellow directors were the Prince Regent, the two royal dukes of Cumberland and Cambridge, and the Earls of Uxbridge, Fortescue, Darnley and Wilton. The patrons were King George III and Queen Charlotte, who both attended regularly. The conductor from 1793 to 1831 was the noted organist, composer and astronomer Thomas Greatorex, who no doubt assisted the directors in their choice of music and performers. The programmes were dominated by pieces from Handel's oratorios and operas. Mozart's music was included from 1826 and Beethoven's from 1835. When Greatorex died in 1831, he was replaced by William Knyvett from 1832–40.[3] The directors chose their own conductor as well as the music and principal performers in 1841 and 1842. However, in 1843, the directors decided it was best to appoint a regular conductor, and Sir Henry Bishop (Composer of "Home Sweet Home"), took the role. He had conducted several Ancient Music concerts prior to his appointment in 1843.

According to the author of *Strawberry Fair*, the Archbishop had a high opinion of his own musical knowledge. Prior to his concert in March, he

---

[2]   The information on the Ancient Concerts is taken from copies of the printed programmes. A background note by John Parry in the 1847 programmes provides a history of the concerts.

[3]   William Knyvett was a noted countertenor and composer to the Chapel Royal, and also a lay clerk at Westminster Abbey. He conducted a number of festivals, including Birmingham and York. He and his wife had sung at Ancient Concerts on many occasions before he was appointed conductor.

had "with great condescension written a number of little notes suggesting to Braham the best way to sing his various songs. The fantastic conceit of it had tickled the incomparable singer." John Braham was one of the leading tenors of the day and in September of the previous year had sung at the York Music Festival. The singer's amusement did not apparently please the Archbishop, who was less than supportive when his eldest son George proposed some nine years later to marry Braham's daughter Elisabeth Countess Waldegrave as her third husband.[4]

It was the practice of all directors to hold a pre-concert dinner for their fellow directors. *The Times* of 12 March 1812 noted: "Yesterday the Prince Regent attended by Col Bloomfield dined with the Archbishop of York to meet the other directors of the Concerts of Ancient Music prior to attending the concert." When the king and queen attended, special arrangements had to be made:

> On account of his Majesty honouring the concert this evening, subscribers are required to enter at the door in Hanover Square and to desire their coachmen to drive round the square and to set down and take up with their horses' heads towards George Street.[5]

One night in February 1820, the Archbishop was hosting a dinner for the directors at his house in Grosvenor Square when Lord Harrowby was also to host a dinner for cabinet members in the adjacent house. The Cato Street conspirators planned to assassinate the cabinet at Lord Harrowby's dinner. Fortunately for the Archbishop and his fellow directors, an informer had passed the details of the conspirators' plans to the government. The ministers dined elsewhere and, at the appointed hour, George Canning is supposed to have joked to his fellow cabinet members: "The Directors of the Concerts of Ancient Music are being

---

4   O. W. Hewett, *Strawberry Fair: A Biography of Frances, Countess Waldegrave 1821–1879* (London: John Murray, 1956), pp. 12 and 60.

5   *The Times*, 21 March 1821.

assassinated in the name and on behalf of His Majesty's Ministers." The conspirators were arrested before reaching Grosvenor Square.[6]

The concerts were financed by subscribers, who paid a fixed sum for all 12 concerts. Between 1811 and 1816 there were around 680 subscribers, although the secretary reported in 1813 that some of those who had promised to subscribe failed to pay up. Numbers of subscribers exceeded 700 in most years from 1816 to 1826, when a decline set in. By 1833, they had fallen to only 323 and, to generate more revenue, the subscribers were permitted to buy additional tickets for single concerts at one guinea. With the decline in subscribers, the directors reduced the number of concerts to eight in 1834. The costs were substantial. A typical concert involved over 100 performers; in addition to eight principal singers, there were around 50 choristers and more than 50 instrumentalists.

On 18 May 1836, the then Princess Victoria attended an Ancient Music Concert organized by the Archbishop. At 6 p.m., the Princess went to Grosvenor Place, where she dined with Archbishop Harcourt, some of his fellow directors and several members of his family.[7] A little before 8 o'clock, the party went on to the concert where they were joined in the directors' box by the Duchess of Cambridge and Lady Westminster. The Princess sat between Lord Cawdor and Lord Burghersh. The party left the concert at 11.45 p.m.[8]

When Queen Victoria ascended the throne in 1837, she became patron, and in 1840 Prince Albert became a director. *The Times* announced on 16 May 1838: "Her Majesty will honour the performance of Ancient Music with her presence tonight." The following day the paper reported: "The Duke of Cambridge gave a dinner as director at Cambridge House for HRH Princess Augusta and the Duchess of Gloucester, the Archbishop of York and Miss Vernon, the Duke of Devonshire, Earl Howe, Lord and Lady Burghersh and Mr Knyvett. All including Prince George of

---

[6] George Canning was at the time President of the Board of Control. He was subsequently Foreign Secretary and Prime Minister. HP, Vol. XII, pp. 206–7.

[7] Sir John and Lady Johnstone (son-in-law and daughter), Mr Granville Harcourt Vernon (son), Colonel Francis Vernon-Harcourt (son) and Miss Vernon-Harcourt (daughter Georgiana).

[8] *Queen Victoria's Journal*, 18 May 1836.

Cambridge went to the concert."[9] In spite of the queen's patronage and attendance, subscriber numbers remained low. In the three years 1839–41, there were around 300. By 1846, there were only 214 subscribers, with 457 single tickets sold and a further 370 for rehearsals. The final concerts were held in 1848, the year after Archbishop Harcourt's death.

By modern standards the concerts were very long, and patrons did not always stay to the end. One of the factors which may have influenced attendance was the lack of variety in the performances. The final concert of 1840 was directed by the Archbishop for Earl Fortescue. The programme included items from Handel's *Messiah*, the *Dettingen Te Deum* and an aria from *Sosarme*, as well as arias and duets from three Mozart operas—*La Clemenza di Tito, Le Nozze di Figaro* and *Don Giovanni*. Other composers included Paisiello, Horsley, Haydn and Mehul. Horsley's glee was the only item encored: "Most of the pieces were well known; indeed, many of them were almost too familiar for the occasion. The selection from Mozart was too predominating for so modern a composer and none of the pieces illustrated the early history of the art."[10] The queen dowager (Queen Charlotte), the Duchess of Cambridge and the Duke of Wellington were present. "The concert was over by nearly 12 o'clock but the company began to disperse some time before."[11]

The Archbishop clearly enjoyed his responsibilities as a director and was happy to plan additional concerts when a director was too busy to organize his own. His knowledge of early music must have been considerable if he was able to develop between two and four different programmes each year for 36 seasons. He continued in the role from 1810 till his death in 1847. Most years he compiled programmes for one or two concerts for himself and at least one for another director. In 1827, for example, he directed four concerts. In addition to his own concert, he directed two for the Duke of Cumberland and one for Earl Fortescue. In

---

[9]   Following Lady Anne's death in 1832, the Archbishop's daughter Georgiana accompanied him to social functions.

[10] William Horsley (1774–1858) was a composer and organist. He was famous for the composition of glees, English part songs popular in the Georgian era.

[11] *The Times*, 28 May 1840.

his ninetieth year, the Archbishop directed his own concert on 19 May, when Prince Albert was present, and a second for the King of Hanover on 3 June, only five months before his death.[12]

York Music Festivals

By the time he was appointed Archbishop of York, Harcourt had already had some experience of music festivals. As a canon of Gloucester, he had welcomed George III and Queen Charlotte to the Three Choirs Festival in 1787.[13] Twenty years later, he was lead patron of the first Carlisle Music Festival in September 1807. Three Handel oratorios were performed in the cathedral and two "miscellaneous concerts" in the Assembly Rooms. The conductor was the noted Polish-born composer Felix Yaniewicz.[14]

Dean Markham had opposed the use of York Minster for music festivals. It was not therefore until Markham's death in 1822 and Cockburn's appointment in 1823 that an approach could be made to organize a festival in the Minster. The Archbishop was amongst the first to write to congratulate the new dean and suggest a music festival should be organized "in the magnificent temple over which he was called to preside". The dean immediately agreed.[15]

Archbishop Harcourt and Dean Cockburn met in May 1823 to agree the date for the festival. After checking with the Birmingham and Liverpool festivals to avoid a clash of dates, it was agreed to hold the York festival in September 1823. In planning the festival, the Archbishop could draw on his experience of organizing other concerts in York, his nephew George Vernon's experience as president of the fourth Derby

---

[12] *The Times*, 20 May 1847. The Duke of Cumberland became King of Hanover on the death of William IV. Under Salic law, Queen Victoria could not become Queen of Hanover.

[13] See Chapter 1.

[14] *York Herald*, 22 August 1807.

[15] John Crosse, *Grand Music Festival Held in September 1823 in the Cathedral Church of York* (York: John Wolstenholme, 1825), pp. 138–9.

Festival in 1819 and his contacts with performers as a director of the Ancient Music Concerts.[16]

The Archbishop played a major role in organizing the 1823 Festival. He secured the services of John Raper, a local banker, to chair a committee of 18, which included the Archbishop's chaplain, W. H. Dixon, as well as the dean and Archdeacon Eyre. There were representatives from Hull, Sheffield and Leeds, whose hospitals were to receive a share of the profits, as well as the York infirmary. The Archbishop was responsible for securing the patronage of the aristocracy: 111 patrons were obtained, of whom 70 attended the festival. They included five dukes, two marquises, seven earls, four viscounts, ten lords and 19 baronets. A guarantee fund was established to which the Archbishop contributed £200. A total of £2,850 was raised to guarantee the festival.[17]

Choosing the lead conductor would be critical to the festival's success. The Archbishop secured the services of Thomas Greatorex, conductor of the Concerts of Ancient Music. Greatorex had been conductor of the Birmingham Music Festival since 1819 and was also involved with Derby festival. In late June, the Archbishop invited Greatorex to stay at Bishopthorpe to determine the scope of the York festival. Members of the committee were invited to Bishopthorpe to discuss the plans. The organists from the Minster, Dr and Mr Camidge, who had been involved in planning earlier concerts in York, were appointed assistant conductors. Greatorex spent about two weeks at Bishopthorpe, leaving on 7 July.[18]

The York newspapers were enthusiastic about the festival and kept readers abreast of the plans, which involved four performances in the Minster, two concerts in the Assembly Rooms and two balls. The

---

[16]   The Archbishop had been to two concerts at St Michael-le-Belfry adjacent to York Minster in 1810 (Crosse, *Grand Music Festival*, p. 95), and Lady Anne had been patron of a concert in January 1819 which raised £265 for York Hospital. The Hon. George Vernon of Sudbury had presided over the third Derby Festival, which had been attended by Prince Leopold, the widower of Princess Charlotte, the Prince Regent's daughter (John Crosse, *Grand Music Festival 1823*, p. 121).

[17]   Crosse, *Grand Music Festival 1823*, pp.141–2 and pp. 145–6.

[18]   *Yorkshire Gazette*, 12 July 1823.

Lord Mayor had given permission for a Mr Sadler to ascend in a large
balloon during the festival. The committee invited local residents to tell
them of accommodation available for "strangers". Tickets for the four
performances in the cathedral cost £3 13s 6d in the West Gallery, which
was installed for the festival, and £2 15s on the floor of the Great Aisle.
Single tickets were from 7s in the side aisles to £1 1s in the West Gallery.
Concert tickets in the Assembly Rooms were 15s.[19]

The 1823 festival was an outstanding success. The Archbishop
preached at a well-attended service in the Minster on the Sunday at
10.30 a.m. He spoke about the interdependence of the various classes of
society and of the benevolence required of the wealthy and the claims
of the public hospitals for their support. On Tuesday 23 September,
"the Archbishop rose from his seat in the Gallery and signified by the
waving of his hat that the performance should begin".[20] There were 3,052
in attendance at the Minster on the first day, and over 4,400 attended on
each of the subsequent three days. The two evening concerts attracted
about 1,500 each, and the first ball 1,400. The second was less successful
with an attendance of 900. The *York Herald* commented that the event
had substantially exceeded all expectations and that the organizers had
assembled "one of the most numerous and superlative collections of talent
which ever was assembled".[21] The Archbishop's role in developing the
festival was widely recognized: "The Committee considers itself under
the deepest obligation to His Grace the Archbishop of York for promoting
and forwarding the Yorkshire Music Festival and for his Grace's zealous
exertions towards its success." The Archbishop was subsequently voted
the Freedom of the City of York.[22]

Financially the 1823 festival also achieved its objective. The total
income was £15,878 and the profit to be shared between the four hospitals
was £7,200. The musicians had cost £5,810, erecting the galleries in the
Minster £1,700. Printing and advertising cost £600 and other expenses

---

[19] *York Herald*, 19 July 1823.

[20] Crosse, *Grand Music Festival 1823*, p. 179; and *Yorkshire Gazette*, 20
      September 1823.

[21] *York Herald*, 27 September 1823.

[22] Crosse, *Grand Music Festival 1823*, Appendix IV, pp. XV and XIX.

£330.[23] It was reckoned that visitors to the festival had spent £50,000 in the city in addition to the £15,000 on tickets.

In 1825, a second music festival was held. The Archbishop asked King George IV to be patron, to which the monarch agreed. The Archbishop was president, and his chaplain, W. H. Dixon, took on the committee chairmanship. Greatorex was retained as conductor. A new concert hall had been constructed, and the proceeds from the evening concerts were to be used to meet the costs of its building. Although attendances held up and the concerts were well received, the surplus on events in the Minster was only £1,900. The share for each hospital was £475, well down on the £1,800 of 1823. The committee, however, had a problem. The receipts for the concerts did not cover the costs of building the new concert hall, and the committee was left with a deficit of £4,000, which could not be met from the guarantee fund. There were suggestions the hospitals might repay their donations, but in the end a public appeal was launched.[24]

The third festival in 1828 was again presided over by the Archbishop. Dixon remained chairman and Greatorex the conductor. Once again there were over 600 performers. The financial outcome was also an improvement on 1825. A profit of £2,550 was available from the main festival for sharing between the four charities and a further £1,400 surplus from the events in the concert hall, giving a total of £987 to each hospital.

There were no further music festivals in York Minster until 1835. The fire of 1829 prevented any repeat festival till the Minster was reopened in 1832. By the time the festival was revived, Greatorex was dead and a new conductor was required. Dixon was replaced by the dean as chairman of the organizing committee. The Archbishop was now in his late seventies and might also have expected to play a lesser role. However, Princess Victoria and the Duchess of Kent agreed to attend and the Archbishop entertained the royal party at Bishopthorpe. Most of his family played a part in the proceedings, with his daughter Georgiana acting as hostess following her mother's death three years earlier.

---

[23]   *Strangers Guide through City of York and its Cathedral* (York: Bellerby's New Circulating Library, 1825), p. 34.

[24]   *Leeds Intelligencer*, 1 September 1825 and 23 March 1826.

The dean chaired the committee, which continued to include Dixon and the Archbishop's son William Vernon-Harcourt. After some debate the committee agreed to share the surplus equally between the four county hospitals and the Minster, where £3,000 to £4,000 was still required to pay for the restoration following the fire. Mr Knyvett and Mr Camidge were the conductors. The festival would take place over four days from Tuesday 8 September.[25] There were complaints that the programme contained "the most hackneyed pieces of Ancient Concerts strung together with an utter disregard of style". The programme was dominated by Handel, with little music from Beethoven or Mozart.[26]

Financially the festival made a surplus. Ticket prices were unchanged from 1828 at a guinea for the West Gallery and 5s for the North Transept. The list of patrons remained impressive, and the Princess and the Duchess of Kent donated £100 each. The surplus exceeded £3,500, giving £1,750 to the Minster funds and £437.50 to each hospital. The Archbishop came in for some criticism for supporting a festival which many would deem profane due to the inclusion of a fancy dress ball.[27] The general outlook had become more puritanical in the period since the previous festival.

The Archbishop must have found the week-long visit of the Duchess of Kent and Princess Victoria exhausting even with the support of many members of his family. The Princess and her mother arrived at Bishopthorpe on Saturday 5 September in time for lunch at 2 p.m. This was largely a family party; in addition to the Archbishop and his daughter Georgiana, his sons Granville, Francis and Egerton were present and staying in the house, plus the Archbishop's daughter Louisa and her husband Sir John Johnstone, also Lady Norreys, the Archbishop's recently married granddaughter by his eldest son George. Granville was accompanied by his wife Frances and daughter Marianne. The Archbishop's son Charles was staying with his brother William and his wife Matilda, and they joined the party for dinner, when Lady Norreys

---

[25]   *Yorkshire Gazette*, 28 February 1835, 14 March 1835; *York Herald*, 9 May 1835.

[26]   *York Herald*, 15 August 1835.

[27]   Pippa Drummond, *Provincial Music Festivals in England 1784–1914* (Farnham: Ashgate, 2011), p. 82.

and her cousin Marianne Harcourt-Vernon sang a duet. Princess Victoria noted that the two girls were pupils of Tamburini.[28] The Princess remarked that they were both "extremely pretty" but liked Marianne's voice best.[29]

The next day, a Sunday, the princess and the rest of the party at the Palace went at 11 a.m. to Bishopthorpe church, where William Vernon-Harcourt preached. The princess visited the vicarage and was introduced to William's children, before returning to the palace for lunch. The party made a second visit to church at 3 o'clock. After dinner, during which there was much discussion of the forthcoming festival, two representatives of the singers Grisi and Rubini came to talk to the Archbishop's daughter Georgiana about their treatment by the festival committee.[30] It was agreed that Colonel Harcourt, the Archbishop's son Francis, would go over to York the next morning to "settle things amicably".[31]

The following day the Duchess of Kent received an address from the Mayor and Corporation of York and another from the inhabitants of York in the dining room at Bishopthorpe before the royal party, including the Archbishop and his family, went to the Mansion House to join the mayor and corporation for lunch. In the afternoon, William Vernon-Harcourt showed the party around the Yorkshire Philosophical Society's museum—"a very curious collection of Geology, Mineralogy and Natural History in excellent order"—before going to the Minster to watch a rehearsal. Grisi and Rubini were there, and the latter sang a Handel aria. Princess Victoria was "well tired" on arrival back at Bishopthorpe but recovered sufficiently to meet an enlarged party of guests for dinner.[32]

---

[28] Antonio Tamburini (1800–1876) was a noted Italian operatic baritone. Between 1832 and 1843, he sang regularly in both London and Paris.

[29] *Queen Victoria's Journal*, 5 September 1835.

[30] Giulia Grisi (1811–1869) was a leading operatic soprano. Giovanni Battista Rubini (1794–1854) was the leading Italian operatic tenor of his day. Grisi and Rubini sang regularly together in London and Paris during the late 1830s and 1840s.

[31] *Queen Victoria's Journal*, 6 September 1835.

[32] *Queen Victoria's Journal*, 7 September 1835.

For the subsequent four days, the Princess and her mother attended the concerts in the Minster. Most of the party at Bishopthorpe went every day, though whether the Archbishop always attended is not clear from the princess's diary. Performances started at 12 noon, and there was a break after Part 1 with the Bishopthorpe party lunching either with the dean and Mrs Cockburn at the deanery or with William Vernon-Harcourt and his wife at the canon's residence. The princess enjoyed much of the music but found the *Messiah* on the Tuesday "very heavy and tiresome", except for some of the choruses. She was immensely impressed with the Minster, stating that "the effect was much finer than Westminster Abbey". The princess attended an evening concert on the Wednesday and the ball on the Friday evening. The Archbishop avoided the ball.[33]

After a week at Bishopthorpe, the princess and her mother moved on to Harewood House for two nights. The Archbishop and Georgiana accompanied them, and the next day, a Sunday, the Archbishop preached in Harewood Church. Princess Victoria wrote:

> The Archbishop is an extraordinary person for his age. He is nearly 78 years old, has all his teeth, has a very powerful voice and is extremely active and his mind is as perfect as any young man's.

The Archbishop and Georgiana continued to accompany the royal party for a further two days, visiting Earl Fitzwilliam at Wentworth House before returning home. Although the Archbishop had stayed many times at Harewood and Wentworth, he must have been tired by the long royal visit. Of Harewood the Princess stated: "The house is fine but not near so comfortable as Bishopthorpe."[34] The visit had enabled the Archbishop to develop a firm friendship with his future queen.

There were no further music festivals at the Minster during the Archbishop's final 12 years at York. The second fire in the Minster in 1840 and the Archbishop's visitation to the dean and chapter of York Minster in

---

[33] *Queen Victoria's Journal*, 8–11 September 1835.

[34] *Queen Victoria's Journal*, 12–15 September 1835.

1841, which questioned the dean's behaviour, might well have precluded any possibility of a festival centred there after 1840.[35]

Hymn singing in Book of Common Prayer services

There was no provision for singing hymns in Book of Common Prayer services. The psalms and canticles could be sung and an anthem in "Quires and places where they sing".[36] Metrical psalms had been used in parish churches since the sixteenth century. However, by the 1820s, many Church of England churches, including Bishopthorpe parish church, used books which included metrical psalms and more modern hymns.[37]

On 6 July 1820, a case came before Granville Harcourt-Vernon, as chancellor of the York diocese, in the ecclesiastical court in York. Daniel Holy and Samuel Broomhead Ward, churchwardens of St Paul's Sheffield, alleged that their incumbent, Thomas Cotterill, was acting contrary to the rules of worship of the Church of England by introducing a book of metrical psalms and hymns not authorized by the Book of Common Prayer. Cotterill had been a fellow of St John's College Cambridge and in 1817 was appointed perpetual curate of St Paul's Sheffield, a chapel of ease to Sheffield parish church. Cotterill had compiled and introduced his first *Selection of Psalms and Hymns* in 1810, when he was incumbent of Lane End in Staffordshire. In 1819, Cotterill introduced to his congregation at St Paul's the eighth edition of his *Selection*, which included 25 psalms

---

[35]   Dean Cockburn was accused of simony—the practice of selling the presentation to livings of which he was patron. He was convicted in the Archbishop's Court, but the conviction was set aside as the proceedings had not met the requirements of the Church Discipline Act 1840.

[36]   Rubric in the orders for Morning and Evening Prayer in the Book of Common Prayer of the Church of England.

[37]   In the preface to 1819 edition of Thomas Cotterill's *Selection of Psalms and Hymns*, Cotterill had written: "At Bishopthorpe, of which the son of the present Archbishop is Vicar and which His Grace usually attends, a selection of psalms from various versions is used, with a supplement containing more than 100 hymns."

and hymns written by Cotterill himself. It was this edition which was the subject of the case before the Archbishop's son Granville.

After both sides had presented their case, Granville Harcourt-Vernon commented that the question posed was a very important one. "There is perhaps not a clergyman in the Kingdom who has not violated the law if Mr Cotterill has done so, and nothing has been said to satisfy my mind that, if this selection is illegal, those of Tate & Brady and Sternhold & Hopkins are not equally so." Granville presumed that the prosecution could have no universal objection to hymns and psalms but only to some part of this selection. He had looked at the selection and could see none to which there could be a reasonable objection. He concluded by saying that the Archbishop had offered to act as mediator and he considered it would do much for the cause of religion if a compromise could be reached. He would reserve judgement.[38]

Granville Harcourt-Vernon pronounced his judgement on 4 August. He had made a detailed study of all the relevant legislation. Nothing could be introduced into the services of the Church unless sanctioned by the king in council or by legislation. The use of the psalms and hymns in Cotterill's book had not been so sanctioned. He did not intend to allocate costs for what was in his opinion a technical irregularity. "I feel that the promoters of these articles were fairly entitled to a decision of the legal question to the best of my judgement, but if they proceed to call for sentence on this cause and decline the mediation I before suggested, I shall consider them as wanting not only in a sense of their own interest but in regard to the Christian Church and practical religion."[39]

Cotterill agreed to withdraw his hymn book. The Archbishop proceeded immediately with his role as mediator. On 26 September 1820, Cotterill wrote to his printer enclosing the selection of hymns agreed with the Archbishop and requested the printer to move with all speed and keep the work confidential. By 12 October, proof sheets were to go to the Archbishop. "His corrections must be strictly adhered to." Four thousand copies were to be printed. The Archbishop would pay for

---

[38]   *Yorkshire Gazette*, 6 and 8 July 1820, and numerous other newspapers.

[39]   *Stamford Mercury*, 4 August 1820; *Statesman*, 8 August 1820, and many other newspapers.

1,000 copies for St Paul's and St James's churches. Cotterill would pay for the rest. He emphasized that the Archbishop was a busy man and must be allowed time "for his valuable remarks". The preface to the 1820 and subsequent editions of the *Selection* states: "To the Most Reverend Edward, Lord Archbishop of York, this collection of psalms and hymns is, with his Grace's permission, inscribed, by his most faithful and obliged servant the Editor."[40] Cotterill advertised the hymn book for sale with some success for by 1822 it was in its third edition.

The Archbishop's strategy was successful. It may not have officially changed the law, but in practice it enabled clergy throughout the Church to introduce hymn books without fear of reprisal. "The Archbishop's decision in the Cotterill case effectively opened the door fully to the use of hymns in public worship in the Church of England".[41] The Archbishop's endorsement of Cotterill's hymn book is probably his most significant contribution to the reform of worship in the Church of England. It undoubtedly had a more lasting impact than his work as a director of the Ancient Concerts or his development of the York Music Festivals. The Archbishop may not have initiated the de facto change in the law on hymn singing but he saw the opportunity presented by the Cotterill case and used it to good effect.

---

[40] Staffordshire Archives: William Salt Library, S. MS 428/3/104; 14 letters between Thomas Cotterill and Thomas Caddell, his printer, 28 September to 13 December 1820.

[41] G. Parsons and J. Wolffe, *Religion in Victorian Britain* (Manchester: Manchester University Press 1988) vol. 5, p. 63.

7

Politics, royalty and reform

Archbishop Harcourt recognized the need to shape the Church of England for the rapid growth in population during the first half of the eighteenth century. He spoke in his first visitation in 1809 of the need to increase the value of poor livings. He pointed out the requirement for more church accommodation for those of limited means in growing industrial towns. During his early years, he actively promoted the building of new churches. He recognized that vast confirmation services were not conducive to orderly worship and increased the frequency of confirmation tours. He supported the introduction of hymn singing in Prayer Book services and was happy to appoint evangelical clergy and use them to train ordinands. Harcourt was pragmatic and not afraid of change.

His ability to lead on matters of Church reform was, however, hampered by the day-to-day responsibilities of his huge and distant diocese. York diocese was much larger in terms of number of parishes and area and was subject to much greater population growth than that of his fellow archbishop. Both Archbishop Howley of Canterbury and Bishop Blomfield of London, who were to lead Church reform in the 1830s, had fewer parishes and were more conveniently placed to combine their duties in their dioceses with attendance at Court and in Parliament.[1]

---

[1] In 1835, York diocese was 5,300 sq. miles with 891 parishes and a population of 1,464,000. London was 1,942 sq. miles with 635 parishes and a population of 1,689,000, and Canterbury 1,152 sq. miles with 343 parishes and a population of 403,000. G. F. A. Best, *Temporal Pillars, Queen Anne's Bounty, the Ecclesiastical Commissioners, and the Church of England,* (Cambridge: Cambridge University Press, 1964), Appendix 6, p. 545. Howley was Archbishop of Canterbury 1828–48, and Blomfield Bishop of London 1828–56.

Archbishop Harcourt's diocese was not reduced to a manageable size until 1836, when the Diocese of Ripon was created and the county of Nottinghamshire transferred to the Diocese of Lincoln.

In a speech to the House of Lords, Archbishop Harcourt explained that he gave precedence to the interests of religion and his clergy over voting in the Lords.[2] The journey from London to York would typically take four days. It was not until 1840, when Dr Harcourt was in his eighties, that travel by train between London and York became possible. The Archbishop and his party usually travelled to and from Bishopthorpe in his own carriages. On one occasion he arrived at the Old Bell Inn at Barnby Moor in Nottinghamshire for the night. The landlord apologized for not being able to accommodate him as all the accommodation had been booked in the name of a gentleman called Ebor.[3]

Harcourt was 51 when he took up his duties as Archbishop of York in 1808. By the time, the reform movement had gained momentum some 20 years later, he was of an age when his physical energy was likely to be declining. Nonetheless being in his seventies did not prevent him attending and sometimes chairing meetings of the Ecclesiastical Commission in the 1830s and 40s. He was more open to reform of both Church and Parliament than many of his fellow bishops.

Although the Archbishop took a keen interest in political developments, he sought to avoid pronouncing publicly on controversial political issues where they did not have a direct impact on the Church.[4] He also showed his concern regarding social issues. He presented many petitions for the abolition of slavery. In August 1817, he wrote to Lord Sidmouth, the Home Secretary, suggesting that the wives of convicts sent to New South Wales should be allowed to accompany their husbands. Lord Sidmouth

---

[2]   *Hansard: House of Lords* (18 May 1832), vol. 12, col. 1044.

[3]   HP Vol. XII, p. 212. The Archbishop of York signs himself "Ebor". Eboracum was the Roman name for York.

[4]   An undated letter to his sister the Dowager Countess Harcourt shows the archbishop was following closely the problems of the Duke of Portland's administration shortly before the duke's death in October 1809. The archbishop was aware of the attempts by Spencer Perceval and Lord Liverpool to bring Lord Grenville into the administration, HP, Vol XII, pp. 151–2.

made it clear that wives could not be allowed to go if they would be a charge on the government of the colony. They would only be allowed if a "prisoner, who is desirous of his wife and children joining him, has conducted himself properly in the Colony and has the means of taking care of them".[5] In 1832, the Archbishop gave his warm support to the Factory Bill, which would control the terms of employment of children.[6]

Electing the chancellor of Oxford University

Archbishop Harcourt was prepared to be involved in quasi-political matters if he could help a friend without compromising his own views. In September 1809, Thomas Grenville, a close friend since their days together at Christ Church, wrote to him to ask for his support for his brother Lord Grenville for the post of chancellor of Oxford University. The post would fall vacant on the soon-to-be-expected death of the third Duke of Portland. Thomas Grenville wrote to express his hopes that "if there should be any question of Lord Grenville's name being put into nomination, he may receive the powerful assistance of your good wishes and support, the early assurance of which might probably tell with great effect upon the result of the nomination". Thomas Grenville went on to say that if the election were to be decided by political motives rather than personal esteem, he would have been reluctant to approach the Archbishop. Lord Grenville would only agree to be nominated if he knew he had the support of his friends.[7]

The Archbishop's support for Lord Grenville would be very important to his campaign. The electors were predominantly clergymen. Having the Archbishop of York on Lord Grenville's side would influence many votes. Furthermore, the Archbishop's endorsement would demonstrate

---

5   Lord Sidmouth to the Archbishop of York, 16 August 1817, HP, Vol. XII, pp. 205–6.

6   *London Evening Standard*, 21 September 1832; *Leeds Intelligencer*, 20 September 1832.

7   T. Grenville to the Archbishop of York, 18 October 1809, HP, Vol. XII, pp. 159–62.

that Grenville's support for Catholic Emancipation did not make him unacceptable to those who most valued the special position of the established Church. On the issue of Catholic emancipation, the Archbishop and Lord Grenville were in opposite camps. The Archbishop, despite their different views on one of the key issues of the time, told Thomas Grenville: "For myself I have always considered Lord Grenville from his talents and literary attainments, from his rank and character as a statesman and from his religious and moral habits, the properest man for the University's choice." He believed Grenville to be "as firmly attached to the Protestant Establishment as I am myself and that he would as zealously defend it in time of need". The Archbishop's letter acknowledged that Grenville's stance on the Catholic question would be a considerable difficulty.[8]

The third Duke of Portland died on 29 October 1809, and the election of a new chancellor was expected to take place in December. In addition to the Archbishop, Lord Grenville had secured the support of the Bishops of Oxford, St Asaph and Norwich, and six other bishops. Thomas Grenville was grateful to the Archbishop for his support, which had been given before he knew if any other bishops would be supportive.[9] The Archbishop was in York and busy with arrangements for his December ordinations. When he learnt that Archdeacon Markham was supporting the Duke of Beaufort's candidacy, the Archbishop proposed that they should pair off and both avoid the round trip of almost 400 miles to Oxford and back. However, the Grenvilles were of the view that the Archbishop's personal appearance in Oxford could be crucial, particularly as there were three candidates. Eventually the Archbishop concluded that he could review his ordination papers in time to get to Oxford for the election.[10]

The press took considerable interest in the election of the chancellor of Oxford. The three candidates were Lord Grenville, Lord Eldon and

[8] The Archbishop of York to T. Grenville, 23 October 1809, British Library Add. MS 41857, f. 156.

[9] T. Grenville to the Archbishop of York, 15 November 1809, HP, Vol. XII, pp. 164–5.

[10] The Archbishop of York to T. Grenville, 24 November 1809, British Library Add. MS 4185, f. 111, f. 222 and f. 224.

the Duke of Beaufort. Some newspapers speculated incorrectly that the Archbishop was supporting the Duke of Beaufort, who was married to Lady Anne's half-sister: "We lament the name of this excellent prelate should have been prostituted to such mean purpose. His Grace has given unqualified support to Lord Grenville."[11] To sort things out with the Duke of Beaufort, the Archbishop stayed with the duke for two days on his visit to Oxford to apologize for the press confusion. The duke was sure most of his friends would have voted for Grenville if he had withdrawn.[12]

The Archbishop approached the Dean of Christ Church to see whether the college would give support to any specific candidate. The dean advised the Archbishop that the college as a body was not planning to get involved in the election.[13] The Archbishop, however, refrained from encouraging his clergy to vote for Grenville. Writing to the Revd Robert Croft, the Archbishop stated he had uniformly refrained from making any application to his clergy. He felt that "the more willing they might be to gratify my wishes, the more incumbent it was upon me not to press them on a point on which, in the honest exercise of their own judgements, they might differ with me in opinion".[14]

The election took place on 13 December and was a close contest due to Lord Grenville's support for Catholic emancipation. *The Times* stated that Lord Grenville possessed every great and good quality but "it is objected to him that he has supported Catholic Emancipation". The final result was Lord Grenville 406 votes, Lord Eldon 393 and the Duke of Beaufort 238.[15] The Archbishop was back in York by 23 December in time to ordain ten deacons and seven priests the following day.

---

[11]   *British Press*, 15 November 1809.

[12]   The Archbishop of York to Thomas Grenville, 18 December 1809, British Library, Add. MS 59003, f. 177.

[13]   The Archbishop of York to the dean of Christ Church, 4 November 1809, HP, Vol. XII, p. 176.

[14]   The Archbishop of York to the Revd Robert Croft, undated, HP, Vol. XII, p. 177.

[15]   *The Times*, 15 December 1808.

Governor of the Charterhouse

The following year Archbishop Harcourt stood for a governorship of the Charterhouse with the support of Lord Grenville.[16] The 14 governors had overall responsibility for running the charity and, when a governor died or resigned, had the right to elect a replacement. Governors were predominantly bishops and members of the House of Lords. Its school provided free education and accommodation for 44 boys, as well as offering day and boarding places to another 100-plus who paid fees. Governors took it in turns to offer free places as they became vacant. The Charterhouse also provided accommodation for up to 80 carefully selected pensioners, mostly professional men over 50 who had fallen on hard times.

In the 1810 election, the Archbishop stood against the then prime minister, Spencer Perceval. Archbishop Harcourt had approached the Bishop of London to secure his vote. The bishop thought it likely the majority would vote for Perceval, as ministers had traditionally been elected.[17] The result was close: the Archbishop secured six votes including Lord Grenville and the Bishop of London. Perceval secured seven votes including the vote of the Archbishop of Canterbury. Writing to Archbishop Harcourt with news of the result, Thomas Grenville indicated the archbishop's campaigning had nearly been successful: "If Sidmouth had not been Sidmouth, or, being so, if he had voted for you instead of making you all his palavering speeches, we should have carried your election."[18] Two years later, following Spencer Perceval's assassination, Archbishop Harcourt was elected.[19]

---

[16] A former Carthusian monastery in the City of London, the Charterhouse was and is a charitable institution founded by Thomas Sutton in the seventeenth century to provide accommodation for up to 80 pensioners and to run a school.

[17] The Archbishop of York to Thomas Grenville, 10 June 1810, British Library Add. MS 41858, f. 102.

[18] Thomas Grenville to the Archbishop of York, 20 June 1819, HP, Vol. XII, pp. 180–181.

[19] The Prime Minister Spencer Perceval was assassinated in the lobby of the House of Commons on 11 May 1812 by a disgruntled Liverpool merchant.

When a governor's turn to appoint a boy to one of the 44 free places occurred, he might offer it to another governor if he had no one in mind. In July 1813, Lord Grenville had the right to appoint and offered the place to the Archbishop, who proposed to appoint the son of a Gloucestershire clergyman with a large family. The clergyman had only a small living and himself had been to Charterhouse and Christ Church, Oxford. In 1830, the Archbishop again planned to take up one of Grenville's places, but the boy was of indifferent health and the mother declined the offer.[20] The governors also set the rules for the admission of pensioners and might play some part in their selection.

Member of Queen's Council during George III's final illness

Some two years after his appointment to York, the Archbishop was invited to join the council to support Queen Charlotte during George III's final illness. On 25 October 1810, the king had been on the throne for 50 years. He was aged 72, and his health was poor. His sight had failed and he walked unsteadily. The mood at court was sombre, for his favourite daughter, Princess Amelia, was dying. The king and his family expected that his mental health would again fail due to his anxiety about Amelia. Previous mental breakdowns had occurred at periods of great stress. Princess Elizabeth wrote to the Archbishop's sister, the Dowager Countess Harcourt: "This one is owing to the overflowing of his heart for the youngest and dearest of his children; a child who never caused him a pang, and whom he literally doted upon."[21] Lady Harcourt was a Lady of the Bedchamber to Queen Charlotte. The king and queen were

---

[20]   The Archbishop of York to Lord Grenville, 8 and 21 July 1815 and March 1830, British Library Add. MS 59003, ff. 196–8 and ff. 199–200.

[21]   Princess Elizabeth to Lady Harcourt, quoted in Janice Hadlow, *The Strangest Family: The Private Lives of George III, Queen Charlotte and the Hanoverians* (London: William Collins, 2014), p. 536.

personal friends of the Harcourts and had regularly stayed at Nuneham with their children.[22]

By January 1811, the king's mental health had deteriorated so far that the government were preparing a Regency bill, which provided for "the administration of royal authority and for the care of his Majesty's royal person during the continuation of his Majesty's illness".[23] The Prime Minister, Spencer Perceval, wrote to the Archbishop of York to invite him to join the council to be appointed to assist Queen Charlotte in the discharge of her responsibilities under the bill.[24] The other seven council members were the Archbishop of Canterbury, three members of the royal household—the Duke of Montrose, who was Master of Horse, the Earl of Winchelsea, Groom of the Stole and the Earl of Aylesford, Lord Steward—and three members of the government—the Earl of Eldon, Lord Chancellor, Lord Ellenborough, Chief Justice, and Sir William Grant, Master of the Rolls. Writing to Sir Robert Peel some years later, the Archbishop described his appointment as "of a very delicate and responsible nature requiring frequent attendance at Windsor during nine years—more especially in the early years of the king's illness".[25]

The first meeting of the council took place at Windsor on Saturday 6 April 1811, with all the members present except the Duke of Montrose, who had gout. While the three physicians were giving their reports, the Archbishop of York and Lord Winchelsea went into the park to watch the king, who was walking on the terrace. Once briefed by the physicians, the council met the queen before returning to London, where the Archbishop was to preach at the Chapel Royal the next day, Palm Sunday.

---

22 Lady Harcourt originally introduced Dr Francis Willis and his son Dr John Willis to King George III and Queen Charlotte in 1788, when the king had suffered his first breakdown. Dr Francis Willis had treated Martha Lady Vernon, the mother of the Archbishop and Lady Harcourt. Roy Porter, *Francis Willis, physician* (Oxford: Oxford Dictionary of National Biography), 4 October 2012 version, accessed 31 July 2023.

23 The Regency Act 1811 (51 Geo. III c. 1).

24 L. Perceval to the Archbishop of York, 14 January 1811, HP, Vol. XII, p. 182.

25 The Archbishop of York to Sir Robert Peel, 21 September 1841, British Library Add. MS 40489, f. 286.

The council's report, which was published in the press, confirmed that: "His Majesty was not yet restored to a state of health as to be capable of resuming the personal exercise of his Royal Authority."[26]

Although the members of the council only reported to Parliament and the Prince Regent at three-monthly intervals, they received daily reports from the doctors and, in the early days, met monthly when there was still hope that the king might recover sufficiently to take up his duties again. In May 1811, the king was sufficiently well to see the Archbishop of York and Lords Winchelsea and Aylesford and for the council to conclude that the king "be entrusted with moderate exercise of his duties".[27] The apparent recovery did not last.

In August 1811, Archbishop Harcourt was at Bishopthorpe and could not attend the council. The Archbishop of Canterbury asked the Archbishop of York for his opinion on calling in Dr Simmons, who had attended the king during a previous bout of ill health. Dr Harcourt was "firmly persuaded that his Majesty's mind is at present incapable of being improved by what is termed management and which can mean only the proper application of reasoning, admonition or restraint". Archbishop Harcourt was concerned that the present doctors would not be willing to continue to treat the king if Dr Simmons was introduced. He did not therefore favour pressing the queen to accept Dr Simmons' services, particularly if she was reluctant.[28] What transpired at the council is not recorded, but Dr Simmons was consulted as well as Dr John Willis and his three regular doctors when the council prepared their quarterly report in January 1812. The report concluded that it was the unanimous opinion of his doctors that recovery was improbable but not impossible.[29]

---

[26] *Morning Post*, 8 April 1811.

[27] *National Register*, 5 May 1811.

[28] The Archbishop of York to the Archbishop of Canterbury, 26 August 1811, and the Archbishop of York to the Duke of Portland, 6 September 1811, HP, Vol. XII, pp. 184–7.

[29] *Pilot*, London, 6 January 1812. The report took account of the views of two visiting physicians, Dr Simmons and Dr Monroe, the king's three regular doctors, Sir Henry Halford, Dr Baillie and Dr Heberden, plus Dr John and Dr Robert Willis and a surgeon, Mr Dundas. The Archbishop of York was

Queen Charlotte expected at least one member of the council to stay at Windsor Castle when she was away. In January 1813, the queen asked the Archbishop to come and stay at Windsor "from tomorrow till Friday" as he was nearby. She reminded him that his sister Lady Harcourt would be there "to render this short stay less dull". Some two years later the queen asked the Archbishop to sort out with the Duke of Montrose who would stay at Windsor as she wanted to prolong her visit to the Prince of Wales and his daughter. "Much good may arise by indulging both father and daughter. I hope by possibly doing some good by my presence, I shall not be blamed by the world."[30] Other members of the council, including the Archbishop of Canterbury, shared the responsibility for attending on the king when the queen was away, but this was a duty which Archbishop Harcourt had to perform on at least one occasion every year till the queen's death in late 1818. In March of that year, for example, the Archbishop of York, the Duke of Montrose and Sir William Grant had all attended the king when the queen was away in London. Archbishop Harcourt was less involved when the Duke of York presided at the council for the last two years of the king's life; he died in January 1820.

Religious toleration and the established Church

Like most bishops at this time, Archbishop Harcourt actively supported the special position of the Church of England. The advantages to the established Church were considerable. Church rates maintained the fabric of the buildings and were paid by all, whether members or not. Baptism and marriage had to take place in an Anglican church. Only an Anglican minister could conduct a burial in a parish churchyard. Only Anglicans could take degrees at Oxford and Cambridge. Many public

---

amongst the signatories to the report, although he would normally have been at Bishopthorpe at the time of year.

[30] Queen Charlotte to the Archbishop of York, 5 January 1813, British Library Add. MS 3862, f. 162; and 10 January 1816, British Library Add. MS 3830, f. 144.

appointments could only be held by Anglicans.[31] The sovereign must be a member of the Church of England. The Church's many privileges were enshrined in law.

Church and State were seen in the eighteenth century as inter-dependent. This interdependence was brought to the fore in the 1790s by the revolution in France. There was a real fear that without religion providing moral guidance, civilization would collapse, as had happened in France. Religious establishment was politically essential: "Without the moral basis that only such an establishment could provide, the centre would not hold and everything would split apart. Crown and Church would fall together and the tremors caused by their mutual collapse would turn to dust and rubble the edifice of a civilised life."[32] As explained in Chapter 2, Harcourt, then Bishop of Carlisle, decided in 1792 to remain in his diocese rather than go to London as seditious pamphlets had been circulating in Carlisle. He supported the view that it was the role of the Church to provide a moral framework and thus to ensure good order.

By the start of the nineteenth century, the situation had become more complex. The Church of England was struggling to maintain its position in growing towns and cities. The Church's legal framework made it difficult to adjust its structures to meet changing needs. Construction of new churches and the creation of new parishes was made complex by the need for parliamentary legislation and by the system of patronage. Dissenting churches and chapels could be developed more swiftly than Anglican places of worship. No statistics were available, but clergy and politicians recognized that the Church of England's dominant position in growing towns was threatened. A few politicians were now querying the Church's established position. Others were arguing for the government to provide funds for the building of new churches and, as we saw above,

---

[31]   An annual indemnity Act enabled dissenters but not Roman Catholics to sit in Parliament and hold public office. Some individuals made occasional attendance at Church of England services to satisfy the legal requirement when in reality they were non-conformists.

[32]   Peter Virgin, *The Church in an Age of Negligence: Ecclesiastical Structure and Problems of Church Reform 1700–1840* (Cambridge, James Clarke & Co, 1989), p. 16.

some £2.6m was provided between 1809 and 1824. Never before or since has the Church received so much financial support from government.

A more profound problem arose from the Act of Union with Ireland in 1801. With this Act, the Parliament at Westminster became directly accountable for Irish affairs. By 1831, the population of England and Wales was about 15 million and of Ireland about 7 million. Around 5.5m of the Irish population were Roman Catholics, who therefore numbered almost a quarter of the total UK population following the Act of Union. To maintain the special disabilities of Roman Catholics appeared "in the long view to have been impractical or preposterous. Home rule was out of the question; and therefore the establishment of the Church of England and Ireland must be altered; and must be altered by a Parliament in which many members wanted strongly to maintain the established Church. Either the establishment of the Church of England must be modified, or the Union must be ended and home rule given to Ireland."[33]

As the century progressed, the calls for Catholic emancipation strengthened. Archbishop Harcourt, in his first speech in the House of Lords as Archbishop of York on 27 May 1808, set out his views in reply to a petition for Catholic emancipation:

> If this petition had only sued for toleration the most extended, he would have felt no difficulty in acceding to its prayer: for toleration was the key-stone of the reformed church. But no complaint of this sort had been made. The Catholics enjoyed their rights under the protection of the law, and he was glad of it; but he hoped parliament would always resist their attempts at acquiring political power; because, however temporal and spiritual power might be disjoined in theory, they could not be practically separated. It had been said that Catholics ought not to be judged now by the sentiments which had been formerly held by people of that persuasion. If any material alteration in their articles of faith had taken place, it became them distinctly to shew it. But it was a well-known rule of that church, that all

---

[33] Owen Chadwick, *The Victorian Church Part One: 1829–1859* (London: SCM Press, 1971), p. 9.

the canons remained in force that were not repealed by a general council; and, certainly, there were many objectionable points, that by this rule must be still considered as part of the Roman Catholic faith. He allowed that many Catholics had been eminent for virtue and piety. Who could hear the name of Fenelon without veneration? He admitted that men might live together very well in society, notwithstanding differences of opinion on speculative points, but he denied that parliament could be opened to the Catholics as long as they owned a foreign jurisdiction, and maintained that there was no salvation beyond the pale of their own church. Impressed with these sentiments, though he by no means regretted what the Catholics had already obtained, he thought it inconsistent with wisdom and sound policy to break down the remaining barriers.[34]

The Archbishop of York's views were widely supported by the English population as a whole. However, as already shown, there were politicians such as Lord Grenville and the Archbishop's friend and neighbour Lord Harrowby who supported Catholic emancipation, whilst being prominent Anglicans. Amongst the bishops, only the Bishop of Norwich consistently voted to remove Roman Catholic disabilities.[35] George III believed his coronation oath made it impossible for him to give his assent to any bill which gave Catholics political power. However, the subject of Catholic relief was regularly raised in the House of Lords in spite of the king's opposition. In May 1817, both the English archbishops and the Archbishop of the Church of Ireland opposed petitions from both the English Catholic nobility and the Catholic priests and people as a whole.

---

[34] *Hansard: House of Lords* (27 May 1808), vol 11, col. 681, accessed 30 July 2023.

[35] Henry Bathurst was appointed Bishop of Norwich in 1805 on the translation of Manners-Sutton to Canterbury. He was a Whig and consistently supported Catholic emancipation. He died aged 90 in 1837.

The Roman Catholic Relief Bill of June 1819 was defeated by 59 votes in the House of Lords.[36]

Although the Prince Regent had initially been more sympathetic than his father to granting political power to his Catholic subjects, his opposition had hardened by the time he became king as George IV in January 1820. The Roman Catholic Disability Removal Bill of April 1821 failed in the House of Lords by 39 votes. Both archbishops opposed the measure in 1821 and again in 1825, when a similar bill was defeated by 48 votes. Only two bishops—Norwich and Rochester—supported Roman Catholic relief.[37]

The accession of George IV to the throne created a new issue for the Church of England. The king's estranged wife now became Queen Caroline. She expected her name to be included in the list of members of the royal family for whom prayers were said in morning service in the Church of England and to be crowned with the king in Westminster Abbey. The king, however, wished not only to exclude her name from the prayers and her person from the coronation, but also to divorce her on the grounds of her immoral behaviour in Italy where she had been living. The bishops were inevitably involved when the proposals for divorce came before the House of Lords in the Bill of Pains and Penalties in the summer of 1820.

The Bill of Pains and Penalties effectively put Queen Caroline on trial before the Lords. The Queen's Counsel was not entitled to a list of witnesses nor to cross-examine them. The bishops were divided on how to proceed. When Lord Harrowby produced a motion to allow the Queen's Counsel to cross-examine immediately after the examination-in-chief and to call back witnesses, the Archbishop of York and seven bishops gave support, but the Archbishop of Canterbury and seven bishops opposed the motion, which was lost by 103 votes.

---

36 *Hansard: House of Lords* (16 May 1817), vol. 36, col. 678, and (10 June 1819), vol. 40, col. 1067, accessed 30 July 2023. The 1819 bill attracted 83 votes in favour and 141 against.

37 *Hansard: House of Lords*, (17 April 1821), vol. 5 col. 356, and (17 May 1825), vol.13, col. 766, accessed 31 July 2023.

The Archbishops of Canterbury and York were also on opposite sides when it came to the divorce clause in the bill. Archbishop Harcourt argued that divorce was contrary to biblical teaching:

> He could not therefore have this clause retained. If, however, this clause was expunged and the other elements of the bill agreed to, their lordships would exhibit to the world the monstrous spectacle of a degraded queen still continuing the spouse of the sovereign. From this dilemma he saw no way of escape but by rejecting the bill altogether. In voting against the second reading yesterday, he had this difficulty in contemplation.

He considered the bill should be dropped:

> The interests of religion and morality must be still more vitally injured by persevering in a measure which was derogatory to the honour of the crown and injurious to the best interests of the empire; which gave the utmost pain to every good man and tended most effectually to forward the views of a party whose object was to vilify the constituted authorities, and to bring into disgrace all that was most sacred and venerable in the laws and constitution of the country.[38]

Three days after Harcourt spoke, the bill came up for its third reading. The Archbishop of Canterbury, who had argued the Bible allowed divorce even if the Church of England did not, considered Queen Caroline's guilt had been established and supported the bill together with nine other bishops. The Archbishop of York, the Archbishop of Tuam and eight other bishops opposed. The bill was carried by nine votes. The Earl of Liverpool decided not to press on with the bill in the light of the small majority.

Archbishop Harcourt preached the sermon at the coronation of George IV. His text was 2 Samuel 23:3–4: "He that ruleth over men must

---

[38] *Hansard House of Lords* (6 November 1820), vol. 3, col. 1698, accessed 31 July 2023.

be just ruling in fear of God; and he shall be as the light of the morning when the sun riseth, as a morning without cloud." The Archbishop spoke of good government and the effect it produces. He spoke warmly of the righteousness of George III:

> The ruler who will be just to his people will preserve their minds from vice and irreligion by withholding his favour from the base and licentious and by exalting the wise and the good to distinction and honour.[39]

The queen attempted to get into the coronation service in Westminster Abbey but failed and died some three weeks later. Whether it was the tone of the sermon or his vote on the divorce clause, the king is said to have turned his back to Archbishop Harcourt at the first levee after the coronation.[40]

It was to be another seven years before progress was to be made on religious toleration. In August 1827, prime minister George Canning, who had agreed not to repeal the Test & Corporations Acts, died and was replaced by a ministry led by the Duke of Wellington. In February 1828, Lord John Russell introduced the Sacramental Test bill, which would replace the Test & Corporations Acts.[41] The government agreed not to oppose the proposed legislation and Robert Peel was given the task of bringing the bishops on side. The Archbishop of Canterbury organized a meeting with Peel, the Archbishop of York and the Bishops of London, Durham, Chester and Llandaff. The meeting agreed a declaration to replace the test under the old legislation and Peel wrote to Archbishop

---

[39]   Edward Vernon, Lord Archbishop of York, *A Sermon preached at the Coronation of George IV in the Abbey Church of Westminster, 19 July 1821* (London: published by His Majesty's Command, 1821).

[40]   HP, Vol. XII, p. 209.

[41]   The Test Act of 1673 required all holders of military and civil offices under the crown to take the oath of allegiance and the sacrament of Holy Communion in the Church of England. The Corporation Act of 1673 placed similar obligations on mayors and municipal officials. The Sacramental Test Act repealed the requirement to take communion in an Anglican church.

Harcourt with a revised copy of the bill, making clear that the decision on who should take the declaration should be determined by the king in council.[42]

When the bill to repeal the Test & Corporations Acts came before the House of Lords, the Archbishop of Canterbury was ill and the Archbishop of York had to take his place. "It is with great reluctance that I at any time offer myself to your Lordships' notice." He realized he could not confine himself to a silent vote. He stated that the Test & Corporations Acts had been designed to safeguard the Church of England and that the Church had the right to expect that something should be substituted for the act. He concluded:

> Whether the provisions in this bill, as they now stand, may prove sufficient for that purpose, or what amendments it may be right to make to them, will best be ascertained when the bill itself shall come into the committee—and in the earnest hope that the measure may eventually be rendered such as to afford satisfaction to all parties, I shall give my vote for the second reading of the bill."[43]

The wording of the declaration was subject to revision in committee. Ultimately the bishops were dissatisfied, and Archbishop Harcourt voted against the bill. In spite of the opposition of most bishops, the repeal of the Test & Corporations Acts was achieved on 9 May 1828. It was an early sign of the challenges to come to the unique position of the Church of England.

In March 1829, less than a year later, the issue of Roman Catholic relief came again before the House of Lords. The Archbishop of York's position had modified. He was concerned at the protection afforded to the established Church. He could not say whether he would support the Roman Catholic Relief bill until he saw it: "That is whether I feel

---

[42]   Peel to the Archbishop of York, 27 March 1828, British Library, Add. MS 40396, f. 96.

[43]   *Hansard House of Lords*, (17 April 1828), vol. 18, col. 1482, accessed 31 July 2023.

justified in giving my support to it or be compelled by my sense of duty as a protestant bishop to oppose it."[44] The Archbishop of Canterbury held a meeting on 17 March to try and get the bishops to vote together but to no avail. It was agreed each would vote as his conscience dictated.

A month later the Archbishop of York again spoke:

> He was minded to support the bill if safeguards were sufficient. He has lived happily for many years with Roman Catholics in his neighbourhood and they are men to be honoured for their integrity and their social and domestic virtues. He could see no objection to bringing catholic peers into House of Lords; to introduce to parliament English Catholics generally would be no threat to the English Church. The case my Lords is however widely different in Ireland—the paramount influence of the Catholic clergy over the minds of an ignorant and credulous peasantry will always be a most formidable instrument for effecting what must be to them their first great objective—the restoration and aggrandisement of their own church ... The accomplishment of this measure will eventually tend to endanger the Church of Ireland. He is not satisfied with the safeguards and cannot vote for the bill. He is most reluctant to vote against the Duke of Wellington's proposals—this is the first time he has done so and is persuaded it will be the last.[45]

Ten bishops voted for emancipation and 19 against. The bill passed, and the Duke of Wellington with much difficulty obtained George IV's assent.

---

44   *Hansard: House of Lords*, (3 March 1829), vol. 20, col. 671.
45   *Hansard: House of Lords* (3 April 1829), vol. 21, col. 143.

Parliamentary reform

In spite of widespread agitation for reform, the Tory administration under the Duke of Wellington was firmly opposed to any change to the distribution of parliamentary seats. Any change would reduce the ability of the peers to control the make-up of the House of Commons. Following the November 1830 general election, precipitated by the death of George IV and the accession of his brother William IV, a Whig administration was returned under Lord Grey, who was pledged to secure reform. A bill was presented to the House of Commons in March 1831 and passed by one vote. It was defeated in committee. Grey resigned, but in the ensuing general election he secured a significant majority and introduced a second reform bill.

1831 Reform Bill

The second 1831 Reform Bill passed through the House of Commons with ease, but its passage through the House of Lords was expected to be challenging. The temporal peers were predominantly Tory. The spiritual peers had largely been appointed under Tory administrations and were expected to be hostile to reform. A significant minority were, like Archbishop Harcourt, sons of peers. Others had been tutors to members of the peerage and owed their episcopal appointments to their connections to the aristocracy.

There was much speculation in the press as to how the bishops would vote. The *Morning Advertiser* reckoned the Archbishop of York and the Bishops of Norwich, Worcester, Llandaff, Chichester, and Bath and Wells would support the bill, and the Bishops of London and Winchester would abstain.[46] The Archbishop of York was intending to vote by proxy, as he was at Bishopthorpe and had, it was said, sent his proxy to the Archbishop of Canterbury.[47] It was therefore thought by some that the Archbishop

---

[46] *Morning Advertiser*, 27 September 1831.

[47] Archbishop Harcourt was in York. He was involved with the York Meeting of what was to become the National Association for the Advancement of

of Canterbury would support the bill.[48] Other papers suggested that the bishops might, at the suggestion of the Archbishop of York, leave the decision to the temporal peers and not vote.[49]

When it finally came to the vote, the 1831 Reform Bill was lost by 41 votes. The Archbishop of York and the Bishops of London, Chester, Ely, Hereford, Worcester and St Davids did not vote. The Archbishop of Canterbury and 20 bishops voted against the bill. The point was soon made that, if the Archbishop of Canterbury and the 20 bishops had voted for the bill, it would have been carried by one vote. In subsequent weeks, many bishops were hustled in public and went in fear of their lives.[50] The bishop's palace in Bristol was burnt down. A Huddersfield mob burnt an effigy of the Archbishop of York in place of Guy Fawkes.[51]

Some newspapers suggested the Archbishop of York had attended the debate and only left to avoid voting. Others noted he was in York on diocesan business. So concerned was Archbishop Harcourt at the press speculation that the *York Courant* and several other papers carried the following report: "We are authorised to state the Archbishop of York having necessarily been detained in Yorkshire during discussions on the Reform bill in the House of Peers sent his proxy in favour of the bill to the Bishop of London who was prevented from attending in his place on that occasion by the unexpected death of his father."[52] *The Leeds Intelligencer* commented with reference to the above statement: "So states a Whig journal, but his Grace's opinion is still a matter of mystery."[53] However, the Archbishop must have been pleased at a letter from a York dissenter who confirmed the Archbishop was in York and concluded: "There is

---

Science. He was also committed to consecrating a new church at Thornes near Wakefield on 11 October. The vote in the House of Lords was to take place on 11 October.

48   *Globe*, 4 October 1831.

49   *Brighton Gazette*, 6 October 1831.

50   *Times,* 15 October 1831 and many other newspapers.

51   *Cumberland Pacquet*, 15 November 1831.

52   *Globe*, 27 October 1831, quoting the *York Courant*.

53   *Leeds Intelligencer*, 27 October 1831.

no individual in the church or in the peerage whose general conduct as a Christian is more to be admired."[54]

The press continued to speculate on Archbishop Harcourt's position during November. "The Bishop of London should explain why the Archbishop of York's proxy was sacrificed and why he did not place it in hands which would have carried into effect his Grace's wishes."[55] It appeared the Bishop of London only received the proxy on the morning of the vote. As he decided not to attend the House of Lords, the proxy could not be passed on to another bishop favourable to reform. The Bishop of London had been in London on the morning of the vote to preach the sermon at the opening of King's College, London. His father's death, which had taken place on 28 September, had no impact on the Bishop of London's ability to vote.[56] It was further suggested that the Archbishop of York had left the decision on whether to cast his proxy to the Bishop of London. *The Times* reported: "We cannot believe this statement is correct; surely his Grace would not do anything so weak as to follow in the train of Dr Blomfield [Bishop of London]."[57]

1832 Reform Bill

Following his failure in October 1831, Grey immediately started to try and persuade the bishops to change their votes. Bishop Blomfield of London saw his position was untenable and agreed to support reform. He expected some other bishops to come over. Grey was less successful with the Archbishop of Canterbury and sought William IV's help to bring more bishops and Tory peers into line, but the king was reluctant to exert pressure. When the bill's second reading came before the House of Lords on 13 April 1832, it was passed by nine votes. The Archbishop of

---

[54]   *Hull Packet*, 1 November 1831.

[55]   *Globe*, 8 November 1831.

[56]   *London Courier*, 9 November 1831; *Evening Mail*, 9 November 1831; *The Times*, 7 November 1831.

[57]   *The Times*, 8 November 1831.

York, the Bishop of London and ten other bishops voted for the bill. The Archbishop of Canterbury and 15 bishops voted against.

The passage of the Reform Bill was, however, still to be challenged. On 7 May 1832, Lord Lyndhurst put forward a motion for the postponement of Schedule A of the bill. This was the schedule which disenfranchised a number of boroughs. Archbishop Harcourt, together with the Archbishop of Canterbury and 13 other bishops, voted for the postponement, since Archbishop Harcourt believed enfranchisement should come before disenfranchisement. The motion was carried by 151 votes to 116. The Archbishop of York had not appreciated that this was a procedural device to prevent the Reform Bill going forward. He was labelled as hypocritical. The *Sun* stated: "How the conduct of these tricksters must lower the character of the hierarchy in the opinion of the country! The Archbishop of York too of all men after his pretended zeal for reform."[58] On 8 May, Lord Grey asked the king to create peers. The king refused and Grey resigned. The Duke of Wellington attempted to form a government but failed. On 15 May, Grey returned after the king agreed to create peers.

A riotous debate took place in the House of Lords on 17 May. The Archbishop of York declined to participate till the following day. He expressed his horror at the violence and excitement which had prevailed in the debate the previous night and hoped he would never see such conduct again. He informed the house that he would have voted for the 1831 bill if he had been present and that he had given his vote for the second reading of the current bill. He believed that a bill which related solely to the constitution of the House of Commons, had been supported by a large majority of the House of Commons and was approved by the king, should receive the support of the House of Lords. He supported enfranchisement before disenfranchisement and had not appreciated the consequences of his vote in committee:

> As to the propriety of an extensive enfranchisement, the connection he had had for a period of twenty-four years with the great manufacturing towns in Yorkshire afforded him abundant opportunity of being convinced of its expediency. He alluded to

---

58   *Sun*, 9 May 1832.

Leeds, Halifax, Huddersfield, and Bradford; all of which places, from their population, wealth, and intelligence, were fit to be intrusted with the elective franchise: and this, of which he so much approved, would be done by the Bill.

He concluded by stating he had that morning had a letter from the mayor of York, who had sent out the militia to defend his house at Bishopthorpe.[59]

On 22 May, Archbishop Harcourt voted for enfranchising the metropolitan districts, "this undoubtedly proving by deeds the sincerity of his intention with regard to the reform bill".[60] On 4 June 1832, the bill was passed by 106 votes to 22. No bishops voted against the bill, but the public did not so readily forgive them. When the Archbishop of Canterbury went to conduct his visitation on 7 August, he was met by a hissing crowd. Hats, caps and cabbage stalks were thrown at his carriage.

Church reform

"To abuse the Church of England was not new. What was new was the amount of vituperation and the number of people who listened. In 1831 pamphleteers against the establishment commanded an unusually avid public."[61] The torrent of anger over the bishops' failure to back parliamentary reform increased the demand for reform of the Church of England. Pamphlets which sold in limited numbers in the 1820s now commanded much wider audiences.

The Black Book by John Wade had been first published in 1820. The book attacked not just the Church of England and Ireland but also other institutions of government. Its facts may have been inaccurate, but there were no alternative official sources of information to enable corrections to be made. The 1820 edition suggested that Earl Harcourt, who was

---

[59] *Hansard: House of Lords* (18 May 1832), Vol. 12, col. 1044. Accessed 31 July 2023.

[60] *Hull Advertiser*, 1 June 1832.

[61] Chadwick, *The Victorian Church Part One*, p. 32.

described as brother to Lord Vernon and the Archbishop of York, and Countess Harcourt between them earned £8,100 from their royal duties.[62] The Archbishop of York was said to receive around £14,000 from the see of York. In the 1831 edition, John Wade reckoned the total income of the Church of England was £9.5m. The first three editions sold about 14,000 copies but the later editions for 1831, 1832 and 1835 sold 50,000.[63]

The twelfth edition of R. M. Beverley's *Letter to the Archbishop of York on the Corrupt State of the Church of England* was published in 1831. The *Christian Guardian* of December 1831 observed:

> In ordinary times it would have excited little attention ... it would scarcely have called forth and certainly not deserved any reply. Appearing however when reform was the watchword of the day and when the Papist, the Infidel and the Dissenter are uniting in one common exclamation 'Down with it, Down with it even to the ground' Mr B's epistle has met with most extensive circulation.

Between 25,000 and 30,000 copies were published. The *Christian Guardian* described the forty-page pamphlet as "a most intemperate account against the church, its ministers, its resources and in short our whole ecclesiastical system, which he describes as almost entirely corrupt and abominable".[64] Numerous clergymen published replies to Beverley defending the Church.

Beverley was a landowner and magistrate who had once been a Quaker but subsequently joined the Plymouth Brethren. "The timidity of my friends compels me to become your Grace's correspondent; and to invade the slumbers of Bishopthorpe with sounds not usually addressed to archiepiscopal ears ... High honour of an answer I do not desire nor expect ... England is thoroughly sick of the Church establishment and

---

[62] John Wade, *Black Book or Corruption Unmasked* (London: John Fairburn, 1820), p. 402.

[63] Chadwick, *The Victorian Church Part One*, p. 33.

[64] *Christian Guardian*, December 1831, p. 481

your Grace's diocese reckons more persons who feel this nausea than any other in England." Of Archbishop Harcourt's family he wrote:

> Neither do I much complain of the aggrandisement of the metropolitan family, they have certainly received some gentle irrigations of personal bounty, but their characters, I am told, deserve it, and it is not very monstrous for a father to reward his sons, if the reward is not excessive. There is general respect voluntarily paid to your Grace's private character and a general opinion prevails that you honourably rule your diocese.[65]

Other publications took up the theme of the Archbishop's family. Under a heading "Beauties of the Venerable Church", the *Poor Man's Guardian* set out its estimate of the amount the Archbishop and his family had made from their various roles in the Church. The figures were undoubtedly a substantial exaggeration as subsequent research was to show:[66]

Poor Man's Guardian's Estimates of income of the Archbishop and his family

Family member	Remuneration	Total to date
Hon. Edward Vernon, Archbishop of York	23 years at £26,000 a year	£638,000
Rev Leveson Vernon, chancellor, Prebendary and 2 Rectories	10 years at £3,000 a year	£30,000
Rev William Vernon, Prebendary and 3 Rectories (1 sinecure)	10 years at £2,500 a year	£25,000
Rev Charles Vernon, Rectory	10 years at £2,000 a year	£20,000

---

[65]   R. M. Beverley, *A Letter to the Archbishop of York on the Corrupt State of the Church of England*, 12th edition (Beverley: W. B. Johnson, 1831), p. 11.

[66]   *Poor Man's Guardian*, 30 June 1832.

Family member	Remuneration	Total to date
Mr Granville Vernon, chancellor of diocese	10 years at £1,800 a year	£18,000
Mr Egerton Vernon, registrar	10 years at £2,000	£20,000
Total per year	£37,300	£751,000

There were several more serious papers setting out how the Church might be reformed. Probably the most influential was Lord Henley's *Plan of Church Reform* of 1832.[67] It underwent a number of editions, but in essence proposed to set up a fund from the revenues of bishops, deans and other dignitaries, from which fund fixed remuneration should be paid to the bishops and other senior posts in the Church. Any surplus would be used to augment poor livings. Henley aimed to eradicate pluralism, non-residence and sinecures and would create two new dioceses. He had been an MP and was married to Sir Robert Peel's daughter. A plan by Dr Arnold, the renowned headmaster of Rugby School, also attracted much attention.[68]

A paper on reform which may well have been of particular interest to Dr Harcourt was produced by Dr George Wilkins. Wilkins had been vicar of St Mary's Nottingham since 1817, and the Archbishop appointed him archdeacon of Nottingham on 24 April 1832. Wilkins's *Letter to Earl Grey* was published in December 1832 and emphasized the need for speedy alterations and amendments if the Church "is to provide an adequate supply of religious knowledge and services to meet the demands of the community at large". Wilkins pointed out the discrepancies in his archdeaconry. He had to try and meet the needs of a population of 41,000 with two churches and two assistants. At the other extreme there were four rectories with populations of less than 400. He emphasized

---

[67] Lord Henley (Robert Henley Eden), *A Plan of Church Reform* (London: Roake & Varty, 1832).

[68] Thomas Arnold, *Principles of Church Reform* (London: B. Fellowes, Printer, 1833).

the lack of a fair relationship between the income of the clergy and the population they served.[69]

In 1831, Archbishop Howley of Canterbury introduced two bills proposing modest reforms. The first was designed to tackle the question of pluralities. It was deemed so feeble by the press that it went nowhere. The second, the Augmentations Act 1831, enabled ecclesiastical corporations to augment livings worth less than £350 with which they were connected. Several bishops took advantage of the legislation to supplement the income of some of their poorer livings from their own resources. In 1834, for example, Archbishop Harcourt augmented the perpetual curacy of Whitby by voluntarily giving £30 per year in addition to the regular stipend.[70] However, such modest changes were not going to satisfy the demands of those who wished for more radical reform of the Church of England.

The outcry against the supposed wealth of the Church could not be refuted due to the absence of facts. The need for an enquiry to establish reliable information was recognized both by radical reformers and Tory churchmen. The prime minister, Lord Grey, supported an established Church and realized it should be reformed by churchmen. On 23 August 1832, he published a list of the names of the Royal Commission to "inquire into the Ecclesiastical Revenues of England and Wales". There were 24 members including the two archbishops, the Bishops of London, Durham, Lincoln and Bangor, two deans, a canon of Westminster, and two archdeacons. The laymen included Lord Harrowby and others who Grey considered sympathetic to the Church. The intention was solely to gather information. Writing to Archbishop Harcourt in January 1834, Lord Grey stated the cabinet's views on Church reform "are purely of a conservative character and tend to the support of the Church

---

[69]   George Wilkins, *A Letter to Earl Grey on the Subject of Ecclesiastical Reform* (London: Longman, Rees, Orme, Brown & Longman, 1832).

[70]   *Hull Advertiser*, 7 November 1834. The perpetual curate of Whitby received £150 according to the Ecclesiastical Commission report of June 1834. Whitby parish had a population of 11,725.

establishment by the removal of some causes of complaint".[71] The report for the first time provided a comprehensive picture of the revenues of the bishops, cathedral dignitaries and the clergymen in the parishes. The report established that the total income of all the bishops was £157,737 but was expected to fall to £148,875 due to the agricultural recession. The episcopal income of the York diocese was £12,629. This was expected to fall to £10,600 due to the agricultural recession and the supplements Archbishop Harcourt was planning to give to the smaller livings in his diocese.[72]

The report considered that all bishops should have an income of £4,500 to £5,500 to enable them to provide themselves with appropriate housing and to meet travel costs. The archbishops and the Bishops of London, Durham and Winchester would receive more. Bishops would no longer be allowed to hold canonries or livings "in commendam", as Archbishop Harcourt had done when Bishop of Carlisle. He had retained the living of Sudbury and his canonry of Christ Church to supplement the modest income of £1,400 from the Diocese of Carlisle. The report concluded that, if the total expected episcopal income was redistributed as suggested, it would be insufficient.[73]

When Peel succeeded Grey as prime minister in 1834, he decided to set up a commission to make specific proposals to reform the Church. When writing to Lord Harrowby to invite him to become a member of his commission, Peel stated: "I am convinced of the absolute necessity of taking some effectual and practical steps with a view not only to the satisfaction of the public mind, but to the higher objective of promoting the spiritual efficiency of the Church and the great moral and religious purpose for which the Church was founded." Peel had

---

[71] Earl Grey to Archbishop of York, 25 January 1834, Durham University Archives, GRE/B60/11/3.

[72] *First & Second Reports from His Majesty's Commissioners appointed to consider the state of the Established Church with reference to Ecclesiastical Duties and Revenues* (London: Gilbert & Rivington, Printers, 1836), p. 29 and p. 36.

[73] *Ecclesiastical Duties and Revenues Commission*, First Report, 17 March 1835, p. 29.

communicated with the Archbishop of York and the Bishop of London, who both supported Peel's proposal. Commission members included both archbishops, the Bishops of London, Lincoln and Gloucester, plus a number of government ministers and laymen.[74]

Peel moved fast. The first meeting took place on 9 February 1835 with the Archbishop of Canterbury in the chair. Archbishop Harcourt was present. Utilizing the information obtained by Grey's commission, Peel's commission was to consider more equal distribution of episcopal duties and revenues and to examine the state of the cathedrals and collegiate churches. It could make whatever recommendations it thought necessary to make the Church more efficient. It should look for the best method for providing for the cure of souls "with special reference to the residence of clergy on their respective benefices". The commission had 21 meetings between 11 February and 10 April 1835. The Archbishop of York was present for 15 of the 21 meetings and in the chair for two meetings.[75]

With the fall of Peel's government on 8 April 1835, the Archbishop of Canterbury had discussions with the new Prime Minister, Lord Melbourne, with a view to continuing the work of the commission. The commission was reconstituted and resumed meeting in June 1835. The five bishops and three laymen were unchanged. The five government ministers were replaced by Lords Lansdowne, Melbourne and Cottenham, Lord John Russell, and Thomas Spring Rice. There were some 23 meetings between June and the end of January 1836. Both archbishops and Lord Harrowby were amongst the most regular attendees, with Dr Harcourt present for 13 of the 23 meetings.[76] Blomfield, Bishop of London, was the dominant

---

[74] Robert Peel to Lord Harrowby, 12 January 1835, quoted in Norman Gash, *Sir Robert Peel: The Life of Sir Robert Peel after 1830* (London: Longman, 1986).

[75] *Ecclesiastical Duties and Revenues Commission* minutes, 11 February to 10 April 1835, Lambeth Palace Library, EDR2/1/1.

[76] *Ecclesiastical Duties and Revenues Commission* minutes, Lambeth Palace Library, EDR/2/1/1; Best, *Temporal Pillars*, p. 300.

force. Dr Harcourt later stated: "Till Blomfield comes, we all sit about and mend our pens and talk about the weather."[77]

The Ecclesiastical Duties and Revenues Commission became the Ecclesiastical Commissioners for England in February 1836 and were incorporated under an Act of Parliament. The members of the commission and their task remained unchanged; they worked remarkably quickly and had produced their first four reports by June 1836. The first proposed the creation of two new dioceses of Ripon and Manchester, the union of St Asaph with Bangor and Llandaff with Bristol, and the redistribution of episcopal incomes to make them more equal. The second proposed a reduction in the number of residentiary canonries and the abolition of non-residentiary canonries in cathedrals and collegiate churches. It also sought to address the issues of pluralism, residence and the employment of stipendiary curates. The third and fourth reports looked more fully at diocesan reorganization and the legislation needed to implement the proposals.[78]

By September 1836, the commission had developed a proposal for the new Diocese of Ripon. It intended "with the consent of the Archbishop of York to lay a scheme before his Majesty to transfer to the new see part of the endowment, lands, messuages and tenements which are at present the property of the see of York, the average income of the latter see being £10,000".[79] The Archbishop was asked to provide a description of the estates to be transferred and an estimate of their value. The aim, with an additional transfer of estates from the Diocese of Durham, was to give the see of Ripon an income of £4,500 in line with Winchester. Archbishop Harcourt's diocese would become a more manageable size, with the number of livings reduced from about 900 to around 550, through the establishment of Ripon and the transfer of the archdeaconry of Nottingham to the Diocese of Lincoln.

---

[77] A. Bloomfield, *Memoir of Charles James Blomfield, D. D., Bishop of London* (London: John Murray, 1864) p. 167.

[78] For a fuller summary of the scope of the first four reports see Best, *Temporal Pillars*, pp. 302–5.

[79] *Ecclesiastical Commission* minutes, 26 September 1836, Lambeth Palace Library, Volume 1, pp. 43–4.

Whilst the legal arrangements for the formation of the Diocese of Ripon were proceeding, discussions had already taken place between the Archbishop of York and Prime Minister Melbourne concerning the appointment of Dr Charles Longley to the new see. Melbourne wrote to Archbishop Harcourt in early July, asking whether he would mind if Melbourne offered another see to Longley due to the delays in the creation of the new diocese. The Archbishop stated he did not want to act unfairly or unkindly, but he was much looking forward to working with Longley and hoped he would be happy to wait. Melbourne concluded that Longley would wait, and Archbishop Harcourt wrote to Longley: "Were I not too sensitive, in this case, that my joy must be your sorrow, I should say and say truly that I never received greater delight than from the information I have received from Lord Melbourne." Longley had been a tutor at Christ Church and was presently headmaster of Harrow. Archbishop Harcourt invited Longley to come to London in July to meet him and his daughter Georgiana, who knew Longley. He advised Longley that the Dean of Ripon was looking for a house for him; meanwhile Longley and his family were welcome to use Bishopthorpe as their headquarters for as long as necessary. He congratulated Longley on the birth of another child and said he was very used to children of all ages at Bishopthorpe. Longley was consecrated Bishop of Ripon in York Minster on 6 November 1836.[80]

The main proposal contained in the commission's second report was the abolition of non-residentiary canonries and the reduction in the number of residentiary canonries in most instances to four. All sinecure rectories would also be abolished. This would release funds from around 400 prebends and produce revenues of over £130,000 a year for redistribution to poor livings. The revenues would accrue gradually as stalls were vacated. The bishops hoped that, by setting their own house in order, they would encourage the government to give more financial support to the Church. As Owen Chadwick stated: "They were in fact,

---

[80]   Archbishop Harcourt to Charles Longley (Bishop of Ripon), 9 July to 25 August 1836, Lambeth Palace Library, Longley 1, ff. 135, 139, 149 and 151.

tinkering to defend."[81] No financial help was forthcoming from the government.

Charles Greville observed in his diary:

> The great reformer here is Lord Harrowby. The prelates have grasped at patronage with all their might and have taken to themselves that which appertains to the Chapters, much to the disgust of the latter. John [Lord John Russell] wrote on a slip of paper which he threw across the room to the Archbishop of York "I don't object to your robbing one another, but I can't let you rob the Crown." The AB of Y replied "That is just what I expect from you." This shows at least the good humour that prevailed amongst them.[82]

Legislation to put through the changes to the number of prebends and for the abolition of sinecure rectories was not achieved until the Dean and Chapter Act of 1840. However, in the meantime bishops and the crown were encouraged not to replace prebends when a stall became vacant. By 1841, Archbishop Harcourt had left vacant seven prebends at York Minster, and at least 60 canonries and prebendaries were vacant in other cathedrals and collegiate churches.[83]

The Archbishop, regardless of his advancing years, continued to attend and sometimes chair meetings of the commission, which had been put on a permanent basis by the 1840 Act. In 1845, at the age of 88 and two years before his death, he attended a meeting in June to discuss the grant of mineral leases in the Diocese of Ripon; he and Bishop Longley agreed to abide by the decision of the board. In December of the same

---

[81] Chadwick, *The Victorian Church Part One*, p. 130.

[82] 27 June 1836 in P. W. Wilson (ed.), *The Greville Diary*, Vol. 1 (London: William Heinemann, 1927), p. 438. Charles Fulke Greville (1794–1865) was head of the Privy Council office from 1821 to 1859. The role brought him into contact with politicians of all parties. His diaries cover the period 1817–37 and were published ten years after his death.

[83] *Clergy List* (London: G. Cox, Strand 1841).

year, he chaired four meetings.[84] Even if he was physically less able, his mental faculties would seem to have been unimpaired.

Archbishop Harcourt took his political responsibilities seriously. Although he seldom spoke in the House of Lords, he attended regularly and, when he could not attend, used his proxy.[85] He was an active supporter of reform of the House of Commons in spite of his aristocratic background and Tory alignment. He appreciated the need for reform of the Church of England and was prepared to devote time to the issues raised. He was glad to see his diocese reduced in size and welcomed the creation of the Diocese of Ripon. He did not allow his age to excuse him from undertaking the duties expected of an archbishop at a time of reform.

---

[84]   *Ecclesiastical Commission* minutes, December 1845, ECE 2/1/1/8.

[85]   Hansard indicates he spoke on only eight occasions in the House of Lords.

8

The later years (1830-47)

Archbishop Harcourt was aged 73 in October 1830. As the focus moved from parliamentary to Church reform, his workload increased at an age when most men reduce their responsibilities. His attendance at Ecclesiastical Commission meetings added to his duties when resident in London. He continued to attend the House of Lords to present petitions from different areas of Yorkshire for the abolition of slavery, for the better observance of the Sabbath and for the protection of the established Church.[1] He attended levees and other functions at Court. He compiled programmes for and attended the Ancient Concerts. He contributed to and often chaired the monthly meetings of the National Schools Society, which managed church schools and distributed grants to them.[2] He continued with regular ordinations in York, consecrated new churches and burial grounds, preached the sermon at the York assizes and handled the day-to-day business of his diocese. He still conducted weddings for family and friends.

His circumstances, however, changed significantly in two ways during the early 1830s. He inherited the Harcourt estates at Nuneham on the death of his cousin the third Earl Harcourt in June 1830 and commenced a major programme of improvements. He also became more dependent on support from his large family following the death of his wife, Lady Anne, in November 1832. His youngest daughter, Georgiana, his sixteenth child, was then aged 25 and became her father's regular companion at dinners and social engagements in London, Nuneham

---

[1] Petitions presented in 1831 on 2 February, 7 March, 14 and 15 April, and 7 May; in 1832 on 8 June and 14 June. Source: Hansard.

[2] *Morning Post*, 5 April 1832.

and Bishopthorpe.[3] Two of his sons also played an important role in supporting the aging Archbishop. William, his third surviving son, was at the time of his mother's death a residentiary canon of York Minster, rector of Wheldrake and Etton and sinecure rector of Kirkby in Ashfield, all appointments in the gift of the archbishop. William and his family lived at Wheldrake, some nine miles from York. Support was also provided by his youngest son, Egerton, who lived 14 miles from York. Egerton was a barrister on the northern circuit and made registrar of the Diocese of York by his father. He was to act as his father's secretary in connection with the Archbishop's visitation to the dean and chapter of York Minster in 1841.[4]

Lady Anne's death

Lady Anne died at Bishopthorpe on 16 November 1832. She had been on a visit to York Museum, contracted an infection and died of peritonitis some days later.[5] She had anticipated she would not live to an advanced age. In a letter to her son Henry dated 25 December 1831, she wrote: "I have always wished not to live to an advanced age and I am therefore ready to say with Simeon 'Now O Lord let thy servant depart in peace.'" She contemplated not seeing Henry again and entreated him to pray for the assistance of the Holy Spirit in his life.[6]

---

[3]   Georgiana was born in 1807. She corresponded with the Duke of Wellington and Sydney Smith. She translated a number of works from their German originals, including Martin Luther's *Letters to Women*. On 4 December 1845, she married General George Malcolm. She lived with her father until her marriage and continued to support him thereafter.

[4]   Egerton was born in 1803, attended Christ Church, Oxford, and was called to the bar in 1830. He served as a member of the council of King's College, London, and was a Deputy Lieutenant of the East Riding. He married in 1859 Laura Milner, daughter of Sir William Milner. He had no children. He lived at Whitwell-on-the-Hill, some 14 miles from York.

[5]   *Harcourt Papers* (HP), Vol. XII, p. 223.

[6]   Lady Anne to her son Lt. Col. Henry Vernon-Harcourt, 25 December 1831, HP, Vol. XII, p. 324.

The Archbishop's distress at his wife's death is evident in a letter to his nephew George, Lord Vernon. Written from his son William's rectory at Wheldrake some eight days after Lady Anne's death, Archbishop Harcourt thanked George for his sympathy and wrote:

> I prayed to God for support earnestly and fervently. I put my whole trust in Him, and I was not disappointed of my hope. I felt sensibly that my prayers had met with acceptance; every disposition to repine ceased; calmness was restored to my mind; and I could say without faltering 'the Lord gave and the Lord has taken away; for ever blessed be the name of the Lord.' I confidently believe that the spirit of her who for so many years constituted the joy and comfort of my life . . . has been received into the Divine Presence.[7]

Lady Anne was buried in the vault at Bishopthorpe church until 1847 when her body was removed to Stanton Harcourt to be placed alongside that of her husband. Archbishop Harcourt and his daughters Georgiana and Anne stayed with William at Wheldrake until 18 December, when they moved to Hackness Hall near Scarborough, the home of his daughter Louisa and her husband, Sir John Vanden-Bempde-Johnstone, and their five children for Christmas. Archbishop Harcourt enjoyed the company of his grandchildren even while grieving for Lady Anne.[8]

Nuneham

The Archbishop's great-grandfather, the first Viscount Harcourt, purchased the Nuneham Park estate in 1712. The present house had been built in 1756 by the first earl. His son, the second earl, employed "Capability" Brown to remodel the landscape and William Mason to

---

[7]   Archbishop to his nephew George, Lord Vernon, 28 November 1832, HP, Vol. XII, pp. 223–4.

[8]   Archbishop to his daughter-in-law Matilda, 19 December 1832, HP, Vol. XII, p. 226.

The Archbishop in 1821 aged 64

Lady Anne Vernon-Harcourt in 1831, the year before her death

Nuneham Courteney, as it was when the Archbishop inherited in 1830

lay out a picturesque flower garden. When the Archbishop inherited the estate on the death of the third earl in 1830, the house had not been updated for some time. The Archbishop and his eldest son George agreed that improvements were needed. The house was extended under the direction of Sir Robert Smirke to make it suitable for occupation by both the Archbishop and his eldest son's family. About £40,000 was spent on construction and a further £30,000 on refurbishing the interior. The gardens and park were reorganized under the direction of the landscape gardener Gilpin. Additional land was subsequently purchased to improve access to the railway station. A new village school was built, and Dr Harcourt established the Arboretum on land exchanged with Queen's College Oxford and Sir Henry Willoughby.[9]

Archbishop Harcourt enjoyed entertaining family and friends at Nuneham. The Harcourt papers suggest he spent about two months in the summer and two in the winter at the house. He spent Christmas at Bishopthorpe before going to Nuneham in January. In the summer, he went to Nuneham directly from London and then to Bishopthorpe sometime in late summer. His friend from his days at Oxford, Thomas Grenville, and his London neighbour, Lord Harrowby, were among his regular visitors. Politicians including Lords Grey and Melbourne mixed with high church clergy and Oxford dons including Bishop Wilberforce, Dr Walter Hook and Dr Buckland.[10]

Nuneham once again became a place to entertain royalty.[11] On Thursday 14 August 1840, the Archbishop welcomed the Queen Dowager, widow of William IV, and her sister Ida, Duchess of Saxe-Weimar. Queen Adelaide had been staying with the Duke of Buckingham, a member of the Grenville family, at Stowe. She was escorted from Oxford by

---

[9]   HP, Vol. XII, pp. 219–22.

[10] HP, Vol. XII, p. 222. Bishop Wilberforce was the fifth son of William Wilberforce. He became Bishop of Oxford in 1845. Dr Hook was vicar of Leeds and subsequently dean of Chichester. Dr Buckland was a lecturer at Oxford, a noted geologist and sometime dean of Westminster.

[11] The second Earl and his wife, the Archbishop's sister Elisabeth, had regularly entertained King George III and Queen Charlotte and their family at Nuneham some 25 years earlier.

the Oxfordshire Yeomanry, who were captained by Lord Norreys, the husband of the Archbishop's grand-daughter Lavinia.[12] Queen Adelaide was welcomed by a large crowd of "yeomanry, farm labourers and poor working men, who were regaled with a good dinner at the venerable prelate's expense". Her Majesty much admired the state of the garden and the beautiful scenery.[13]

A year later, the 83-year-old Archbishop and Georgiana entertained Queen Victoria and Prince Albert, when Albert came to Oxford to attend the annual commemoration of the founders and benefactors of the university. Queen Victoria and Prince Albert arrived at Nuneham at about 3 p.m. on 14 June 1841 and were enthusiastically received by local families and a large party of Oxford students, who had rowed up the river. The royal couple had a bedroom, two dressing rooms and a sitting room. The Archbishop escorted the queen to dinner at 7.45 p.m. The Duke of Wellington, then chancellor of the University, Lord Liverpool and many members of the Archbishop's family attended.[14] After dinner, the party was joined by representatives from Oxford University including Thomas Gaisford, Dean of Christ Church, Dr William Buckland and Dr Joseph Phillimore.[15]

The following day, Queen Victoria stayed at Nuneham, whilst Prince Albert and the Archbishop left for Oxford at 10 a.m. They were received by the Duke of Wellington, who had left Nuneham early. After honorary degrees had been conferred and speeches made, the prince

---

[12]   Elisabeth Lavinia was the daughter of the Archbishop's eldest son, George, and Lady Elisabeth Bingham, daughter of the Earl of Lucan. She had married Lord Norreys, the son of the Earl of Abingdon. The marriage was conducted by the Archbishop in the parish church at Nuneham on 9 January 1835.

[13]   *St James Chronicle*, 15 August 1840; *Oxford Chronicle*, 14 and 15 August 1840.

[14]   Family members at the dinner included the Duke and Duchess of Sutherland, Lord and Lady Norreys, Sir John and Lady Johnstone, and Col Francis and Lady Catherine Harcourt. Lady Catherine was a daughter of the Earl of Liverpool. Source: *Queen Victoria's Journal*, 14 June 1841.

[15]   Dr Phillimore was Regius Professor of Civil Law and chancellor of the Diocese of Oxford. He was the Archbishop's commissary for his 1841 visitation of York Minster, as discussed later in this chapter.

went to the town hall to receive addresses from the mayor and council. Following lunch at St John's College, he visited the Bodleian Library, Christ Church college, the University Press and "Dr Buckland's Museum", before attending a service in New Hall chapel. The Archbishop and the Prince then returned to Nuneham for dinner, where the party included the Bishop of London and the Archbishop's son Egerton. After dinner, more guests came out from Oxford including Dr Hampden, the Regius Professor of Divinity. "Some of the ladies sang." On 16 June, Prince Albert made a short early morning visit to Blenheim before the royal party left Nuneham at 11 a.m. for Buckingham Palace.[16]

The Archbishop continued to welcome royal visitors till almost his final year. In August 1844, Prince Wilhelm, Crown Prince of Prussia, stayed at Nuneham. The Duke of Wellington was again present to introduce the prince to the Archbishop and his family. The royal party walked in the grounds before dining at 8 p.m. with the prime minister, Lord Melbourne, the Vice Chancellor of Oxford University and his wife, and the Dean of Christ Church and his wife, as well as several members of the Archbishop's family. The following morning, Prince Wilhelm and his entourage rode around the park before leaving for the Duke of Buckingham's estate at Stowe.[17]

The last royal visitor to Nuneham was Prince Adolphus, Duke of Cambridge. He stayed at Nuneham from 24 to 26 March 1845. He was well known to the Archbishop, as both were directors of the Concerts of Ancient Music. Egerton and Georgiana accompanied Prince Adolphus to Oxford rather than the 88-year-old Archbishop. The Prince made his final visit to Nuneham from 29 to 31 July 1846, when he was accompanied by his sister Princess Mary, Duchess of Gloucester.[18]

There was a possibility that Prince Albert might stay at Nuneham in connection with a British Association for the Advancement of Science

---

[16] *Queen Victoria's Journal*, 15 and 16 June 1841, and *The Times*, 16 June 1841.

[17] *The Times*, 22 August 1844. Members of the Harcourt family included Egerton, Georgiana and Henry, who was accompanied by his wife, Lady Francis.

[18] *The Times*, 29 March 1845 and 1 August 1846. The Duke of Cambridge was the youngest son of George III.

meeting at Oxford in 1847. However, he came down from London by train for the day. The Archbishop provided a "fat buck for an ordinary at the Star Hotel" to be used for Prince Albert's visit.[19]

York Minster—Fires and visitation

York Minster was a cause of serious concern to the Archbishop during his final years. A fire on 2 February 1829 had destroyed the choir. It had been started by Jonathan Martin, who had hidden himself in the Minster when it was closed. The Archbishop contributed £2,000 and new communion plate. Two of his sons, Francis and Octavius, each gave £25. The restoration was completed in 1832 with funds raised by a committee led by Earl Fitzwilliam and supported by the Archbishops of York and Canterbury.[20]

Eight years later, on 20 May 1840, the Minster suffered a second fire. Between 8 and 9 o'clock at night a light was seen in the north-west tower. A clockmaker from Leeds had left a lighted candle, which set fire to some dry twigs brought in by birds. The nave roof was destroyed as well as the bells in the tower. A committee of 12 including the Archbishop and chaired by the Earl of Harewood was established to raise funds. The Archbishop contributed £1,000 and his sons Granville and Egerton £50 each. Sir Robert Smirke was appointed architect on the recommendation of the Archbishop and with the support of the dean and chapter.[21]

In the months following the second fire, it became clear to some members of the Minster chapter that Minster funds were not only wholly inadequate to deal with the consequences of the fire but that they had been poorly administered. The dean appeared in some instances to have acted without the authority of the chapter. Research into the Minster accounts was conducted by the Archbishop's son William, who was supported by a second residentiary canon, W. H. Dixon. Dixon was one

---

[19]   *Daily News*, 30 June 1847, and *Oxford Journal*, 3 July 1847.

[20]   W. Hargrove, *A New Guide for Strangers and Residents in the City of York* (York: W & J Hargrove, 1844), pp. 36–7; *The Times*, 19 and 21 March 1829.

[21]   *The Times*, 1 July 1840.

of the Archbishop's two chaplains and vicar of Bishopthorpe.[22] These two men provided the Archbishop with the information which led him to instigate his 1841 visitation. The Archbishop's other chaplain, Stephen Creyke, chaired the Minster Restoration Committee.

On Monday 18 January 1841, the Archbishop summoned to the chapter house of the Minster all the dignitaries of the cathedral for his Primary and Metropolitan Visitation. The dean, Sir William Cockburn, who spent most of his time in his parish at Kelston in Somerset, was present, together with the four archdeacons and most of the resident and non-resident canons. The Archbishop announced he planned to conduct an enquiry into the management of the Minster. He explained that, due to his infirmity, he would not conduct the visitation himself, and had appointed Dr Joseph Phillimore as his commissary.[23] The dean objected to the appointment of Phillimore, as he did not consider him an impartial assessor. The dean complained he had not had a chance to go through the Minster books himself, as he lived far away in a small country village, whilst William Vernon-Harcourt had had much opportunity to scrutinize the books, make extracts and brief his father. William explained everything had been reviewed at chapter meetings. The dean stated he was surrounded by enemies and left the meeting, which continued without him. The Archbishop had provided a list of 20 "articles" which he wished chapter members to review. The chapter started to discuss the Archbishop's questions on 20 and 21 January. The meeting agreed to refer some aspects of the enquiry, which concerned Minster administration and on which the dean and chapter disagreed, to an arbitrator for adjudication. To allow time for the arbitration and for the investigation of other questions raised by the Archbishop, the Visitatorial Court was adjourned to 25 February.[24]

---

[22] Dixon was also rector of Etton, a valuable living in the gift of the Archbishop; he had been a residentiary canon of York since 1831.

[23] Phillimore was Regius Professor of Civil Law at the University of Oxford and Advocate in the Court of the Arches.

[24] *Leeds Mercury*, 21 January 1841; *Leeds Intelligencer*, 23 January 1841; *Sheffield Iris*, 26 January 1841; Robert Phillimore, *A Report of the Proceedings of the Visitatorial Court at York*, (London: S. Sweet Law, 1841), pp. 81–7.

Dr Phillimore had hoped to conclude proceedings at the February meeting, but this was not to prove possible. The arbitrator, Sir William Follett, had decided not to proceed, as he did not think he had the dean's confidence. The dean wrote from his parish to say he had not been told the date of the February meeting and would not attend. The issue, however, which made any conclusion impossible was the reply Canon Dixon gave to the Archbishop's nineteenth question: "Are the chancels of the churches and chapels belonging to the Dean and other members of your body in good and sufficient repair?" Dixon had written to Phillimore to say presentations to vicarages in the dean's patronage were usually sold, and it was not known if the money was used to fund repairs. Phillimore was astonished and declared "it was neither more nor less than a charge of Simony". Phillimore encouraged Dean Cockburn to attend the court as the charge was so serious. "No heavier charge could be brought against a dignitary of the Church of England."[25]

The February meeting of the court continued without the dean. Dr Phillimore stated that the evidence he had received from the chapter members confirmed the need for the visitation. He hoped that the venerable Archbishop might see peace restored to the chapter of the Minster. To achieve this end the Archbishop had produced a set of "injunctions" as to how the Minster should in future be managed.[26] Canon Dixon then presented his case for charging the dean with selling presentations to benefices and provided examples. Dean Cockburn did not deny that benefices had been sold but stated he believed it was lawful at the time. The meeting concluded with Dixon stating that the dean and chapter accepted the Archbishop's proposals for the future administration of the Minster but suggested some small amendments.[27] The court was adjourned to 23 March.

---

[25] Phillimore, *A Report of the Proceedings of the Visitatorial Court at York*, pp. 90–5.

[26] Phillimore, *A Report of the Proceedings of the Visitatorial Court at York*, pp. 99–104.

[27] Phillimore, *A Report of the Proceedings of the Visitatorial Court at York*, pp. 105–8.

Following the meeting Phillimore and Cockburn continued to correspond. He complained: "I am a poor man having suffered severely in purse as well as reputation by the ceaseless malice of Mr Harcourt [William, the Archbishop's son]." The dean encouraged press attention to the case by having letters published in *The Globe* and *The Yorkshireman*. What private discussions took place between the Archbishop, his son William and Canon Dixon are not recorded. However, on 11 March the Archbishop instructed his secretary to write to Cockburn to say he considered it indispensable that the dean should be present at the adjourned meeting of the court on 23 March, so that he could answer Canon Dixon's charges.[28]

Dean Cockburn was present at the start of the meeting of the court on 23 March. He immediately objected to Phillimore's jurisdiction and said he could not plead his case without acknowledging Phillimore's authority. Members of the chapter asked him not to interfere, but Cockburn refused and withdrew. A lawyer then presented Canon Dixon's case and called witnesses. On the second day the court (in the Dean's continuing absence) discussed issues of Minster administration, including the occasions when the dean had acted without the authority of the chapter. One of the most recent was the sale of the lead and bell metal following the fire; Cockburn had sold these materials for £200 without the authority of the chapter and had not paid the funds received into the Minster accounts.[29]

The court resumed on Thursday 1 April. The public galleries were crowded and included many members of the Archbishop's family. A barrister asked to speak on behalf of Dean Cockburn, but Phillimore refused to hear him, stating only the dean could speak. Dr Phillimore then read out the Archbishop's revised injunctions for administering the Minster. On the following day, again with a large audience, the dean failed to appear and Phillimore again refused to let the dean's barrister speak. The commissary then read his judgement on the simony charges. The court adjourned to the chapter house, where the Archbishop was present to deliver his sentence depriving Cockburn of his office. The

---

28 Phillimore, *A Report of the Proceedings of the Visitatorial Court at York*, pp. 111–16.

29 *London Evening Standard*, 25 March 1841.

Archbishop explained he found the whole proceedings most painful. "Nothing but the strongest sense of the paramount duty I owe to the Church in general and to the Church in York in particular could induce me to sign the sentence which has been submitted to me." He had no doubt that simony had been committed. The dean himself had written to the chapter clerk to say that if he had 100 livings, he would sell them all. He felt duty bound to deprive Cockburn of his dignity and privileges. After the deputy registrar had read the sentence, Archdeacon Corbett read an address from the non-resident canons assuring the Archbishop of their esteem and regretting that he had been required to make such a visitation at his advanced age. The Archbishop thanked the canons for their address: "To possess the confidence and good opinion of my clergy has ever been the dearest wish of my heart."[30]

The court was then adjourned until May when some further "injunctions" were issued. During this period, Cockburn appealed to the Court of Queen's Bench against his sentence of deprivation. The Court of Queen's Bench concluded that the Archbishop had the right to conduct the visitation, but that the right of the Visitatorial Court to pronounce a sentence of deprivation had been removed by the Church Discipline Act of August 1840.[31] In all other respects, the visitation had been conducted properly. Dr Phillimore's knowledge of the law was out of date.

The final meeting of the Visitatorial Court took place at York Minster on 20 July. The dean was present and apologized: "I wish again to be admitted to the friendship of the Archbishop; and I am sorry if I have said or done anything which has given him dissatisfaction."[32] He admitted no pecuniary considerations should have influenced the

---

[30] *Leeds Mercury*, 3 April 1841; *York Herald* and *York Gazette*, 3 April 1841. Family members present included William, Egerton, Georgiana, William's wife Matilda and the Archbishop's son-in-law Sir John Johnstone.

[31] Act for Better Enforcing Church Discipline 1840 (3 & 4 Vict c. 86).

[32] The dean was restored to friendship with the Archbishop. Writing to William Vernon-Harcourt on 23 May 1845, the Archbishop stated, "the Dean has just been with me for some time, more gracious and agreeable in all respects than I ever saw him." The dean was on his way to York and asked if the Archbishop had "any commands I can execute for you there". HP, Vol. XII, p. 258.

disposal of benefices. He accepted that the Archbishop had every right to investigate the conduct of his clergy in the Visitatorial Court. Phillimore absolved Cockburn of his contempt. The dean, however, continued to object that the Archbishop's new rules for administering the Minster had been agreed in his absence and that they might contradict the cathedral statutes. Phillimore assured him the new "injunctions" did not contradict the cathedral statutes. He advised the court that the dean had now paid into the cathedral fabric fund £520 he had received in rent. William Vernon-Harcourt stated that the original objective of the visitation had been achieved and new arrangements had been made for the efficient administration of the Minster. He noted that the dean had also paid into the fabric fund the £200 bell metal money and a further £100 of rent.[33]

While William Vernon-Harcourt and Canon Dixon were assisting the Archbishop with the visitation, the Archbishop's second domestic chaplain, Stephen Creyke, was chairing the Minster Restoration Committee.[34] The restoration could only proceed as funds allowed. By February 1841 just over £13,000 had been raised and committed to the repair of the fabric of the tower and the nave roof. More damage had been found than first thought. By the time of a public meeting in York in April 1842 the total funds still only amounted to £14,337 and had all been committed. The committee needed a further £9,000 to restore the nave vault and bases of the piers, make good the woodwork and stained glass and repair the pavements.[35]

A second public meeting was held in October 1842 chaired by Lord Wharncliffe. The Archbishop's sons William and Granville attended and spoke. The Archbishop himself wrote to express his regret that his infirmity prevented him from attending. He promised a further £1,000. The dean and chapter agreed to put up £4,000, but William explained that the chapter was already spending £6,000 on repairs to other parts of the

---

[33] *York Herald*, 24 July 1841; *Yorkshire Gazette* 8 May and 31 July 1841.

[34] Creyke had been rector of Wigginton, one of the Lord Chancellor's livings, since 1834. The Archbishop had added Sutton-on-the-Forest in 1837. Creyke employed curates in both parishes. The Archbishop had made Creyke a non-resident canon of York Minster in 1841.

[35] *Yorkshire Gazette*, 13 February 1841 and 2 April 1842.

Minster and that the architect has indicated a total of £47,000 needed to be spent to put the whole building in good order. The dean and chapter were raising £26,000 through a mortgage to undertake the most urgent repairs to parts of the building not affected by the fire. The £4,000 the chapter was putting towards fire repairs would otherwise have been used to repair other parts of the building.[36]

Following the October meeting further funds started to flow in, with many of the original supporters making a second contribution. The Archbishop's sons Egerton and Octavius donated, and by November 1842 an additional £6,311 had been raised. By August 1844, sufficient funds had been raised without drawing on the £4,000 promised by the dean and chapter. The repairs had largely been completed and the restoration committee was dissolved.[37] Stephen Creyke, possibly in recognition of his success as chairman of the restoration committee, was appointed archdeacon of York by the Archbishop in 1845.

Dr Hampden, Regius Professor of Divinity at Oxford University

Some four years before the York Minster visitation, Archbishop Harcourt was involved in another controversy. The Whig government of Lord Melbourne wished to appoint Whig sympathizers to bishoprics and other prominent positions in the Church of England and had difficulty finding candidates with the desired political views. In 1836, the position of Regius Professor of Divinity at Oxford became vacant. William Howley, the high church Archbishop of Canterbury, had submitted a list of suggested names to Melbourne including Pusey, Newman and Keble.[38]

---

[36] ³6 *Yorkshire Gazette*, 8 October 1842.

[37] *Yorkshire Gazette*, 19 November 1842 and 31 August 1844.

[38] Edward Pusey, John Henry Newman and John Keble were all Fellows of Oriel College, Oxford, and leaders of the Oxford Movement in the Church of England. Newman was received into the Roman Catholic Church in 1845 and became a Catholic priest and subsequently a cardinal. He was beatified in 2019.

Melbourne unsurprisingly ignored this list of Tory high churchmen and offered the post to Renn Dickson Hampden, who was Professor of Moral Philosophy.[39]

However, before the appointment was confirmed, news of it reached Oxford. A petition against Hampden was organized and signed by more than half the resident MAs for presentation by Archbishop Howley to the king, William IV. Hampden's views were deemed unorthodox by the high church petitioners. One of the Regius Professor's main responsibilities was to give a series of lectures to ordinands and attendance at the lectures was a requirement for ordination. The petitioners were fearful that Hampden's supposedly unorthodox views would be passed on to all future ordinands from Oxford.

Hampden refuted the claims of the petitioners, whose case was weakened by the fact that Hampden's appointment to the chair of Moral Philosophy two years earlier in 1834 had been uncontroversial. However, both Archbishop Howley and Archbishop Harcourt went to see Melbourne to try and persuade him that Hampden's position would be fatally compromised if he was appointed. Howley had further discussions with the king but, in spite of the opposition, Hampden's appointment was made.[40]

In 1840, Lord Melbourne explained the case to Queen Victoria: "When we made Dr Hampden Regius Professor at Oxford, [Archbishops Howley and Harcourt] certainly behaved abominably; they came and remonstrated ... They said his opinions were heterodox (which they are not)." Some six months after her discussions with Lord Melbourne, Queen Victoria was introduced to Dr Hampden by Archbishop Harcourt at Nuneham.[41]

---

[39]   In 1833, Hampden had been nominated principal of St Mary Hall by Archbishop Harcourt's friend Lord Grenville, who was then chancellor of Oxford University.

[40]   Dr Hampden's appointment is described in Owen Chadwick, *The Victorian Church Part One* (London: SCM Press, 1971), pp. 112–21.

[41]   *Queen Victoria's Journal*, 28 December 1840 and 15 June 1841. Hampden was appointed Bishop of Hereford in 1847, where he proved to be a conscientious and uncontroversial diocesan bishop.

Appointment of rural deans

The ancient office of rural dean had been an important feature of the
medieval church but had all but disappeared from the Church of England
by the eighteenth century. Where it did survive, it was largely a title
without any formal duties. The revival of the role in the early nineteenth
century was driven by the desire of individual bishops to raise clerical
standards.

The scope of the role was determined by the bishop and varied
from diocese to diocese. The publication in 1835 of the first edition of
William Dansey's *Horae decanicae rurales*, a comprehensive two-volume
history of the office, did much to stimulate interest in and discussion
of the role of the rural dean, although by this date the office had been
revived in many dioceses. Rural deans had been appointed in two Welsh
dioceses and in Salisbury, Ely and Gloucester by 1811. The revival was
often encouraged by translation of bishops between dioceses. Bath and
Wells, Bristol, Lincoln and Oxford all had rural deans by 1831. Bishop
Blomfield appointed rural deans in London and Archbishop Howley in
Canterbury in 1833. The Bishop of Worcester followed suit in 1834. By
the time Dansey produced a second edition of his book in 1844, another
six dioceses, including York, had appointed rural deans.[42]

Archbishop Harcourt was encouraged to appoint rural deans by the
archdeacon of the East Riding, Samuel Wilberforce. Wilberforce was
vicar of Burton Agnes, near Hull, and had succeeded his father-in-
law, Francis Wrangham, as archdeacon in 1841. The Archbishop's son
Egerton, as Diocesan registrar, assisted Wilberforce with his research into
the role of the rural dean and may well have drawn up "the [Archbishop's]
instructions to be observed by rural deans in the Diocese of York". The
rural dean's prime role was to assist the archdeacon in the performance
of his duties. The rural dean was to make enquiries about the clergy,
churchwardens and other parish officers. Information was to be obtained
on clergy residence, performance of divine service and attendance at

---

[42]   The revival of the office of rural dean is described in Arthur Burns, *The
Diocesan Revival in the Church of England c. 1800–1870* (Oxford: Clarendon
Press, 1999), pp. 75–107.

communion, benefice vacancies, fabric of the churches, parochial schools and maintenance of the parish registers. The rural dean might be asked to call the clergy together to meet the archdeacon. The archdeacon would collate the information received from his rural deans and make a report to the Archbishop once a year.[43]

The Archbishop appointed 13 rural deans in March 1842. Amongst the five appointed for the West Riding were the vicar of Doncaster and the vicar of Sheffield. Six rural deans were appointed in the archdeaconry of Cleveland including his son William's brother-in-law, the Revd William Gooch, and the Archbishop's chaplain Canon Stephen Creyke. Only two appointments were made in Robert Wilberforce's archdeaconry of the East Riding. All the appointed clergy received a copy of the Archbishop's instructions.[44]

Education

Some two years later in October 1844 the Archbishop took up "a matter of pressing and paramount importance to the spiritual interests of the diocese [of York]". He wrote to all the clergy in his diocese to ask for their support for the provision of better facilities for teacher training. The aim was to build a new training school to meet the needs of the dioceses of Ripon and York. The present accommodation was too small for the existing number of students and there was no provision for the training of schoolmistresses, "an object of scarcely less importance than the training of masters". Ripon and York dioceses each needed to raise £2,500. The Privy Council had promised £3,500; the project would cost £8,500. Every clergyman was asked to preach a sermon on the subject and use such other means as seemed appropriate to raise funds.[45]

---

[43] William Dansey, *Horae Decanicae Rurales*, 2nd edition (London: J. G. F. & J. Rivington 1844), pp. 349–50; *English Chronicle*, 19 March 1842.

[44] *Globe*, 11 and 31 March 1842; *Patriot*, 3 March 1842.

[45] The Archbishop of York to the clergy of his diocese, 8 October 1844, HP, Vol. XII, p. 255.

The fundraising in York diocese went well. The Archbishop contributed £300, his son William £50, and his son-in-law Sir John Johnstone another £50. By the end of December 1844, £2,340 had been raised. York diocese achieved its target by May 1845, but Ripon struggled and had not reached £2,500 by October 1845, when the new building was well under way. It was completed in April 1846 at a cost of £11,910.[46] The Archbishop funded two exhibitions each for trainees worth £10 a year.

Archbishop Harcourt continued to play an active role in educational and other political issues which would affect his diocese and the wider Church of England. In 1840, he corresponded with the Earl of Carlisle concerning the issues dividing the Church and the government. He reminded his nephew that the national schools supported by the Church of England accepted the children of dissenters. In a division in the National Schools Committee some 25 years earlier, he had voted to open the schools to dissenters. Children should not be required to attend church services, "provided their parents from time to time undertake for their attending some place of divine worship on Sundays". He explained to Lord Carlisle that the Church Schools system could not be financed without lay support. The division between Church and State had been driven by the withdrawal of grants to the Society for the Propagation of the Gospel for missionaries in the colonies, a cause dear to the Archbishop, and by the failure of the government to push through a settlement of the "Church Rates" question. The proposal had been supported by both Archbishops and the Bishop of London but opposed by dissenters. Instead, the government had put forward plans for taking over ecclesiastical leases and for a national education system, which were not acceptable to the Church.[47]

---

[46]   *Yorkshire Gazette*, 14 December 1844, 28 December 1844; *York Herald*, 3 May 1845; *Yorkshire Gazette*, 25 April 1846.

[47]   The Archbishop of York to William Vernon Harcourt, 19 January (1840), HP, Vol. XII, pp. 259–62. The letter summarizes the points the archbishop made to the Earl of Carlisle. The year is unstated but assumed to be 1840, as the letter refers to Lord Carlisle's resignation as Lord Lieutenant, which took place in 1840.

The future of the Harcourt estates

Knowing he must be coming towards the end of his life, in September 1841, the Archbishop set about trying to restore the Harcourt peerage. He had made his first attempt shortly after succeeding to the Harcourt estates in 1830. He had had a meeting with the then prime minister, the Duke of Wellington, to request his permission to approach the new king, William IV, to restore the peerage. The Archbishop believed he had a good relationship with the king but did not want to make the approach without the consent of the government.[48] The duke accepted the Archbishop had a good case and asked him to leave matters in his hands. The Archbishop agreed, but Wellington went out of office before he could do anything.[49]

In 1839, the Archbishop appears to have made a second attempt to obtain a peerage from Lord Melbourne. Melbourne told Queen Victoria that the Archbishop of York was a cunning old man: "He always has some purpose—wants a peerage for himself and his son."[50]

The Archbishop made a third attempt in September 1841. He wrote to Sir Robert Peel setting out his case for a peerage. He reminded Peel that Queen Victoria had stayed with him, that he was the sole surviving member of the council which had advised Queen Charlotte, that his predecessors had had close links with royalty and that the estates had been given to the Harcourts by William the Conqueror. He emphasized he did not want the title for his own sake but in justice for his family.[51]

---

[48]   William IV told Lord Holland that Edward Harcourt, Archbishop of York, was an agreeable man to talk to and a statesman—a conclusion he had drawn from his willingness to vote for the second reading of the Reform Bill. Source: A. D. Kriegel (ed.), *Holland House Diaries 1831–1840: The Diary of Henry Richard Vassall Fox, Third Lord Holland* (London: Routledge & Kegan Paul, 1977), p. 155.

[49]   Earl Harcourt died 17 June 1830 and the Duke of Wellington left office on 30 November 1830.

[50]   *Queen Victoria's Journal*, 17 March 1839.

[51]   The Archbishop of York to Sir Robert Peel, 21 September 1841, British Library Add. MS 40489, f. 286.

Sir Robert's reply was swift and clear. He regretted it was not in his power to give the Archbishop what he asked, though it would be "personally gratifying if he could". Peel had had many requests for peerages. The House of Lords had already increased in size, and he could see no need to increase it further. He would not propose any increases to the queen. If there ever was a need for more peerages, he would consider claims at the time.[52]

A few months before his death, the Archbishop encountered another issue concerning the future of the Harcourt estates. The Archbishop's eldest son George intended to remarry. George's first wife, who had been a favourite of the Archbishop until he found out about her affairs, had died in 1838. George's intended bride was Frances, Countess Waldegrave, a widow and the daughter of the famous singer John Braham. She was aged 25 and had an income of about £20,000 a year. George was aged 61, with an income of about £12,000 a year, an insufficient sum to keep Nuneham and a town house. Both had an interest in politics, poetry, painting and sculpture. George could help her run her estates and coal mines. Her income would enable them to live in a manner similar to George's cousin, the Duke of Sutherland. Marriage to a staid and somewhat pompous man like George Harcourt would give Frances the position in society that she craved.[53]

The Archbishop did not support the marriage. He had largely forgotten the failings of George's first wife. He had fallen out with the bride's father; he recalled that Braham had laughed at him when he made suggestions as to how Braham should sing a certain aria. The Archbishop, however, had a more serious concern. George proposed that Lady Waldegrave should have the right to live at Nuneham after his death. The Archbishop wrote to his son William, "A deep sense of gratitude to my beloved brother-in-law [2nd Earl Harcourt] will never allow me to be a party to so unrighteous a proceeding." He went on to say that he trusted William would never agree to such a proposal after his death and he was sure his grandson Edward,

---

52   Sir Robert Peel to the Archbishop of York, 24 September 1841, British Library Add. MS 40489, f. 288.

53   O. W. Hewett, *Strawberry Fair: A Biography of Frances, Countess Waldegrave 1821–1879* (London: John Murray, 1956), pp. 56–63.

William's eldest son, would not agree with the proposal either. If the proposal had been adopted, William would never have had possession of Nuneham. Lady Waldegrave died in 1879 and William in 1871.[54]

George and Frances were married on 30 September 1847 at Aveley parish church in Essex, where old friends of the Waldegraves and John Braham lived. Only George's daughter and her husband, Lord and Lady Norreys, and some Braham relations attended. The couple went immediately to stay at Bishopthorpe. Frances was introduced to the recently married Georgiana, who became a close friend, and to George's brothers and sisters based in Yorkshire. "With the single exception of the Archbishop, all the meetings were successful and in most instances the brothers and sisters preferred Frances to George."[55]

Consecration of Leeds parish church

After the traumas of his visitation to York Minster in early 1841, the Archbishop must have been pleased to be able to attend a more joyous event in late summer of the same year. The new Leeds parish church was to be consecrated on 2 September 1841. Leeds had been part of his diocese till the formation of the Diocese of Ripon in 1836. The Archbishop had championed the enfranchisement of Leeds and other growing cities in his diocese in the debate on the Reform Bill. As Metropolitan, he was determined in spite of his age to play a full role in the service. Responsibility for the formal consecration would fall to Bishop Longley as diocesan bishop, but the Archbishop would preside at Holy Communion.

The Archbishop, Georgiana and his chaplain Canon Dixon stayed the night before the service with William Beckett at Kirkstall Grange. Bishop Longley and the Archbishop headed a large procession of clergy, who entered the new church at 11 a.m. After the formalities of consecration had taken place, the vicar, Dr Hook, read the service of Morning Prayer.

---

[54]   The Archbishop of York to William Vernon Harcourt, 1 August 1847, Bodleian Library, HP 3863 f. 133.

[55]   Hewett, *Strawberry Fair*, p. 62.

The Archbishop then took his place by the altar and led the service of Holy Communion:

> It was gratifying to witness the earnest devotion and the clearness with which his Grace enunciated the prayers, commandments and collects. It was undoubtedly a great effort for the venerable prelate, who is now in his 85th year; yet owing to the excellent construction of the church and his Grace's sonorous voice, he was distinctly heard even in the most distant parts of the spacious edifice.

The administration of communion took about two hours, as around 1,000 of the 2,000 congregation received the sacrament.

The service was followed by a lunch in an adjacent hall and more speeches. Dr Hook read an address to the Archbishop. In his reply, the Archbishop expressed his joy that, though his diocesan ties were broken, the clergy of Leeds still retained a kind remembrance of his former connection. He congratulated Dr Hook for his successful accomplishment of "the splendid temple now dedicated to the glory of God". The Archbishop thanked the Bishop of New Jersey for coming so far to demonstrate the bond between the church in England and the church in America. Archdeacon Musgrave thanked the Archbishop, and the Bishop of New Jersey concluded the speeches. The Archbishop and Georgiana eventually left Leeds at 6.30 p.m.[56]

Accident at Bishopthorpe

The Archbishop's robust constitution was further demonstrated a year later. On the morning of 2 June 1842, the Archbishop, with his son Egerton, Canon Dixon and the deputy registrar, Joseph Buckle, had been to Ardsley near Barnsley to consecrate the new church. Following their return by train, Canon Dixon and the Archbishop were walking in the garden when a drain collapsed. They both fell into the water. Egerton,

---

[56]   *Leeds Mercury*, 4 September 1841, and *Leeds Intelligencer*, 4 September 1841.

who was walking behind, attempted a rescue, which proved difficult due to the high sides of the drain. However, after a wash and change, the Archbishop attended dinner as usual and joked that "their sudden intrusion into the domain of the frogs and tadpoles must have occasioned much consternation". The following day the Archbishop travelled 14 miles to consecrate the new church at Clifford.[57] He conducted an ordination in Bishopthorpe chapel on 12 June before returning to London to attend a dinner on 15 June, at which the Duke and Duchess of Sutherland entertained Queen Victoria and Prince Albert.[58]

The accident had no impact on the elderly Archbishop's summer programme in 1842. On 23 June, he and Georgiana attended the Duchess of Buccleuch's fete in Richmond, Surrey, at which Queen Victoria was present. They then travelled to the Isle of Wight to stay with the Archbishop's son Col. Francis Harcourt and his wife, Lady Catherine, at their house, St Clare Castle. Returning to Nuneham in early July, they entertained the Duke and Duchess of Sutherland and their son and daughter for a week. In August, they were back in London, where the Archbishop conducted two weddings at St George's Hanover Square. He did not stay for the wedding meal as he needed to catch a train to York, where he held his usual four public dinners at Bishopthorpe Palace in successive weeks in September. He concluded the month with a visit to Bishop Longley at Ripon.[59]

Final five years, 1843–7

With the continuing extension of train services, the Archbishop could travel more readily and swiftly between his three residences in London, Nuneham and York and to the homes of family members. In spite of his advanced age, his pattern of life was maintained largely unchanged in his final years. On his return to London each March, he would attend

---

[57]   *Morning Herald*, 14 June 1842.

[58]   *Morning Herald*, 16 June 1842.

[59]   *Morning Herald*, 24 June, 7 July, 20 July, 23 August, 26 August, 27 September 1842.

Ecclesiastical Commission meetings and appear at levees. He organized and attended grand dinners, especially in connection with the regular programme of Ancient Concerts, where he continued to be happy to take responsibility for the concerts of directors who were too busy to plan a programme. He made sure he attended the christenings of Queen Victoria's children. He did not like to miss out on parties for visiting royalty, such as the dinner for the visit of the Emperor of Russia and the King of Saxony in June 1844.[60] He opened Nuneham to the public for several days in the summer.

Even if he was becoming physically frailer, his voice remained strong, and he continued to marry family members. In September 1843, he married his granddaughter Marianne Harcourt-Vernon to Mr St John Mildmay at Bishopthorpe. In early October, he travelled to Trentham to marry Lady Evelyn Leveson Gower, the eldest daughter of the Duke and Duchess of Sutherland, to Lord Blantyre. In August 1844, he married another Sutherland daughter to the Marquess of Lorne, the eldest son of the Duke and Duchess of Argyll. Perhaps the family wedding which gave him the greatest pleasure was the marriage of his own daughter Georgiana to Col. George Malcolm at Bishopthorpe on 5 December 1845. The ceremony was conducted by Georgiana's eldest clerical brother, Leveson Vernon-Harcourt. Her sister Louisa Johnstone's children were bridesmaids. Eight of her brothers were present, as well as numerous members of her extended family. The honeymoon was spent at the Johnstones' house, Hackness Hall.[61]

The Archbishop's increasing infirmity meant that extended confirmation tours and the consecration of most churches and burial grounds was passed out to other bishops, principally the Bishop of Ripon. Between 1843 and 1847, 17 churches and burial grounds were consecrated. Of these the Archbishop consecrated three in 1843 and one, the new burial ground at Bishopthorpe, in 1845. He continued regular ordinations at Bishopthorpe and opened his palace for four public dinners every September till 1846, when the practice ceased.

---

[60] *Morning Herald*, 8 June 1844.

[61] *Morning Herald*, 11 and 23 September 1843, 1 August 1844, 9 December 1845; *York Herald*, 6 December 1845.

He continued to take an active interest in other issues affecting his diocese. Sir Robert Peel, while prime minister, consulted him on appointments to new district churches until Peel went out of office in 1846. When the Ecclesiastical Courts Bill was being considered in 1843–4 and threatened to close the court in York, he received a deputation and indicated his support for the court at York. He used his sons Egerton as registrar and Granville as judge of the York court to advance the case for retention.[62]

Although a supporter of the railways—he invested £5,000 in the York and North Midland[63]—the Archbishop opposed the building of a line close to Bishopthorpe. Egerton appeared on his behalf at the committee on the proposed route of the London & York line, which would have cut off Bishopthorpe Palace from the home farm.[64] Egerton stated the Archbishop opposed the line not for his own sake but for his successor, for the Archbishop would not be alive when the line opened.[65]

In January 1846, he appointed a new archdeacon of Cleveland. He had spent Christmas as usual at Bishopthorpe and made a short visit to Nuneham before coming up to London at the end of March. In April, he decided he could not undertake a family wedding and handed the task to his nephew, the Dean of Lichfield, a member of the Howard family.[66] There was some press speculation about his health, but the *Morning Herald* noted in May that the Archbishop of York was not suffering from extreme debility. He was able to take his accustomed walks. Although he did not attend the dinner given by the Archbishop of Canterbury for all the bishops in May, he was able to make a call on Queen Victoria two days later to congratulate her on the birth of another baby.[67] He continued to write letters complaining about the proposed line of the London & York railway, but could not attend the laying of the foundation stone

62 *Yorkshire Gazette*, 20 May 1843, 24 June 1843 and 28 December 1844

63 Undated letter in the author's collection from the Archbishop asking his adviser to purchase £5,000 of shares.

64 *Morning Herald*, 7 June 1845.

65 *Morning Herald*, 24 March and 25 May 1846.

66 *Morning Herald*, 30 April 1846.

67 *Morning Herald*, 8 May, 22 May and 27 May 1846.

of the new chapel for the Bishop of Ripon. The foundation stone was engraved: "This chapel is the gift of Rt. Hon. & Most Rev Edward Vernon Harcourt, Lord Archbishop of York, to the see of Ripon." Following the last Ancient Concert, he left London with Georgiana for Nuneham, where his visitors included the Duke of Cambridge and Thomas Grenville. He and Georgiana travelled to Bishopthorpe on 17 September.[68]

The Archbishop's arrival at Bishopthorpe in 1846 was cause for a major celebration. More than 400 parishioners greeted him like a hero. They gathered at the new boys' school, which the Archbishop had financed, and, led by the village band, made their way to Middlethorpe. When the 89-year-old Archbishop arrived, a large body of villagers removed the horses from his carriage, attached ropes to it, and physically drew him to the Palace. At the entrance, a decorated triumphal arch bore the inscription, "God Save our Gracious Benefactor". The vicar, Canon Dixon, read an address, and the Archbishop replied that it was his duty to provide a school and pay for repairs to the church. He concluded, "I am in enjoyment of tolerable health, saving some of those infirmities which are inevitable in old age." The Archbishop retired to his palace with the crowd cheering loudly and the band playing. He was fit enough to receive a visit from the Duchess of Gloucester a fortnight later.[69]

The Archbishop did not return to London till April 1847 and was accompanied by his daughter Georgiana and her husband Col. Malcolm. The Archbishop's engagements were much fewer than usual. He focused on the programme of Ancient Concerts. On 19 May, the Duchess of Kent dined with him, and Prince Albert joined them for the concert. In June, he directed a concert for the King of Hanover. The final concert was on 30 June, when the Duke of Wellington hosted the preconcert dinner. The Archbishop left London for his last visit to Nuneham in early July for a two-month stay.[70]

On 20 September, the Archbishop travelled to Bishopthorpe. He celebrated his ninetieth birthday with members of his family on Sunday

---

[68] *Morning Herald*, 6 July, 28 July, 31 August and 19 September 1846.

[69] Bishopthorpe village website, December 2022, and *Morning Herald*, 19 September and 10 October 1846.

[70] *Morning Herald*, 20 May, 25 June, 1 and 12 July 1847.

10 October. Several newspapers carried the story that he had been walking in the gardens at Bishopthorpe with Canon Dixon and fallen into a ditch when a bridge collapsed. His son Egerton took the opportunity at a York diocesan meeting of the Society for the Propagation of the Gospel to explain the story was old news, as the accident had happened five years earlier in June 1842.[71] The Archbishop received a delegation from the meeting and entertained a bishop from the West Indies. On Monday 1 November, the Archbishop visited the newly restored chapter house at the Minster and praised the quality of the restoration. Two days later he fell ill, and a doctor was called. He remained peacefully in bed on the Thursday and died at 1 p.m. on Friday 5 November.[72]

In accordance with his wishes, his funeral took place at Stanton Harcourt. The hearse left Bishopthorpe Palace for York railway station at 12.15 p.m. on Friday 12 November in pouring rain. In spite of the weather, the crowds were huge. The procession included the Bishop of Ripon, the three archdeacons and some 120 clergy, plus the Lord Mayor and representatives of York Corporation. Once the coffin was installed in the train, the clergy and members of the Corporation went to the Minster for a service of thanksgiving.[73]

On arrival at Aylesbury, the coffin was taken through Oxford to Eynsham, where many of the tenants joined the family mourners to process at 12 noon to Stanton Harcourt church. The service was conducted by the vicar of Stanton Harcourt, supported by the rector of Nuneham. The Archbishop was interred in the Harcourt vault. Lady Anne's body and the body of their daughter Caroline were subsequently brought to Stanton Harcourt and interred there. Family mourners included five of the Archbishop's sons and his daughters Louisa and Georgiana and their husbands.[74]

Queen Victoria wrote to Georgiana two days after her father's death: [75]

---

[71] *Yorkshire Gazette*, 11 September 1847; *York Herald*, 16 October 1847.

[72] *Leeds Intelligencer*, 6 November 1847; HP, Vol XII, p. 268.

[73] *Yorkshire Gazette* and *Illustrated London News*, 20 November 1847.

[74] *Leeds Intelligencer*, 20 November 1847. The sons present were Leveson, Frederick, Octavius, Charles and Granville.

[75] Queen Victoria to Georgiana Malcolm, 7 November 1847, private collection.

My dear Mrs Malcolm

I cannot let anyone but myself express our sincere concern at the melancholy event which has just deprived you of a beloved parent and us of a kind friend.

I have experienced so much kindness from the Archbishop that I shall ever retain a grateful recollection of it and the visits to Bishopthorpe and Nuneham will never be forgotten, nor the latter by the Prince.

We beg you to express our sympathy on this mournful occasion to all your family and in the hope that your health may not suffer from the severe shock.

Believe me always

Yours sincerely

Victoria.

Conclusion

Samuel Wilberforce, Bishop of Oxford at the time of Archbishop Harcourt's death, wrote to a friend:

> The old Archbishop had greatly won upon my affections. There was a charming kindness and love about him, and simplicity and absence of selfishness. The want was in depth—in every way; in intellect, in moral purpose, in sense of responsibility, in concentration of affection.[1]

Archdeacon Churton, preaching on the Sunday following the archbishop's death stated:

> The temporal honours and possessions that he succeeded to never made him neglect or forget his spiritual office and charge over the Church of Christ, but rather made him more abundantly consecrate his worldly wealth to the Church's service; his charities increased as his wealth increased; he was still ready, while his active power remained, for every public call; and his easy access to his clergy, and all who sought his aid or counsel, was more remarkable as years came on. It is but giving expression to the common feeling of his diocese and province to say that few could leave his presence without regarding him afterwards as a friend and father, and speaking of him with words that marked at once affection and esteem.[2]

---

[1] Bishop Wilberforce to Miss Louisa Noel, 13 November 1847, quoted in A. R. Ashwell and R. G. Wilberforce, *Life of the Rt. Rev Samuel Wilberforce*, Vol. 1 (London: John Murray, 1880–1882), p. 418.

[2] Edward Churton, Archdeacon of Cleveland, sermon: *The Remembrance of a Departed Primate*, quoted in HP, Vol. XII, p. 267–73.

The Archbishop was undoubtedly held in high esteem at the time of his death. His personal faith was strong, and he recognized his own good fortune. At a meeting with representatives of the York diocesan branch of the Society for the Propagation of the Gospel some two weeks before he died, he said:

> I am now at the close of a life unusually extended and blest with health, kind friends, and an affectionate family—every comfort this world can afford; and I should be most ungrateful if I did not, while life is spared me, assist every effort that I can, and take every opportunity that is offered to me, to extend the knowledge of the Gospel of my Saviour.[3]

An archbishop needs to be more than a well-liked man of faith if his period in office is to be deemed well spent. Good family and political connections had enabled Archbishop Harcourt to climb the episcopal ladder and provided him and his family with wealth and status. He entered his archiepiscopate at the age of 50. He came from a traditional aristocratic and landowning background. He must be judged on the extent to which he helped his diocese and the wider Church adapt to the rapid population growth which occurred in the first half of the nineteenth century. As a political appointee, he must also be judged on his willingness to stand up for what he believed to be right.

With nearly 900 parishes extending over about 5,300 square miles, Archbishop Harcourt could not hope to know his clergy as well as he had known the clergy of the Diocese of Carlisle. Through his formal visitation and confirmation tours in 1809, 1817 and 1825, he gained a good knowledge of the Diocese of York and its clergy. In other years, he visited all parts of his diocese to consecrate new churches and burial grounds and to conduct confirmations. All his clergy had the chance to meet him at the dinners he organized at each location during his tours, as well as at the four public dinners every summer at Bishopthorpe Palace. He ensured he knew his clergy well enough to be able to recommend candidates to patrons. His advice was sought and accepted by prime

---

3   Quoted by Archdeacon Churton in his sermon, HP, Vol. XII, p. 269.

ministers, including Lord Liverpool and Sir Robert Peel. The Lord Chancellor, Lord Brougham, asked Archbishop Harcourt to nominate clergy for all poorer livings. He took seriously his responsibilities to his clergy.

The Archbishop recognized the need for more church accommodation in growing towns, particularly for people of limited means. Following the passing of the first Church Building Act in 1818, he invited his archdeacons to assess the needs in York diocese. He was involved personally in preparing the returns and regularly attended meetings of the Church Building Commission, where he made clear his views on church design. A total of 111 new churches were consecrated during his episcopacy. He secured government funding for all or part of the cost of 47 churches.

It was little help to provide more church accommodation if there were insufficient clergy to minister in them. Archbishop Harcourt recognized that the output of graduates from Oxford and Cambridge was insufficient to meet the needs of his diocese. Incumbent incomes in the diocese of York were below the national average and many parishes had no clergy house. As he had done in Carlisle diocese, he welcomed literates and took steps to ensure they were properly trained. He set up a system of recognized tutors, who combined academic training with practical parish experience. Although he generally favoured high church clergy when choosing archdeacons, he was happy to appoint evangelical clergy and to use them to teach his sons and to tutor ordinands.

On two issues of major concern at the time, pluralism and non-residence, Archbishop Harcourt made some progress. With 200 livings worth under £100, he accepted that pluralism made good sense if two neighbouring small parishes could be served by one incumbent. Where non-residence was wholly unacceptable, he took steps to remedy the situation, as in the case of Sydney Smith. In 1835, a year before the Diocese of Ripon was established, only 49 per cent of parishes in the Diocese of York had a resident incumbent, broadly in line with the Church as a whole. By 1846, the reduced Diocese of York had resident incumbents in 67 per cent of parishes. Where the incumbent was not in residence, there was usually a resident curate.

His policy on appointment to livings was in line with practice at the time. Five of his sons were presented to offices in his gift. Other members of his wider family were also presented to valuable livings. Such nepotism was acceptable early in the nineteenth century but considered less appropriate by the time of his death. He was expected to offer livings in his gift to political allies. However, he also promoted able clergy of more humble origin. He consulted local clergy and his archdeacons before recommending candidates to patrons. He often recommended for promotion clergy already working in the parish.

Music was central to his life. For 37 years, he was a director of the Concerts of Ancient Music. He played a leading role in establishing and securing patronage for the York Music Festivals. His intervention ensured that hymns could be sung without challenge in Church of England services.

Archbishop Harcourt took his political responsibilities seriously. He attended and voted regularly in the House of Lords. He confined his speeches to ecclesiastical issues and avoided making pronouncements on contentious political matters. His opposition to the granting of political rights to Roman Catholics modified over time. He supported reform of the House of Commons, recognizing that the major industrial cities in his diocese deserved to be represented in Parliament. He attended Ecclesiastical Commission meetings more frequently than most bishops and chaired meetings till the age of 88. He approved the reduction in cathedral establishments and refrained from making new appointments to canonries as they became vacant. He supported the creation of the Diocese of Ripon and agreed to the transfer of income from the archbishopric of York. He supported the reform of Parliament and the Church.

He valued his connections to the royal family. He devoted time and care to his responsibilities as a member of the Queen's Council during the final illness of George III. In his sermon at the coronation of George IV, he made plain his disapproval of licentious behaviour and praised George III for his values. He showed his willingness to act upon what he believed to be right and incurred royal displeasure by giving support to George IV's estranged wife Queen Caroline. He welcomed royal visitors to his homes. The Duchess of Kent and Princess Victoria stayed at Bishopthorpe for the York Music Festival in 1835. His guests at Nuneham included the Dowager Queen Adelaide, widow of William IV, the Crown Prince of Prussia, Queen Victoria and Prince Albert. The Duke of Cambridge, a fellow director of the Ancient Concerts, was a frequent visitor.

Archbishop Harcourt valued his family. When Bishop of Carlisle he personally tutored his older sons. He and Lady Anne were deeply distressed at the death of their second son Edward at Oxford at the age of 18. The Archbishop always enjoyed conducting marriages and christenings for the wider family. In his later years, particularly following the death of Lady Anne in 1832, he depended on the help of his children to continue his duties in York diocese and in London. Without the advice of his sons William and Egerton, he would not have been able to conduct his York Minster visitation in 1841. His youngest daughter Georgiana's support enabled him to maintain his social life in London, Nuneham and York.

His generosity to good causes was well recognized in his lifetime. In his years as Bishop of Carlisle, when his funds were limited, he assisted charities by preaching. When he became Archbishop of York, he used his increased income to contribute to organizations concerned with the extension of the Church at home and overseas and to the education and relief of the poor. His position enabled him to secure funds from fellow members of the aristocracy, whilst donating generously himself, for example, to the York Music Festivals and to both restorations of York Minster. He never failed to give Christmas gifts to his tenants and to the poor of Bishopthorpe and York. He was fully conscious of the need to share the wealth he had been so fortunate to acquire.

The many descendants of Archbishop Harcourt can be satisfied that he lived a worthwhile and virtuous life. His sense of duty was based on a sure Christian faith. He undertook his responsibilities with care to the end of his days. He may not have been a leader of reform in either Parliament or the Church, but he was more supportive of change than most of his fellow bishops. He was not afraid to stand up for a cause in which he believed. He was always grateful for his wealth, which enabled him to provide well for his family and to offer support to other less fortunate members of society.

Family members

Parents and siblings of Edward Venables Vernon (Harcourt) 1757–1847

Father: George Venables Vernon, 1st Lord Vernon, Baron of Kinderton (1708–80)

George was the son of Henry Vernon of Sudbury and his wife Anne Pigott, who inherited the Kinderton estates from her mother, Mary, the sole heiress of Thomas Venables. George took the additional surname of Venables in 1728. He married three times, and Edward was the last surviving son of his third wife. He was created Baron Vernon of Kinderton in 1762.

Mother: Martha Harcourt, Lady Vernon (1715–94)

Martha was the daughter of the Hon. Simon Harcourt and Elizabeth Evelyn, granddaughter of the diarist John Evelyn. Martha's brother, Simon Harcourt, was created the first Earl Harcourt. He had two sons, who became successively the 2nd and 3rd Earls Harcourt. Martha married George Venables Vernon in April 1744.

Siblings surviving at Edward's birth

Half-brother: George Venables Vernon, 2nd Lord Vernon (1735–1813)

George was the son of George Venables Vernon's first wife Hon. Mary Howard, daughter of the 7th Lord Howard of Effingham. He married twice. Only a daughter, Georgiana, survived to adulthood. She married Edward Harbord, later Lord Suffield, of Gunton Park, Norfolk.

Half-sister: Mary Venables Vernon, Hon. Mrs Anson (1736–1821)

Mary was also the daughter of George Vernon's first wife, Mary Howard. She married George Adams, who changed his surname to Anson. Mary and George had nine children. The eldest son became the first Viscount Anson. The youngest son, Frederick, was ordained by Edward and succeeded him as rector of Sudbury in 1803.

Elder Sister: Elizabeth Venables Vernon, Countess Harcourt (1747–1826)

Elizabeth was the oldest surviving child of George Vernon's third wife Martha. She married her first cousin, George Simon Harcourt (1736–1809), who was Viscount Nuneham at the time of her marriage in 1765. She was Lady of the Bedchamber and a close personal friend to Queen Charlotte, wife of George III. She became Countess Harcourt in 1777, when her husband succeeded his father as 2nd Earl Harcourt. She had no children.

Brother: Henry Venables Vernon, 3rd Lord Vernon (1747–1829)

Henry married Elizabeth, daughter and heiress to Sir Charles Sedley, in 1779 and changed his surname to Sedley. They lived at Nuthall Temple in Nottinghamshire. He reverted to the Venables Vernon name on succeeding his elder half-brother as the 3rd Lord Vernon in 1813. His eldest son, George Charles, became the 4th Lord Vernon. His youngest son, John Sedley Venables Vernon, was ordained deacon by Edward in 1821 and appointed to the living of Molesworth in 1822 and subsequently Barton-in-Fabis in 1826.

Sisters:

Catherine Venables Vernon (1749–75)
Martha Venables Vernon (1751–1808)
Anne Venables Vernon (1754–1837)

None of these sisters married. Anne died in London at the age of 83. Martha died on 6 June 1808 shortly before Edward made his first entry to York as Archbishop. All three are buried at All Saints Church, Sudbury, Derbyshire.

Parents and siblings of Lady Anne Leveson Gower, Edward's wife, 1761–1832

Father: Granville Leveson Gower, Marquess of Stafford 1721–1803
Known as Earl Gower from 1754 to 1786, he was married three times. His first wife died from smallpox six months after their marriage. He was educated at Westminster and Christ Church, Oxford. He served as Lord President of the Council in several governments and helped Edward progress his career. His main house was Trentham Hall, Staffordshire.

Mother: Lady Louisa Egerton, Countess Gower 1723–1761
Lady Louisa was the daughter of Scroop Egerton, 1st Duke of Bridgewater. She married Granville Leveson Gower in 1748 and had four children. She died shortly after the birth of her fourth child, Lady Anne Leveson Gower, who was to become Edward Venables Vernon's wife.

Stepmother: Lady Susanna Stewart, Marchioness of Stafford 1742–1805
Lady Susanna was the daughter of the 5th Earl of Galloway. She married the future Marquess of Stafford in 1768 and had four children. She developed a close relationship with her stepdaughter, Lady Anne.

Siblings:

Lady Louisa Leveson Gower (Lady Louisa Macdonald) 1749–1827
She married Sir Archibald Macdonald, Chief Baron, and brother of Lord Macdonald.

Lady Caroline Leveson Gower (Countess of Carlisle) 1752–1824
She married the 5th Earl of Carlisle in 1770. They lived at Castle Howard, Yorkshire.

George Leveson Gower, Viscount Trentham (Duke of Sutherland) 1758–1833
George was a close friend of Edward at Christ Church. George married the 20-year-old 19th Countess of Sutherland in 1785. He was known

as Earl Gower from 1786 and Marquess of Stafford from 1803 to 1833. He was created 1st Duke of Sutherland six months before his death. He inherited the Bridgewater estates through his mother and was one of the richest men in Britain.

Half-siblings:

Lady Georgiana Augusta Leveson Gower (Lady Georgiana Eliot) 1769–1806
She married Mr William Eliot, subsequently 2nd Earl of St Germans. They lived at Port Eliot in Cornwall.

Lady Charlotte Sophia Leveson Gower (Duchess of Beaufort) 1771–1854
She married Henry Charles Somerset, the Marquess of Worcester and future 6th Duke of Beaufort, in 1798. Their country home was Badminton in Gloucestershire.

Lady Susan Leveson Gower (Lady Susan Harrowby) 1772–1838
She married Dudley Ryder, Lord Harrowby, in 1795. In 1809 he was created Earl of Harrowby. They lived next door to Edward in Grosvenor Square and their country house was Sandon Park in Staffordshire. Lord Harrowby and the Archbishop were close friends.

Hon. Granville Leveson Gower (Earl Granville) 1773–1846
He married Lady Harriet Cavendish, daughter of the 5th Duke of Devonshire. He was created Viscount Granville in 1815 and Earl Granville in 1833.

Archbishop and Lady Anne's children

Hon. Edward Venables Vernon and Lady Anne Leveson Gower were married in her father's house in Scotland Yard in the parish of St Martin-in-the-Fields on 5 February 1784.

They had 16 children: 11 sons and five daughters. The 16 children were born within a period of 22 years, between 1785 and 1807.

Seven of the sons (George, Edward, Leveson, Henry, Granville, Charles and Egerton) attended Westminster School. All except Henry went on to Christ Church, Oxford. The rest were educated locally and either entered the navy at the age of 12 (William, Frederick and Octavius) or went up to Sandhurst (Francis). William left the navy after five years and went to Christ Church. The daughters were all educated at home.

George Granville Venables Vernon (Harcourt) 1785–1861

George was MP for Lichfield from 1806 to 1830 and for Oxfordshire from 1831 till his death. His first wife was Lady Elizabeth Bingham, daughter of the 2nd Earl of Lucan. They had one daughter, Elizabeth Lavinia, who married Lord Norreys, the future 6th Earl of Abingdon. In 1840, George married as his second wife Frances, Countess Waldegrave, daughter of John Braham, the noted tenor, and widow of the 3rd Earl Waldegrave. George shared Nuneham in Oxfordshire with the Archbishop till the Archbishop's death, when he inherited the Harcourt estates at Nuneham and Stanton Harcourt.

Edward Venables Vernon 1787–1806

Edward died while an undergraduate at Christ Church, Oxford.

The Revd Leveson Venables Vernon (Harcourt) 1788–1860

Leveson was ordained deacon and priest by his father in 1812. He served successively as incumbent of Rothbury, Stokesley and Beckenham, the last from 1835–38. He was appointed a prebendary of York and chancellor of York Minster in 1827 and served as archdeacon of Cleveland from 1828–32. He married the Hon. Mary Peachey, daughter of the 2nd Lord Selsey, in 1815. She inherited West Dean in Sussex and Newsells Park in Hertfordshire. They had no children.

The Revd William Venables Vernon (Harcourt) 1789–1871

William entered the navy at the age of 12, as his father advised he could not become a clergyman. However, following his brother Edward's death, his father agreed he could be ordained, and he left the navy and went to Christ Church. He was ordained deacon and priest by his father in 1813. He was successively incumbent of Etton, Wheldrake and Bolton Percy. He also served two periods as rector of Bishopthorpe. He was a residentiary canon of York Minster from 1821. A noted scientist, he was a founder of the British Association for the Advancement of Science. He married Matilda, daughter of Col Gooch, in 1824 and they had two sons and five daughters. His younger son was Sir William Harcourt, the distinguished politician and sometime Home Secretary and Chancellor of the Exchequer. William inherited the Harcourt estates from his brother George and his descendants continue to live at Stanton Harcourt.

Admiral Frederick Edward Venables Vernon (Harcourt) 1790–1883

Frederick entered the navy as a midshipman at the age of 12. Promoted to lieutenant in 1809, commodore in 1811 and captain in 1813, he served largely in South America and the Pacific. He did not go to sea after 1823 and officially retired as captain in 1846. He was promoted to admiral during his retirement. He married Marcia Tollemache, sister of the first Lord Tollemache. They had two sons and three daughters. The author is descended from their younger son Leveson Francis. Frederick was an ardent Protestant and disapproved of his younger brother Octavius's interest in racing. The family lived in London at 47 Cadogan Place.

Col Henry Venables Vernon (Harcourt) 1791–1853

Henry was a lieutenant colonel in the Grenadier Guards and a JP. He married Lady Frances Harley, daughter of the 5th Earl of Oxford. They lived at Brampton Park, Herefordshire and had no children.

Granville (Harcourt) Vernon 1792–1879

Granville was a lawyer and appointed chancellor of York diocese by his father in 1818. He was MP for Aldborough 1815–20 and for East Retford 1832–47. In 1814 he married Frances Julia Eyre, heiress to the Grove and Headon estates in Nottinghamshire. They had four sons and a daughter.

Admiral Octavius Venables Vernon (Harcourt) 1793–1863

Octavius entered the navy as a midshipman at the age of 12 in 1806. He was promoted to lieutenant in 1814 and captain in 1827. He served till

1836 and, like his brother, was promoted to admiral in retirement. He married Anne, daughter of William Gater and widow of William Danby, in 1838 and they lived at Swinton Park, near Masham in North Yorkshire. They had no children. His horse Ellington won the Derby in 1856.

Caroline Elizabeth Venables Vernon 1795–1815

Caroline died at the age of 20 at the family home in London and was reinterred with her father and mother at Stanton Harcourt in 1847.

Anne Susan Venables Vernon (Harcourt) 1796–1870

Anne was left £10,00 in her father's will. In the 1861 census she was living in Princes Buildings, Clifton, Bristol. Later she lived at Penton Grange, Penton Mewsey, near Andover in Hampshire, where she built a public lecture hall. She never married.

The Revd Charles Venables Vernon (Harcourt) 1798–1870

Charles was ordained deacon and priest by his father in 1822. He succeeded his brother Leveson as rector of Rothbury in 1824, where he built a public library and re-ordered the church. He was a canon of Southwell Minster 1830–37 and of Carlisle Cathedral from 1837. He never married and remained at Rothbury till his death.

Col Francis George Venables Vernon (Harcourt) 1801–80

Francis went to Sandhurst in 1814 and served with the Grenadier Guards from 1816–36. He was equerry to the Duchess of Kent, Queen Victoria's mother, and MP for the Isle of Wight 1852–57. He married Lady Catherine Jenkinson, daughter of the 3rd Earl of Liverpool, in 1837. They had no children. Their houses included St Clare Castle on the Isle of Wight and Buxted Park in Sussex.

Louisa Elizabeth Catherine Vernon 1802

Louisa was born at Rose Castle on 2 February and survived only a few days.

Egerton Venables Vernon (Harcourt) 1803–83

Egerton was called to the bar in 1830. His father appointed him registrar of the Diocese of York. He served on the council of King's College, London, 1856–1868. He was a JP and Deputy Lieutenant of the East Riding. He lived at Whitwell-on-the-Hill near York and married Laura Milner, daughter of Sir William Milner, in 1859. They had no children. He had the use of St Clare Castle in the Isle of Wight following his brother Octavius's death. He acted as executor for most of his siblings.

Louisa Augusta Venables Vernon (Lady Johnstone) 1804–69

Louisa married Sir John Vanden-Bempde-Johnstone, Bart in 1825 and had two sons and three daughters. Her husband was MP for York and subsequently Scarborough. They lived at Hackness Hall near Scarborough.

Georgiana Charlotte Venables Vernon (Mrs Malcolm) 1807–86

Georgiana is best known for her correspondence with the Revd Sydney Smith and for her translation from the German of Martin Luther's *Letters to Women* and the novels and theological works of Gustav Freytag. In 1845 she married Colonel, later Major General, Malcolm. They lived at 67 Sloane Street, London and had no children.

APPENDIX 2

Churches and burial grounds consecrated during Archbishop Harcourt's archiepiscopate

The Archbishop in his 1809 visitation expressed concern that there were insufficient church places, particularly for those who could not afford to rent a pew. Between 1808 and 1847, 111 new churches were consecrated, of which 95 were consecrated by Dr Harcourt personally. Forty-seven of these churches were built with a contribution from government funds under the Church Buildings Acts and are marked with an *. A further church, St Peter's at Hoyland near Barnsley, was rebuilt with some government funding in 1830, but never consecrated. The list was compiled from the Harcourt registers at the Borthwick Institute and checked against newspaper reports, church websites and *Six Hundred New Churches* by M. H. Port.

Dr Harcourt also consecrated 76 burial grounds. A further six burial grounds were consecrated in the York diocese by other bishops between 1845 and 1847. Dr Harcourt's last consecration was an extension to the burial ground at Bishopthorpe on 5 December 1845, when he was aged 88.

Churches and burial grounds consecrated by Archbishop Harcourt

No.	Date	Dedication	Location
1	13 June 1809	St James, Stannard Hill	Nottingham
	24 June 1809	Burial ground	Pontefract

No.	Date	Dedication	Location
2	1 July 1809	St John, Great Horton	Bradford
	29 July 1809	Burial ground	Scarborough
3	28 August 1810	St Luke	Shireoaks
4	18 September 1811	St Helen	Skelton-on-Ure
	11 June 1813	Burial ground	Sutton-in-Ashfield
	30 August 1813	Burial ground	New Malton
	31 August 1813	Burial ground	Bridlington
	28 November 1813	Burial ground	Harewood
5	29 November 1813	St John	Wortley
6	26 December 1814	St Mary	Boston
	9 February 1815	Burial ground	Wakefield
	10 February 1815	Burial ground	Doncaster
7	12 October 1815	Christ Church	Bradford
8	13 October 1815	St John in the Wilderness, Marshaw Bridge	Halifax
9	14 October 1815	St Paul	Drighlington
10	28 August 1816	Christ Church	Liversedge
	9 July 1817	Burial ground	Nottingham
11	14 July 1817	St Margaret	Swinton
	16 July 1817	Burial ground	Sheffield
	15 August 1817	Burial ground	Leeds
	2 September 1817	Burial ground	Sculcoates
	5 October 1819	Burial ground	Gildersome
	5 October 1819	Burial ground	Pudsey
	6 October 1819	Burial ground	Bradford
	6 October 1819	Burial ground	Wibsey
12	7 October 1819	St Anne	Southowram
	8 October 1819	Burial ground	Huddersfield
13	8 October 1819	Holy Trinity	Huddersfield
	15 August 1820	Burial ground	Newark

No.	Date	Dedication	Location
	17 March 1822	Burial ground	Wentworth
	30 July 1822	Burial ground	Brompton
	5 September 1822	Burial ground	Otley
14	26 September 1822	Christ Church*, Sculcoates	Hull
	21 October 1822	Burial ground	Ackworth
15	22 October 1822	St George*	Barnsley
16	22 October 1822	St Mary	Barnsley
	23 October 1822	Burial ground	Attercliffe
	24 October 1822	Burial ground	Hucknall
17	24 October 1822	St Paul	Nottingham
18	28 October 1822	St John	Pockley
19	30 August 1824	St Lawrence*	Pudsey
20	30 August 1824	St John	Bierley, Bradford
	31 August 1824	Burial ground	Haworth
	31 August 1824	Burial ground	Keighley
21	1 September 1824	Christ Church	Sowerby Bridge
	1 September 1824	Burial ground	Lightcliffe
	2 September 1824	Burial ground	Almondbury
22	6 September 1824	St Peter*	Stanley
	7 September 1824	Burial ground	Wheldrake
23	28 October 1824	Christ Church, Woodhouse	Huddersfield
24	2 November 1824	St Mary	Birdsall
25	29 June 1825	St George*	Sheffield
26	1 July 1825	St Paul*	Alverthorpe
	2 August 1825	Burial ground	Horsforth
27	4 August 1825	St Mary*	Low Harrogate
	15 August 1825	Burial ground	Welton
	2 September 1825	Burial ground	Ninebanks
28	5 September 1825	St Mary	Gateforth

No.	Date	Dedication	Location
	5 September 1825	Burial ground	Winksley with Grantley
29	28 September 1825	St John	Sharow, Ripon
30	29 September 1825	St John the Evangelist	Bishop Thornton
31	27 December 1825	St Paul*	Hanging Heaton
32	12 January 1826	Christ Church* Meadow Lane	Leeds
33	13 January 1826	St Mark*	Woodhouse
	14 January 1826	Burial ground	York
34	16 January 1826	St John	Roundhay
35	26 July 1826	Christ Church*	Attercliffe
36	12 October 1826	St Mary*	Quarry Hill
37	1 November 1826	St Matthew*	Wilsden
38	1 November 1826	St Paul*	Shipley
	21 February 1827	Burial ground	York
39	4 September 1827	St John*	Daw Green Dewsbury
	4 September 1827	Burial ground	Birstall
40	5 September 1827	St Peter*	Earlsheaton
	7 September 1827	Burial ground	Heptonstall
	29 October 1827	Burial ground	Hartwith
	29 October 1827	Burial ground	Thornthwaite
41	30 October 1827	St Cuthbert*	Pateley Bridge
42	31 October 1827	Holy Trinity	Dacre, Ripon
43	2 July 1828	St Philip*	Sheffield
44	23 August 1828	Christ Church*	Scarborough
	25 August 1828	Burial ground	Burton Fleming
	25 August 1828	Burial ground	Wold Newton
	25 August 1828	Burial ground	Muston
45	6 October 1828	Christ Church* Linthwaite	Huddersfield
	13 October 1828	Burial ground	Allerthorpe

No.	Date	Dedication	Location
	15 October 1828	Burial ground	Kirkheaton
	16 October 1828	Burial ground	Worsborough
46	17 October 1828	St Mary*	Greasborough
	18 October 1828	Burial ground	Tadcaster
47	27 August 1829	St Peter	Redcar
48	9 September 1829	St Saviour	Retford
49	10 September 1829	Christ Church	Doncaster
	22 September 1829	Burial ground	Topcliffe
	23 September 1829	Burial ground	Ripon
50	25 September 1829	St Stephen*	Kirkstall
	25 September 1829	Burial ground	Guiseley
	25 September 1829	Burial ground	Rawden
	13 October 1829	Burial ground	Beverley
	14 October 1829	Burial ground	Sutton in Holderness
51	22 December 1829	St John	Oulton
	19 July 1830	Burial ground	Barnsley
	19 July 1830	Burial ground	Barnsley
52	20 July 1830	Christ Church*	Stannington
53	21 July 1830	St Mary*, Bramall Lane	Sheffield
	23 July 1830	Burial ground	Nottingham
54	30 August 1830	St Peter*	Morley
	31 August 1830	Burial ground	Baildon
55	31 August 1830	Holy Trinity*	Idle
56	1 September 1830	All Saints*	Paddock
57	1 September 1830	St John*	Golcar
58	1 September 1830	St Stephen*	Lindley
59	2 September 1830	All Saints*	Netherthong
60	2 September 1830	Holy Trinity*	South Crossland
61	2 September 1830	Emmanuel*	Lockwood
62	27 August 1831	St James*	Myton

No.	Date	Dedication	Location
63	21 September 1831	St Mark*	Woodhouse
	21 September 1831	Burial ground	Leeds
64	22 September 1831	St James* Stannary	Halifax
	22 September 1831	Burial ground	Illingworth
65	23 September 1831	St Paul*	Huddersfield
66	23 September 1831	Christ Church*	New Mills
67	24 September 1831	St James*	Heckmondwike
	24 September 1831	Burial ground	Batley
68	26 September 1831	St Martin*	Brighouse
69	27 September 1831	St Paul*	Birkenshaw
70	11 October 1831	St James*	Thornes
71	4 January 1832	St Matthew*	Holbeck
72	22 August 1832	St John*	Cleckheaton
	20 October 1832	St Mary's	Scarborough
	23 January 1833	Burial ground	York
	22 August 1833	Burial ground	Rawmarsh
73	24 August 1833	Holy Trinity	Sunk Island
	13 September 1833	Burial ground	Scarborough
74	23 September 1833	St John	Newland
75	5 October 1833	St James the Great*	Hebden Bridge
76	27 December 1833	All Saints	West Markham
77	30 December 1834	St John	Scofton
78	25 August 1835	Wadsley Parish Church	Wadsley
	26 August 1835	Burial ground	Greasley
	27 August 1835	Burial ground	Nottingham
79	29 September 1835	St Paul, Cross Stone	Todmorden
	30 September 1835	Burial ground	Rothwell
80	26 October 1836	St Andrew	Upleatham
	October 1836	Burial ground	Handsworth
81	7 August 1837	Christ Church	Newark on Trent
	15 September 1837	Burial ground	York

No.	Date	Dedication	Location
	27 October 1837	Burial ground	Whitby
82	4 October 1838	Christ Church	Fulwood
83	9 June 1840	St Paul	Monk Bretton
84	9 June 1840	Holy Trinity	Thorpe Hesley
85	1 October 1840	St John Park	Sheffield
86	1 October 1840	St Thomas	Crookes
	October 1840	Burial ground	Filey
87	17 October 1840	St Thomas	Scarborough
	4 November 1840	Burial Ground	York
88	24 July 1841	St Peter	Leeds
89	18 September 1841	St George	Woodsetts
	18 September 1841	Burial ground	Letwell
90	1 October 1841	St John	Beverley
91	7 October 1841	Christ Church*	Bridlington
	11 October 1841	Burial ground	Horbury
	19 October 1841	Burial ground	Cawood
92	7 June 1842	Christ Church	Ardsley
93	8 June 1842	St Luke	Clifford
	1 August 1842	Burial ground	Pickering
94	6 June 1843	Holy Trinity	Elsecar
	6 June 1843	Burial ground	Darfield
95	7 June 1843	St Thomas*	Kimberworth
	5 December 1845	Burial ground	Bishopthorpe

Churches and burial grounds consecrated by other
bishops during Dr Harcourt's time as Archbishop

No.	Date	Dedication	Location
1	25 September 1840	St Hilda	Middlesbrough
2	22 November 1842	St John	Skipton on Swale
3	4 October 1843	Ascension	Oughtibridge
4	5 October 1843	Christ Church, Gleadless	Sheffield
5	7 August 1844	St Mark*	Sutton
6	8 August 1844	St Anne	Ellerker
7	28 May 1845	Holy Trinity	Leven
	31 May 1845	Burial ground	Great Driffield
8	22 September 1845	St Stephen	Hull
9	14 October 1845	Holy Trinity	Darnall
	15 October 1845	Burial ground	Ecclesfield
10	12 November 1845	All Saints	Rise
11	13 November 1845	St Paul	Tickton
12	14 April 1846	St Michael & All Angels	Cowesby, Thirsk
	10 September 1846	Burial ground	Thirsk
	2 October 1846	Burial ground	Ackworth
	24 October 1846	Burial ground	Rotherham
13	17 November 1846	St James	Fairburn
14	25 November 1846	St Mary	South Milford
15	31 May 1847	St Mary	Sand Hutton
16	27 October 1847	St Paul*	Sculcoates
	28 October 1847	Burial ground	Hull, Cottingham

Appointments in the gift of
the Archbishop of York

The information below is extracted from the Church of England Clergy Database (CCEd), which covers the period up to 1835, the *Clerical Guides* of 1817 and 1836, and the *Clergy List* of 1841. The information on income has been taken from the 16 June 1835 report of the *Commission to Inquire into the Revenues and Patronage of the Established Church of England and Wales*. The income figures are estimates averaged over three years to December 1831. Where there are two figures, the second figure is taken from the 1841 *Clergy List*.[1]

Dignities

In addition to the livings listed below, the Archbishop of York had the right to appoint the dignities in the cathedral church of York and the collegiate churches of Ripon and Southwell, except the deans of York and Ripon. With regard to appointments at Ripon, the dean had the right to present to three vacancies and the archbishop to one. The appointments could be valuable both financially and in terms of status and recognition. The basic stipends were often relatively modest, but were usually enhanced

---

[1] *Clerical Guide* (London: FC & J Rivington) 1817, 1822, 1829 and 1836. *Clergy List* (London: G Cox at the Ecclesiastical Gazette Office) 1841–1867. Both publications contain lists of prelates, dignitaries, incumbents, benefices, cathedral establishments and patrons, with the precise contents varying from year to year.

by a share of the revenues of the cathedral or church. Such revenues fluctuated substantially depending on the value of fines received on the renewal of leases.

At York, the archbishop could appoint the four Canons Residentiary and the 24 prebends. The canons received between £24 and £75 regular income and a share of the Minster revenues, which might amount to £275 each in a typical year. The prebends received a regular income of typically £15 to £50, but could in some years receive very large sums in fines. In the year to December 1831, eight prebends received income from fines. The most fortunate two received £2,500 each. The incomes of the 16 prebends at Southwell ranged from £4 to £75, average about £30. Only two received income from fines in 1835. At Ripon, the sub-dean and the eight prebendaries received a regular payment of £26 6s 8d and a revenue share of about £29.

Archdeacons

The archbishop also had the right to appoint his four archdeacons, as well as his lay staff, including secretary, registrar, deputy registrar and chancellor of the diocese. Such appointments could only be filled by his nominees as they became vacant. The net remuneration after expenses of an archdeaconry was modest. An archdeacon needed additional sources of income. According to the Commission of Enquiry, the average income across all archdeaconries in 1831 was gross £160 and net £140 inclusive of fines, which might amount to about 45 per cent of the total. The fees received for the four York archdeaconries were below average. Figures for fines for individual archdeaconries were not provided.

Anthony Trollope wrote in 1866: "An archdeacon has a great deal to do and very little to get. Indeed as to the matter of getting the archdeacon, as archdeacon, may be said to get almost nothing."[2] For this reason, an archdeacon must have at least one good living. "He is not infrequently a man of means and has been selected for his post partly on that account.

---

2   Anthony Trollope, *Clergymen of the Church of England* (London: Chapman and Hal, 1866), pp. 42–4.

He is one the Bishop can love and trust. He has to be able to keep a curate or two, give a dinner and keep at least a one-horse chaise. He must be able to take his place in county society. He must know his brother rectors and vicars and have an eye on their welfare." Archbishop Harcourt ensured his archdeacons were provided with good livings. They mostly came from aristocratic or county families and were usually prebendaries of York or Southwell, which appointments would provide additional income.

Archdeacons of York: gross £97 net £59 before fines

Robert Markham (1795–1837)
Son of Archbishop Harcourt's predecessor and rector of Bolton Percy (£1,540).

Stuart Corbett (1837–45)
Rector of Bramwith Kirk (£517) and Scrayingham (£662); his uncle was the Marquis of Bute, and he was a cousin of the Earl of Wharncliffe; the Archbishop made him a prebendary of York in 1841.

Stephen Creyke (1845–66)
Creyke came from an old Yorkshire family and had been a successful headmaster of St Peter's School York and chaplain to the Archbishop, who had given him a York prebend in 1841. He was rector of Beeford (£779) and Farlington with Marton (£130).

Archdeacons of East Riding: gross £69 net £51 before fines

Darley Waddilove (1786–1828)
Waddilove was dean of Ripon and had been chaplain to both previous archbishops; he was also a prebendary of York, incumbent of Topcliffe (£600) and Cherry Burton (£887).

Francis Wrangham (1828–41)

Wrangham was the son of a Malton farmer and married to a Creyke of Marton in the East Riding; his career developed through his own abilities; he had been a tutor to the Duke of Manchester. He was chaplain to Archbishop Harcourt from 1814–34 and a prebendary of York 1823. A supporter of the abolition of the slave trade, he was rector of Hunmanby (£350) and Doddleston (£593) in Chester diocese and Prebendary of Chester from 1842. He was succeeded as archdeacon by his son-in-law.

Robert Wilberforce (1841–54)

Wilberforce was the son of William Wilberforce and married to Francis Wrangham's daughter; rector of Burton Agnes (£897), he was a supporter of the Oxford Movement and became a Roman Catholic in 1854. His brother Samuel was Bishop of Oxford and later Winchester.

Archdeacons of Cleveland: gross £36 net £30 before fines

Charles Baillie Hamilton (1806–20)

Married to the daughter of the Earl of Home, he was vicar of Stainton (£323) and Middleton in Teesdale. (No income figure available.)

Francis Wrangham (1820–8)

See archdeacon of East Riding above; his move to the archdeaconry of the East Riding made sense, as his parish of Hunmanby was in the East Riding.

Leveson Vernon Harcourt (1828–32)

In line with the practice of his predecessor, Archbishop Harcourt appointed one of his sons as an archdeacon. Leveson had been rector of Stokesley (£1,026) since 1822 and took over Stainton (£323) from his cousin the Hon. Henry Howard in 1824; his father had appointed him chancellor of York Minster and prebendary of York in 1827. He left Stokesley for Beckenham in Kent in 1835.

Henry Todd (1832–45)

Todd was librarian at Lambeth Palace and rector of Settrington (£1,045) from 1820. The patron was the Earl of Bridgewater, a cousin of Archbishop Harcourt's wife; he was a crown chaplain and prebendary of York from 1830. He died in 1845.

Edward Churton (1846–74)

Churton went to Christ Church and had strong links to the high church Hackney Phalanx. He had been a curate at Hackney and married the rector's daughter. He accepted the incumbency of Craike in Yorkshire from the Bishop of Durham (£672) in 1835. Archbishop Harcourt made him a Prebendary of York in 1841.

Archdeacons of Nottingham: gross £65 net £15 before fines

Sir Richard Kaye (1780–1810)

Kaye was also dean of Lincoln; he was the only archdeacon not to attend Archbishop Harcourt's induction at York Minster due to ill health.

John Eyre (1810–30)

Eyre had received significant preferment from Archbishop Markham and was already a prebend of both York and Southwell. He had been chaplain to the 3rd Duke of Portland. When appointed archdeacon, he was rector of Babworth (£850), sinecure rector of Headon (£178) and vicar of Headon (£200). The Eyre family were patrons of Headon. During his period as archdeacon, he exchanged in 1826 the incumbency of Barton-in-Fabis (£360) for Beelsby (£450). The patron of Beelsby was the Southwell chapter. He became a close friend of Archbishop Harcourt and his family. His niece married Archbishop Harcourt's son Granville Harcourt Vernon, who through his wife inherited the Eyre family estate at Grove in Nottinghamshire.

William Barrow (1830-2)

Barrow came from Sedbergh, where he was involved in running an academy. He had been appointed a canon of Southwell in 1815 and was incumbent of Waltham in Lincolnshire (£331). On appointment as archdeacon, he exchanged Waltham for Beelsby (£450), which had been vacated on the death of Eyre. He resigned after two years due to ill health.

George Wilkins (1832-65)

Wilkins was the incumbent of St Mary's Nottingham (£699). His father had been architect to Earl Manvers, who was patron of St Mary's. Archbishop Harcourt would have known Wilkins through his visitations, confirmations and consecration of churches in Nottingham. He had been made a prebend of Southwell in 1823. He exchanged St Mary's for Beelsby in 1843, by which time Nottinghamshire was in the Diocese of Lincoln.

Livings

The number of livings in the gift of the Archbishop varied during his nearly 40 years in office. Details of the incumbents in 62 livings in his gift for most of the 40 years are given in the schedules below. The average value of the livings, at £250, was the same as the average for the Diocese of York as a whole. "PC" is a perpetual curate, "C" is curate, "V" is vicar and "R" is rector. The first column shows the incumbent listed in the 1817 *Clerical Guide*, his date of appointment and additional appointments shown in the guide or other sources. The next column gives details of any subsequent incumbents in the period up to the date of appointment shown for the incumbent listed in the 1841 *Clergy List*. The information given has been checked against the CCEd for the period up to 1835 and other sources such as the *Gentleman's Magazine*, church websites and family records. The aim was to identify the extent to which the Archbishop accepted pluralism and favoured family members. WVH is Dr Harcourt's son William and LVH is his son Leveson.

Benefice	Type	Value (£)	Incumbent in 1817	Other incumbents 1817–41	Incumbent in 1841 and later	Other livings held in 1841 and comments
Acklam West	PC	44	W M S Preston 1816–23; also PC Middlesbrough (£34) and V Startforth (£150) (Earl of Lonsdale)		I Benson 1824	Middlesbrough PC (£34)
Barnsley St George	PC	123/150	Matthew Mark 1833 (new church); the Archbishop was patron of Silkstone parish, of which Barnsley formed a part. Mark was a literate and had been curate in the parish.		R E Roberts 1838	
Barnsley St Mary	PC	225	B Mence 1798		W Carter 1836; R Willan 1847	
Barton-in-Fabis, Notts	R	360	J Eyre to 1826	Hon. J S Venables Vernon 1826–29 (from Molesworth); also Prebendary of Southwell from 1826—Archbishop's nephew.	F G Wintour 1829	V Rampton (£173) 1838; Prebend of Rampton Southwell 1830—this gave Wintour the right to appoint himself as the vicar of Rampton.

Benefice	Type	Value (£)	Incumbent in 1817	Other incumbents 1817–41	Incumbent in 1841 and later	Other livings held in 1841 and comments
Beeford w Lissett	R	779	W Walbanke Childers 1812–33, also Cantley (£233) 1803–33, a family living in the gift of his brother, and prebendary of Ely 1824 (55 miles apart).		William Tiffin 1833–44 / S Creyke 1845–65 (See Bishopthorpe)	Tiffin—None from Feb 1834; formerly Cambridge, then schoolmaster at Dalston free Grammar School; Chaplain to Lady Lonsdale and curate of Castle Sowerby under J D Carlyle on £30; borrowed £800 to build a parsonage (see below other earlier appointments: Mattersey, Kirkby-in-Cleveland and Hayton).
Birdforth	PC	94	H R Whytehead to 1818; also Nunkeeling (£55).		John Winter 1818	Curate at Husthwaite; died aged 91 in 1873.
Birstall	V	275	W M Heald 1801–35		W M Heald 1836	Heald junior had been curate to his father.

Benefice	Type	Value (£)	Incumbent in 1817	Other incumbents 1817–41	Incumbent in 1841 and later	Other livings held in 1841 and comments
Bishopthorpe	V	134	R Markham to 1814; also Bolton Percy, Archdeacon of York and Canon of Carlisle.	WVH 1814–24; also Etton (V) 1816–37 and Kirkby-in-Cleveland (R) from 1823.	W H Dixon 1837–54	W H Dixon 1824–34; WVH 1834–37. Dixon was canon at York, prebendary of Ripon, AB of Y's Chaplain, Sutton-on-the-Forest (V) 1834–7 and then Etton (V) 1837 till his death in 1854.
Bolton Percy	R	1,540	R Markham 1797–1837 (see above)		WVH 1837–65	Kirkby-in-Cleveland sinecure (see below).
Brodsworth	V	367	R Wilson 1808–27 also lecturer St Benet Fink London		J Sharpe 1827*	Vicar of Doncaster 1817 (£125) where he had been curate for two years; also Doncaster lectureship.

Benefice	Type	Value (£)	Incumbent in 1817	Other incumbents 1817–41	Incumbent in 1841 and later	Other livings held in 1841 and comments
Carlton-in-Lindrick	R	576	R P Goodenough 1819; also Beelsby Lincoln (£260) 1819; Goodenough's wife was a daughter of Archbishop Markham.		Charles Wasteneys Eyre 1826	Babworth (£800) from 1830 (J Simpson patron), prebendary of York and chaplain to the Earl of Scarborough. Had dispensation for Babworth, which he acquired following the death of his father, Archdeacon John Eyre. CWE inherited the Rampton estate, when Granville Harcourt-Vernon inherited Grove. CWE had been curate at Headon where John Eyre was sinecure rector and vicar till his death in 1830.
Carlton Miniot	PC	103/125	J Holmes to 1830	R Lascelles 1830–33; also Thirsk and Huttons Ambo—all close by; the Lascelles were a local land-owning family.	W H Dent 1833; E Jowett 1843	With Sowerby (PC) 3 miles apart (£34).

Benefice	Type	Value (£)	Incumbent in 1817	Other incumbents 1817–41	Incumbent in 1841 and later	Other livings held in 1841 and comments
Conisbrough	V	206	H Watkins 1770–1829 and Barnbrough from 1815 (£640); prebend of York and Southwell; chaplain to Viscount Hamperden.		H S Markham 1830 G Wright 1844	Clifton Notts (£500) 1830; canon at York 1833; Lowther Chaplain.
Crambe	V	180	John Cleaver 1804–23 J Richardson 1823–32	William Richardson from 1832–37 w Huttons Ambo (son of James Richardson); C J Hawkins 1837–39 (see Nunburnholme and Sutton).	Henry Fendall 1839	Nunburnholme from 1828 to 1839—with Huttons Ambo (£93); educated Eton and Cambridge.
Darrington	V	512	J Chaloner 1815–31 with Newton Kyme (£450);Christ Church graduate.		G Pease 1831	
Doncaster	V	125/385	Sir Robert Affleck 1807–17 (to Silkstone)—see below.		J Sharpe 1817	Brodsworth added 1827—see above—promoted from curate. His son R J Sharpe had Liversall PC 1847 in the gift of vicar of Doncaster.

Benefice	Type	Value (£)	Incumbent in 1817	Other incumbents 1817–41	Incumbent in 1841 and later	Other livings held in 1841 and comments
Easington	PC	51	G Inman 1813 with Skeffling (£53) & Kilnsea (£82)—all small adjacent parishes on Spurn Head. His wife was a daughter of the Raines family of Wyton Hall.			
Egton	PC	33/120 in 1848	B Richardson 1806 with Glaisdale and Goathland (see Glaisdale)		G Dixon 1847	
Etton	R	853	WVH 1816–37 with Wheldrake (£450) 1824–34 and Kirkby-in-Cleveland sinecure (R) from 1823 (see below).		W H Dixon 1837–54	Also Bishopthorpe (more information above).
Farlington w Marton	PC	130	Major Dawson 1768–1830		S Creyke 1830 Campion Napper (no date in 1848 guide).	See Sutton-on-the-Forest below.
Felixkirk	C	450	W Dennison 1776–1827		C V B Johnstone 1827	Brother-in-law of Louisa Johnstone, AB of Y's daughter.

Benefice	Type	Value (£)	Incumbent in 1817	Other incumbents 1817–41	Incumbent in 1841 and later	Other livings held in 1841 and comments
Felkirk	V	136	R Hunt 1801–37 with Medmenham (Bucks) 1801 (£133).		John Baines Graham 1837	Burnsall (1st portion) 1832, of which his father was patron (£315), and Holy Trinity Micklegate 1822 (£93), patron Lord Chancellor—he was the son of John Graham, leading evangelical in York.
Fylingdales	PC	98/120	J Harrison 1800, literate—previously Egton Chapel.			
Glaisdale	PC	77/ 120 in 1848 guide	B Richardson 1806 with Goathland (£58) (Dean of York) and Egton (£33).		B Richardson II 1844	B Richardson II was the nephew of B Richardson.
Guisborough	PC	72/176	T P Williamson 1798–1835 with Upleatham chapel 1827 (£57)—also AB of Y patron.	William Leigh Williamson 1835–6 who had been curate for a year. He and his father died of cholera.	H Clarke 1836	Local Guisborough family; he had been ordained by AB of Y and was curate of Wilton.
Haxey	V	550	John Lamb 1792	Reappointed 1810; also rector of Stretton (£300) in Rutland, where he lived and died at the age of 84 in 1842.	John Lamb 1810 J Dobson 1845	Reappointed 1810—lived at Stretton.

Benefice	Type	Value (£)	Incumbent in 1817	Other incumbents 1817–41	Incumbent in 1841 and later	Other livings held in 1841 and comments
Hayton Notts	V	152	W Tiffin[3] 1815–33 (see also Beeford and Mattersey).		J Mason 1833	PC St Helen West Burton—adjoining villages.
					W C Mee 1845	
Hedon	PC	45	W Wasse 1828–1839 (Hedon not listed in 1817 guide); Hedon population 1,080 and Preston 957 (£81), both held by Wasse. Preston was in the gift of the sub-dean of York. Wasse had been a sizar at St Catherine's Cambridge.		J H Wake 1839	Also held with Preston. Wake was married to the daughter of the Revd A W Eyre, vicar of Hornsea and Ritson (1854 Sutton-on-the-Forest).
Hinksey North	PC	105	John Curtis 1778–1820	Fellow, dean and bursar of Magdalene College Oxford; also rector of Wytham and of Albury during this period.	E G Marsh 1820	Appointed by Earl Harcourt—prebendary of Southwell, rector of Waltham 1834 (£331) and vicar of Yardley 1828 (£275).
					R G P Tiddeman 1841	

3   Was from Castle Sowerby in Carlisle diocese where he had been curate to J D Carlyle.

Benefice	Type	Value (£)	Incumbent in 1817	Other incumbents 1817–41	Incumbent in 1841 and later	Other livings held in 1841 and comments
Huttons Ambo	PC	93	J Cleaver 1804–22	William Richardson from 1823; also vicar of Crambe (£180), 4 miles away (Both AB of Y). His father, James, had been at Huttons Ambo for a year and also vicar of Crambe.	H Fendall 1839	Combined this role with Crambe (V, £180) as had his predecessor— previously Nunburnholme (See below).
Keyingham	PC	92	Lamplugh Hird or Wickham 1793–1842 with Paul (see below).		Joshua Smyth 1821	Smyth was a literate who had been curate at Keyingham since 1819 and Paull on £100 a year plus surplice fees when Lamplugh Hird was vicar. Smyth was vicar of Burton Pidsea (£42) from 1842—a gift of the dean and chapter of York.
Kilburn	PC	99	T Barker 1804 also Thirkleby (£210) (see below).			

Benefice	Type	Value (£)	Incumbent in 1817	Other incumbents 1817–41	Incumbent in 1841 and later	Other livings held in 1841 and comments
Kinoulton	V	160	Thomas Hoe 1800 was a literate. He was also rector of Long Clawson (£105) five miles from Kinoulton but in Leicestershire.			
Kirkby in Cleveland sinecure	R	359	Cyril Jackson, Dean of Christchurch to 1819. W Tiffin was vicar from 1812–16.	LVH 1819–23 whilst rector of Rothbury (£1,106).	WVH 1823	Etton and Wheldrake to 1834; Bolton Percy from 1837 and prebendary of York.
Kirk Leavington	PC	63/100	John Graves 1794 with High Worsall.	William Raine 1834–8	Warcup Putsey 1838	Was a literate and curate at Elton in Durham some six miles away. Had been curate at Ormesby following ordination by Harcourt. With Hilton 1847 (£50).
Lythe	V	123/150	T Porter 1780–1826 Literate—no other		W Long 1826	Curate since 1812 and promoted to V in 1826. He was a literate who had been ordained by Harcourt.
Marton	V	122	Daniel Duck 1798–1829		R Fawcett 1829	Also PC of Hilton (£50) about 7 miles away.
					H Taylor 1847	

Benefice	Type	Value (£)	Incumbent in 1817	Other incumbents 1817–41	Incumbent in 1841 and later	Other livings held in 1841 and comments
Mattersey	V	293	W Tiffin 1815–34; Hayton 1815–33; also Kirkby-in-Cleveland (V) 1812–16 and Ormesby 1814–16; Beeford from 1833.		William Carr Fenton 1835	Cowthorpe near Wetherby from 1824 (£130); founder, Doncaster School for the Blind. Mattersey is near Bawtry; he was a literate. He lived at Mattersey and had a curate at Cowthorpe.
Molesworth Hunts	R	228	William Ellis 1775–1821; from 1790 Chaplain to D of Norfolk and his own living of Walton, Bucks (£120).	Hon. J S Vernon from 1822–26, when he moved to Barton-in-Farbis (see above); JSV was Harcourt's nephew.	G H Eyre 1826 J Oxlee 1836	No other living
Myton u Swale	V	150	R S Thompson 1804—also Askham Bryan and Askham Richard (£120 and £200).			

Benefice	Type	Value (£)	Incumbent in 1817	Other incumbents 1817–41	Incumbent in 1841 and later	Other livings held in 1841 and comments
Nunburnholme	R	302	WVH for 9 months in 1816.	W Page 1816–18—Page was a Christ Church graduate and had been the AB of Y's chaplain in Carlisle—he was V of Willen (Bucks, £115) and Steventon (Berks, £192). He was Master of Westminster, prebendary of Westminster and sub-almoner to AB of Y. C Dyson 1818, curate at Warter 1826; H Fendall 1828—no other—moved to Crambe and Huttons Ambo 1839.	Charles James Hawkins 1839–45	Westminster and St John's Cambridge, then deacon 1832 and curate at Bishopthorpe, when Dixon was vicar, and married a Dixon; Crambe and Huttons Ambo 1837–39; Nunburnholme 1839–45; Sutton-on-the-Forest 1845–54; Haxey 1854–61.
					H B Boothby 1846	
Nafferton	PC	139	John Ewbank 1788 w Thornton Steward (£234).	Evan Morgan 1826–36	G Wright 1837	PC of Nun Monkton many miles away;
					F O Morris 1844	Morris was chaplain to the Duke of Cleveland.

Benefice	Type	Value (£)	Incumbent in 1817	Other incumbents 1817–41	Incumbent in 1841 and later	Other livings held in 1841 and comments
Ormesby w Eston	C	167	John Tansh 1762–1814	William Tiffin 1814–16; J Thomson 1816–37	Thomas Irvin 1837	His father was incumbent of Hackness and Harwood Dale, a living in the gift of Harcourt's son-in-law Sir John V B Johnstone.
Paull w Thorngunbald	V	160	Lamplugh Hird 1793–1842; also prebendary of York (see also Keyingham).		James Samuel Jones 1843	Educated at St Bees, he had been curate at Paull since 1832.
Poppleton Nether	PC	155	Thomas Gilpin 1797–1826		C J Camidge 1826	Also curate at St Sampson's York under W Bulmer, he was the son of the organist at York Minster and went on to be vicar of Wakefield in 1855. He died 1878.
Royston w Bretton Monks	V	166	John Fletcher 1791; was promoted from curate and appointed his son John as curate in 1815.	G Fenton 1836–42; he retained his incumbency of Denton (£44) and remained a curate at Ilkley.	W H Teale 1843	
Rudston	V	236	Francis Metcalfe 1783–1823; also V Kirkbride £230.	James Dallin 1823–33, vicar choral at York Minster and rector of Holy Trinity Goodramgate York (see below).	Robert Dallin 1833	Curate since 1824, he was suspended in 1846 for two years for drunkenness.

Benefice	Type	Value (£)	Incumbent in 1817	Other incumbents 1817–41	Incumbent in 1841 and later	Other livings held in 1841 and comments
Sand Hutton in Thirsk	PC	94	Jonathan Holmes 1791; also PC Thirsk (£143) from 1811.		S Coates 1834–43	Also Perpetual Curate of Thirsk (£143); Coates moved to Sowerby in 1843 (also part of Thirsk parish but worth £310).
					W M Lindley 1843	
Skelton w Brotton	C	137	J Parrington to 1816		W Close 1816	Literate—no other
Sheriff Hutton	V	191	Thomas Tate 1782 Literate	No other	B Lumley 1824	Graduate—also Dalby 1806 (£240), Lumley family living; 5 miles apart.
Silkstone	R	272	G D Kelley to 1815; also had Darrington and Featherstone plus York prebendary; J Kelley 1815–17—was a literate and probably son of GDK, and died 1817.	Sir Robert Affleck, Bart 1817–35; also vicar of Westow and chaplain to 3rd Earl Harcourt and prebendary of York (see below).	H Watkins 1835	Beckingham Notts (V) 1802 (£110) gift of Southwell chapter; he had been curate at Conisborough under his father, also Henry (see above). Millett was chaplain to Bishop of Ripon.
					G Millett 1845	

Benefice	Type	Value (£)	Incumbent in 1817	Other incumbents 1817–41	Incumbent in 1841 and later	Other livings held in 1841 and comments
Skipsea	V	96	Joseph Lowes 1791	J Mason 1823–34. His son John was a curate at Skipsea but not promoted on his father's death. Mason was a literate and succeeded by a graduate.	Charles Cory 1834	No other.
Sowerby (Thirsk)	PC	34/310 in 1848	Edward Greenwood 1798–1821; also PC of Over Stilton (11 miles apart).	William Wilkinson 1821–27	W H Dent 1827–43	With Carlton Miniot (£103) 3 miles away. Samuel Coates from 1843 (see Thirsk).
Stainton in Cleveland	V	323	Venerable Charles Baillie Hamilton to 1820—Archdeacon.	Hon. H E J Howard 1820–24; LVH with Stokesley 1824–33.	W Gooch 1833	With Benacre Suffolk 1823 (£440, family living); WVH married Matilda Gooch, his sister); prebendary of York 1845.

Benefice	Type	Value (£)	Incumbent in 1817	Other incumbents 1817–41	Incumbent in 1841 and later	Other livings held in 1841 and comments
Stokesley	C	1,026/ 1,220	George Markham 1791–1822; Markham was also dean of York.	LVH 1822–35—also held Stainton to 1835 and was chancellor of York. He was archdeacon of Cleveland 1828–32.	C Cator 1835	Charles Cator swapped Beckenham in Kent with LVH, who went to Beckenham (£900). Beckenham was a living in the gift of Joseph Cator, father of Charles and of Thomas Cator who was rector of Kirk Smeaton and Womersley and lived at Skellbrook Park near Doncaster. Charles had also given up the living of Carshalton, which went to William Hardy Vernon (No direct connection).

Benefice	Type	Value (£)	Incumbent in 1817	Other incumbents 1817–41	Incumbent in 1841 and later	Other livings held in 1841 and comments
Sutton-in-the-Forest	V	395	E Rice 1803–10 George Talbot 1810–11—he was Chaplain to George 2nd Lord Vernon; left to become rector of Ingestre and Church Eaton.	LVH 1812–13; W Carey 1813–20; G Pellew 1820–24; Hon. H E J Howard 1824–34, also Slingsby (£557)—Dean of Lichfield 1834; WH Dixon 1834–7 (AB OF Y's Chaplain)—also Bishopthorpe 1824–? To Etton 1837.	S Creyke 1837–45	Farlington (£130) (see above) and Ergham (£21) 22 population and no church, and Wigginton £297 (gift of Lord Chancellor): archdeacon 1845. Charles James Hawkins 1845 (see Crambe and Nunburnholme).
Thirkleby	V	210	Thomas Barker 1804	With Kilburn; promoted from curate in succession to his father.		
Thirsk	PC	143	J Holmes 1798–1830 w Sand Hutton 1798–1830.	R Lascelles 1830–33 w Sand Hutton and Carlton Miniott (Lascelles a local Thirsk family).	S Coates 1833–43	With Sand Hutton (£94); W M Lindley 1843 with Sand Hutton, literate ordained by Archbishop Harcourt.
Upleatham	PC	57/80		Joseph Wilkinson 1827, also Redcar (£50); he may have attended St Bees.		

Benefice	Type	Value (£)	Incumbent in 1817	Other incumbents 1817–41	Incumbent in 1841 and later	Other livings held in 1841 and comments
Westow	V	173	Robert Affleck 1796–1833	Affleck was chaplain to 3rd Earl Harcourt and vicar of Silkstone from 1817 (see above). He was a Christ Church graduate.	W T Wild 1833	Does not appear to have any other appointments except evening lectureship at St James Clerkenwell.
Wheldrake	R	474	R Elliott 1798–1824 w Huggate	WVH 1824–34 with Etton and Kirkby-in-Cleveland	R B Cooke 1834	With Owston 1830 (family living) but only till 1837.

Benefice	Type	Value (£)	Incumbent in 1817	Other incumbents 1817–41	Incumbent in 1841 and later	Other livings held in 1841 and comments
Whitby	PC	151/206	Thomas Eglin 1773–1818	Also vicar of Stillingfleet 1768–1818.	James Andrew 1818	Andrew died in 1843 and was replaced by Rev T Trevanion in 1844, who had been rector of Wadworth. According to Yorkshire Gazette 9 Dec 1843 the Archbishop had told the churchwardens he wished to appoint a man of "zeal and activity combined with sound judgement". The Archbishop did not know Trevanion but Wadworth was a living of the dean and chapter of York so may have been known to WVH.
York Trinity w St John & St Maurice	V	138/150	James Dallin 1803–38 with Rudston to 1833		E J Raines 1838	Raines was curate to Dallin on £50 a year for both churches; no other appointment.

Acknowledgements

Cherry Ann Knott and Michael Chandler were kind enough to read the whole manuscript and make valuable comments and corrections. Nicholas Dixon made available to me some of his research material on Archbishop Harcourt, and Sara Slinn found time to meet me in Cambridge to discuss her research into Archbishop Harcourt's training arrangements for literates. Their assistance has been much appreciated.

I am also grateful to the archivists and librarians in the following institutions for their advice and provision of information:

- Bodleian Libraries, Weston Library, University of Oxford
- Borthwick Institute for Archives, University of York
- British Library, Additional Manuscripts
- Cambridge University Library
- Carlisle Archive Centre, Diocese of Carlisle Records
- Christ Church Archives, University of Oxford
- Durham University, Archives and Special Collections
- Gloucester Cathedral, Archives and Library
- Harrowby Manuscripts Trust, Sandon Hall, Stafford
- Lambeth Palace Library, National Library and Archive of the Church of England
- Nottingham University Archives, Manuscripts and Special Collections
- Staffordshire and Stoke-on-Trent Archive Service, Stafford, William Salt Library.

Sources

There were three key sources of information:

Harcourt Papers (HP)

A selection of letters from the Harcourt archive was edited with an accompanying text by the Archbishop's grandson Edward William Harcourt and 50 copies were printed for private circulation between 1876 and 1901. The 15 volumes cover the history of the Harcourt family at Stanton Harcourt from 1200. Volume XII includes letters to and from the Archbishop and his wife. Volumes XI and XIII also include material relevant to Archbishop Harcourt's life. The original letters and others not included in the printed volumes are now in the Weston Library of the Bodleian Libraries, University of Oxford. I am grateful to William Gascoigne, the Archbishop's great-great-great-great grandson, for permission to quote from the unpublished letters and to the Bodleian Libraries for access to the archive.

The British Newspaper Archive online

This online archive of local and regional newspapers contains at February 2023 over 35,000 entries for the Archbishop of York for the years 1808–47. Without this archive it would have been impossible to get a picture of the Archbishop's day-to-day activities in London and in his diocese. The newspapers showed how he was perceived at the time as well as providing information about his travels around his diocese and his social life.

Clergy of the Church of England Database (CCEd)

Launched in 1999, this database makes available the records of clerical careers from 1540 to 1835. It was an essential resource for tracing appointments made during Archbishop Harcourt's time in Carlisle and York dioceses and for identifying clergy mentioned in the Archbishop's letters. I am grateful to Professor Arthur Burns (King's College, London), Project Director for the period 1760–1835.

Bibliography

The only works written by Archbishop Harcourt and published in his lifetime were three sermons:

Harcourt, Edward Vernon, Lord Bishop of Carlisle, *A sermon preached before the Lords Spiritual and Temporal in the Abbey Church of St Peter, Westminster, on Thursday 30th January 1794 being the anniversary of the martyrdom of King Charles I* (London: R. Faulder, 1794).

Harcourt, Edward Vernon, Lord Bishop of Carlisle, *A sermon preached before the Incorporated Society for the Propagation of the Gospel in Foreign Parts in the parish church of St Mary le Bow on 16th February 1798* (London: S. Brooke, 1798).

Harcourt, Edward Vernon, Lord Archbishop of York, *Sermon preached at the Coronation of King George IV in the Abbey Church of Westminster 19th July 1821* (London: Published by His Majesty's Command, 1821).

Other works consulted include:

Anson, Harold, *Looking Forward* (London: Heinemann, 1938).

Arnold, Thomas, *Principles of Church Reform* (London: B. Fellowes, Printer, 1833).

Ashwell, A. R., and Wilberforce, R. G., *Life of the Rt. Rev Samuel Wilberforce* (London: John Murray, 1880–1882).

Aylmer, G. E. and Cant, Reginald (eds), *History of York Minster* (London: Clarendon Press, 1977). Chapter VII by Owen Chadwick covers the period 1822–1916.

Baring-Gould, S., *The Church Revival: Thoughts thereon and reminiscences* (London: Methuen, 1914).

Batey, M. L., *Nuneham Courtenay, Oxfordshire: A short history and description of the house, gardens and estate* (Abingdon: The Abbey Press, 1970).

Beeson, Trevor, *The Canons, Cathedral Close Encounters* (London: SCM Press, 2006).

Best, G. F. A., *Temporal Pillars, Queen Anne's Bounty, the Ecclesiastical Commissioners, and the Church of England* (Cambridge: Cambridge University Press, 1964).

Beverley, R. M., *A Letter to the Archbishop of York on the Corrupt State of the Church of England* (Beverley: W. B. Johnson, 1831).

Blomfield, A., *Memoir of Charles James Blomfield, D. D., Bishop of London* (London: John Murray, 1864).

Bower, David John, *The Church of England in East Yorkshire from 1743 to c. 1840* (University of Hull, PhD Thesis, 2006).

Boyd, W. and Shuffrey, W. A., *Littondale Past and Present* (Leeds: Richard Jackson, 1893).

Brose, Olive J., *Church and Parliament: The Reshaping of the Church of England 1828–1860* (Stanford, CA: Stanford University Press, 1959).

Bullock, F. W. B., *A History of Training for the Ministry of the Church of England 1800–1874* (St Leonards-on-Sea: Budd & Gillatt, 1955).

Burgess, John, *Religious History of Cumbria 1780–1920* (Sheffield University, PhD Thesis, 1984).

Burns, Arthur, *The Diocesan Revival in the Church of England c. 1800–1870* (Oxford: Clarendon Press, 1999).

Burns, Arthur, and Innes, Joanna (eds), *Rethinking the Age of Reform, Britain 1780–1850* (Cambridge: Cambridge University Press, 2003).

Cannon, John, *Parliamentary Reform 1640–1832* (Cambridge: Cambridge University Press, 1972).

Chadwick, Owen, *The Victorian Church Part One: 1829–1859* (London: SCM Press, 1971).

Chandler, Michael, *Queen Victoria's Archbishops of Canterbury* (Durham: Sacristy Press, 2019).

Chenevix Trench, Charles, *The Royal Malady* (London: Longman, Green & Co., 1964).

Clerical Guide or Ecclesiastical Directory (London: FC & J Rivington 1817, 1822, 1829, 1836). The *Clerical Guide* and its successor the *Clergy List* contain lists of prelates, dignitaries, incumbents, benefices, cathedral establishments and patrons, with the precise contents varying from year to year.

Clergy List (London: G Cox at the Ecclesiastical Gazette Office, Strand, 1841–1867)

Cotterill, Rev Thomas, *A Selection of Psalms and Hymns for Public Worship* (London: T. Caddell, 1819).

Crosse, John, *Grand Music Festival Held in September 1823 in the Cathedral Church of York* (York: John Wolstenholme, 1825).

Cudworth, William, *Round About Bradford* (Bradford: T. Brear, 1876).

Dansey, William, *Horae Decanicae Rurales*, 2nd edition (London: J. G. F. & J. Rivington, 1844).

Dasent, A., *A History of Grosvenor Square* (London: Macmillan, 1994).

Dixon, Nicholas Andrew, *The Activity and Influence of the Established Church in England c. 1800–1837* (Cambridge University PhD Thesis, 2018).

Dixon, W. H., *A memoir of W. H. Dixon* (London: British Library reprint, 2010).

Dixon, W. H., and Raine, James, *Fasti Eboracences,* Volume 1 (London: Longman Green, 1863).

Drummond, Pippa, *Provincial Music Festivals in England 1784–1914* (Farnham: Ashgate, 2011).

Evans, Eric J., *The Forging of the Modern State: Early Industrial Britain 1783–1870* (Abingdon: Routledge, 2013).

Fraser, Antonia, *The King and The Catholics: The Fight for Rights 1829* (London: Weidenfeld & Nicolson, 2018).

Frost, Maurice (ed.), *Historical Companion to Hymns Ancient & Modern* (London: W. Clowes for the proprietors, 1962).

Garrard, James, *Archbishop Howley 1828–1848* (Farnham: Ashgate Publishing, 2015).

Norman Gash, *Sir Robert Peel: The Life of Sir Robert Peel after 1830* (London: Longman, 1986).

Gee, Eric, *Bishopthorpe Palace: An Architectural History* (York: Ebor Press, 1983).

Gibson, William, *Church, State and Society 1760–1850* (Basingstoke: Macmillan, 1994).

Granville, Countess Castalia, *Lord Granville Leveson Gower, First Earl Granville: Private Correspondence 1781–1821*, 2 volumes (London: John Murray, 1916).

Grass, Tim, *The Lord's Work: A History of the Catholic Apostolic Church* (Eugene, OR: Pickwick Publications, 2017).

Green, S. J. D. and Horden, P., *All Souls under the Ancien Regime: Politics, Learning and the Arts 1600–1850* (Oxford: Oxford University Press, 2000).

Greville, C. C. F., *Diaries of Charles Greville*, ed. Edward Pearce with Deanna Pearce, (London: Pimlico, 2006).

Hadlow, Janet, *The Strangest Family: The Private Lives of George III, Queen Charlotte and the Hanoverians* (London: William Collins, 2014).

Hargrove, W., *A New Guide for Strangers and Residents in the City of York* (York: W. & J. Hargrove, 1844).

Hedley, Gill, *Free Seats for All: The Boom in Church Building after Waterloo* (London: Umbria Press, 2018, for National Churches Trust).

Henley, Lord (Robert Henley Eden), *A Plan of Church Reform* (London: Roake & Varty, 1832).

Hewett, Osbert Wyndham, *Strawberry Fair: A Biography of Frances, Countess Waldegrave 1821–1879* (London: John Murray, 1956).

Huggins, Mike, *Horse Racing and British Society in the Long Eighteenth Century* (Woodbridge: Boydell Press, 2018).

Jacob, W. M., *The Clerical Profession in the Long Eighteenth Century 1680–1840* (Oxford: Oxford University Press, 2007).

Johnson, Malcolm, *Bustling Intermeddler? The Life and Work of Charles James Blomfield* (Leominster: Gracewing, 2001).

Knott, Cherry Ann, *George Vernon 1636–1702, 'who built this house', Sudbury Hall, Derbyshire* (Stroud: Tun House Publishing, 2010).

Kriegel, A. D. (ed.), *Holland House Diaries 1831–1840: the Diary of Henry Richard Vassall Fox, Third Lord Holland* (London: Routledge & Kegan Paul, 1977).

Larsen, Timothy, *Crisis of Doubt: Honest Faith in Nineteenth-Century England* (Oxford: Oxford University Press, 2006).

Leveson Gower, Hon. Frederick, *Bygone Years* (London: John Murray, 1905).

Loch, James, *Memoir of George Granville, First Duke of Sutherland* (London, 1834, for private circulation).

Mathieson, William Law, *English Church Reform 1815–1840* (London: Longman Green, 1923).

Milner, Mary, *Life of Isaac Milner, Dean of Carlisle* (London, Cambridge: J. W. Palmer, J. J. Deighton, 1842).

Morris, Rev M. C. F., *Yorkshire Reminiscences* (London: H. Milford, 1922).

Ollard, S. L. and Crosse, G. (eds), *A Dictionary of English Church History*, 2nd rev. edn (London: A.R. Mowbray 1919)

Parsons, Gerald and Wolffe, John (eds), *Religion in Victorian Britain*, Vol. 1–5, (Manchester: Manchester University Press in association with the Open University, 1988).

Phillimore, Robert, *A Report of the Proceedings in the Visitatorial Court at York by the Commissary against the Dean of York* (London: S Sweet Law, 1841).

Port, M. H., *Six Hundred New Churches: The Church Building Commission 1818–1856* (London: SPCK, 1961, for the Church Historical Society).

Roberts, Andrew, *George III: The Life and Reign of Britain's Most Misunderstood Monarch* (London: Allen Lane, Penguin Books, 2021).

Queen Victoria's Journals online <http://www.queenvictoriasjournals. org/home.do>, accessed 19 June 2023.

Sack, James J., *The Grenvillites 1801–1829, Party Politics and Factionalism in the Age of Pitt and Liverpool* (Urbana, IL and London: University of Illinois Press, 1979).

Slinn, Sara, *York Clergy Ordinations 1800–1849* (York: Borthwick Institute, University of York, 2001).

Slinn, Sara, "Archbishop Harcourt's Recruitment of Literate Clergymen and his Seminaries for Literates in the Diocese of York", *Yorkshire Archaeological Journal* 80 (2008), pp. 167–87 and 81 (2009), pp. 279–309.

Slinn, Sara, *The Education of the Anglican Clergy 1780–1839* (Woodbridge: Boydell Press, 2017).

Smith, Nowell C. (ed.), *Letters of Sydney Smith* (Oxford, Clarendon Press, 1953).

Smyth, William Henry, *Aedes Hartwellianae*, 2 volumes (London: for private circulation, 1864).

Snowden, William (A Yorkshire Incumbent), *The Case for Non-Graduate Clergy, usually called Literates* (London: Sherwood, Gilbert & Piper, 1830).

Soloway, R. A., *Prelates and People: Ecclesiastical Social Thought in England 1783–1852* (London: Routledge & Kegan Paul, 1969).

Stephenson, A. M. G., *Archbishop Vernon Harcourt, Studies in Church History IV,* Volume 58 (Cambridge: Cambridge University Press for Ecclesiastical History Society, 1967).

Stirling, A. M. W., *The Letter-Bag of Lady Elizabeth Spencer Stanhope* (London, New York: J. Lane, 1913).

Strachey, Lytton and Fulford, Roger, *Greville Memoirs Volume 5* (London: Macmillan, 1938).

Sykes, Norman, *Church & State in England in the XVIII Century* (Cambridge: Cambridge University Press, 1934).

Thompson, H. L., *Christ Church* (London: F. E. Robinson, 1900).

Tindal Hart, A., *Ebor: Archbishops of York from Paulinus to Maclagan 627–1908* (York: Ebor Press 1986).

Trollope, Anthony, *Clergymen of the Church of England* (London: Chapman & Hall, 1866).

Turberville, A. S., *The House of Lords in the Age of Reform 1784–1837 with an Epilogue on Aristocracy and the Advent of Democracy 1837–1867* (Westport, CT: Greenwood Press 1974).

Turnbull, Richard, *Reviving The Heart: The Story of the 18th Century Revival* (Oxford: Lion Hudson, 2012).

Varley, E. A., *A study of William Van Mildert, Bishop of Durham, and the high church movement of the early nineteenth century* (Durham University, Doctoral thesis, 1985).

Virgin, Peter, *The Church in an Age of Negligence: Ecclesiastical Structure and Problems of Church Reform 1700–1840* (Cambridge: James Clarke & Co, 1989).

Virgin, Peter, *Sydney Smith* (London: Harper Collins, 1994).

Wade, John, *Black Book or Corruption Unmasked* (London: John Fairburn, 1820).

Walsh, John, Haydon, Colin and Taylor, Stephen (eds), *The Church of England c. 1689–c. 1833: From Toleration to Tractarianism* (Cambridge: Cambridge University Press, 1993).

Weston, David, *Rose Castle and the Bishops of Carlisle 1133–2012* (Carlisle: Cumberland & Westmoreland Antiquarian and Archaeological Society, 2013).

Wilkins, George, *A Letter to Earl Grey on the Subject of Ecclesiastical Reform* (London: Longman, Rees, Orme, Brown & Longman, 1832).

Wilson, Philip Whitewell (ed.), *The Greville Diary*, 2 volumes (London: William Heinemann, 1927).

Index

EU GPSR Authorized Representative:

LOGOS EUROPE, 9 rue Nicolas Poussin, 17000 La Rochelle, France

contact@logoseurope.eu

www.ingramcontent.com/pod-product-compliance
Lightning Source LLC
Chambersburg PA
CBHW060417100426
42812CB00030B/3217/J